British Merchants in Nineteenth-Century Brazil

Subtlety of differences –
merchants view – needs US
government at home

Tariff 1% lower than
Portugal's

Threat of fleet action –
especially if black revolt

emphasize the nation –
attitudes of pride?
THINK BRAZIL'S VIEW

LUSO - BRAZILIANS

Key story in Brazilian
independence

AVOID FACILE, ONE-SIDED JUDGEMENTS —
April 12, 1832 – height of anti-slavery action

Ultimate suppression of slave trade by 1850's
due to strengthening of central govt – paradigm
for Amazon?

British Merchants in Nineteenth-Century Brazil:

Business, Culture, and Identity
in Bahia, 1808–50

Louise H. Guenther

Centre for Brazilian Studies
University of Oxford

Louise H. Guenther was a Visiting Research Associate at the Centre for Brazilian Studies and a Senior Associate Member of St Antony's College, Oxford, in 2001–2. She received a Ph.D. from the University of Minnesota in 1998 and is currently a faculty member at Pearson College in British Columbia, Canada.

Published by
Centre for Brazilian Studies
University of Oxford
92 Woodstock Road
Oxford OX2 7ND

ISBN 0-9544070-3-2

Cover illustration: *The Bahia Cricket Club at play on the Campo Grande,* in J.J. Wild, *At Anchor* (London, 1878), by permission of the British Library (1786.a.6).
Cover design by Andrew Chapman, Chapman Design.

Typeset by Meg Palmer, Third Column.
Printed by Lightning Source.

To my mother and father

Contents

Preface

The University of Oxford Centre for Brazilian Studies is publishing a series of books on the historical relationship between Britain and Brazil. The first two books in the series were works of reference: Oliver Marshall, *Brazil in British and Irish Archives* (2002), a guide to manuscript sources on Brazil in British and Irish archives, and Leslie Bethell, *Brazil by British and Irish Authors* (2003), a guide to books on Brazil by British and Irish authors from the end of the sixteenth century to the end of the twentieth century.

The Centre is now pleased to publish the first monograph in the series: Louise H. Guenther, *British Merchants in Nineteenth-Century Brazil: Business, Culture, and Identity in Bahia, 1808–50*. It explores the history of a small but influential British community made up mainly of merchants but also diplomats, professionals and clerks – as well as their families – and its interaction with Brazilian society in the port city of Salvador, Bahia, the former capital of the Portuguese empire in America, in the half century after the opening of Brazil's ports to foreign trade in 1808. A significant contribution both to global business history and to social and cultural history, Dr Guenther's book deepens our knowledge and understanding of Britain's economic penetration of Brazil in the nineteenth century and the nature of British enclave communities in areas of the world that did not form part of Britain's formal empire.

Leslie Bethell
Director
Centre for Brazilian Studies
University of Oxford

Oliver Marshall
General Editor
Britain and Brazil Series

Acknowledgments

In writing this book, I have been most fortunate to receive support and encouragement from friends, scholars, academic institutions, and funding agencies in the United States, Brazil, and Great Britain. I am especially indebted to the University of Minnesota's Department of History, in particular my doctoral advisor, Stuart B. Schwartz; to the MacArthur Interdisciplinary Program on Global Change, Sustainability and Justice; to the Fulbright Commission, for a year-long fellowship to carry out archival research in Brazil; to the Institute of Latin American Studies at the University of London and to the Centre for Brazilian Studies at Oxford University, for their vital support throughout the various stages of research and writing. I offer my keenest thanks to Zenita Guenther, Deborah Levison, Allen Isaacman, Robert McCaa, Ted Farmer, João José Reis, Geoffrey Jones, and particularly Leslie Bethell, for their thoughtful insights and generous encouragement over the years. I am grateful to Oliver Marshall for his editorial comments, and to all the other friends at St. Antony's College, Oxford, and London. In their different ways, each helped to make my year as a Visiting Research Associate at the Centre for Brazilian Studies into the remarkably illuminating and productive experience that it was.

My efforts to understand the inner workings of this fascinating community of adventurous expatriates have led me to consider the implications of this sort of historical investigation for the current issue of cross-cultural understanding in an increasingly globalized world. By this I mean, at least, the non-destructive engagement of differences. In his book, *An Intimate History of Humanity* (1994), Oxford historian Theodore Zeldin has suggested that a more human history is needed, one that attempts to place the events of the public sphere – be they political, economic, or social – more in the background, looking instead to discover as much as possible about what he calls "the gossamer world of intimate relations".[1] In seeking such quasi-ecological resonances between the whole person of the past and that of the present, between subject and viewer in dynamic relationship, we may try to find some way through to a more compassionate future.

'Bahia'

The place name 'Bahia' is commonly used to refer to both the city of Salvador da Bahia and the vast rural province surrounding it. In this study, the name in the former sense is used except where otherwise noted.

Introduction

The society of this city is considered superior to that of Rio de Janeiro, and the families appear to maintain a more social intercourse with strangers. [...] Bahia is considered by the English merchants a more agreeable place of residence than any of the maritime towns of the Brazil.

James Henderson, *A History of the Brazil* (1821), pp. 338–46

For what we seek in the study of interpersonal relations is not very different from that which we seek in the study of shocks between antagonistic socio-cultural systems – intercultural shocks – since systems are made up of people, who in turn are inseparable from such systems, within which they change from individuals to persons.[1]

Gilberto Freyre, *Ingleses no Brasil* (1948), p. 34

This book has several objectives. It closely examines how Latin America became incorporated into the world economic and political system of the nineteenth century, which was largely dominated by Great Britain up until World War I. Economic historians have long referred to this process as the British "informal empire" in Latin America.[2] I believe that this implicit analogy to the formal British colonial structures of Africa and Asia later in the century is historically inappropriate in several important ways, not least because it tends to subsume the Latin American experience of independence into the global, sun-never-sets pervasiveness of the mature British Empire.

According to the informal empire thesis, Spanish and Portuguese America underwent a generally linear process through which Iberian imperial dominance was replaced by British imperial dominance during independence, and in its turn this British influence was replaced by that of the United States after World War I. Brazil was a very important

1

trading partner for Great Britain throughout the period with which this study is concerned. The informal-empire model serves to explain many of the overall changes in world trade flows over two or three centuries. However it does not really take into account what was happening between Brazilians and Britons throughout the nineteenth century, and most importantly, *how* this happened on a day-to-day basis, the uncertainties that were constantly struggled with, and the broad changes that took place in relationships over time. I wish to reconstruct, as far as possible, this far messier – and in many ways more interesting – process.

The story of Brazil in the eighteenth and nineteenth centuries is broadly understood as a gradual transition from a colonial, slave-based, Northeastern-centered sugar colony to an independent, Southeastern-centered, 'modernized' nation initially through the expansion of precious minerals extraction, then coffee exports and ultimately financial and industrial development.[3] Existing studies of British influence in Brazil, therefore, have tended to focus on the ways in which British capital – and British political pressure – helped to move this process forward. However, during the early decades of the nineteenth century, precisely the years when Brazil was negotiating its independent status with respect to Portugal, the northeastern province of Bahia had regained its economic preeminence (though temporarily, as it turned out) due to the exhaustion of the richest gold deposits of Minas Gerais. Coffee production in the southeast of Brazil did not become intensely important to the country's economy until the 1840s, and the transatlantic slave trade – Bahia's economic lifeline – would not be fully abolished until the 1850s.[4] The British were well aware of the economic importance of Bahia to the Portuguese empire (Chapter 1), and it is no mystery that many British merchants chose to settle there rather than in Rio de Janeiro or Pernambuco due to the many economic, material, and social advantages Bahia had to offer (Chapter 3). Additionally, in the early 1820s Bahia was the only major city where actual battles were fought between pro-royalist and pro-independence forces, with unpredictable results for British interests, and for British individuals (Chapter 2).

The situation of the British merchant communities in Brazil was both more complicated and better documented than was the case for those in the war-torn nations of former Spanish America. Because of the transfer of the Portuguese court to Rio de Janeiro in 1808, Brazil's transition to political independence was far less violent than for most of

Spanish America; even in Bahia, the fighting did not escalate to the point of complete societal disruption. Therefore the delicate social processes with which this study is concerned were better able to develop in Brazil (without too much discontinuity) and more of the relevant documentation has survived (sources are discussed below). These processes are explored in detail in Chapters 4, 5, and 6. The complexity of the British relationship to colonial Brazil makes it useful to study each side's various moves and countermoves, from the transfer of the court, through Independence, and up until the final abolition of the slave trade.

As a longtime ally of Portugal, the British faced a more restrictive set of options concerning Brazilian Independence than they did for the ex-Spanish colonies. As historian W.H. Koebel remarked in 1917:

> It was surely one of the anomalies of statesmanship that gained for England the simultaneous gratitude of Brazil and the Spanish-speaking States. She had assisted the former in her step from a royal colony to a kingdom; she had aided the latter to divest themselves of royalty and its influence by becoming republics![5]

British strategies for supporting the independence of Portuguese America were more subtle and more risky, because the British government could not afford to alienate Portugal altogether. Brazil holds a unique position in the roster of post-colonial nations. The phenomenon of the transfer of the Portuguese court to Rio de Janeiro, from 1808 to 1821, meant that Brazil was, and still is, the only ex-colony to have served as the seat of government for its own imperial metropole. The political, social, and psychological implications of this are profound, and have been credited with Brazil's ability to remain united as a single nation while most of Spanish America rapidly broke up into multiple independent countries; the United States fought a civil war in response to a similar fracture in the mid-nineteenth century. The British presence in Brazil began with the creation of this unique political circumstance, as thousands of courtiers and all the machinery of government were reliant upon a British naval escort to flee the Napoleonic invasion of Portugal. This circumstance adds to the richness of the historical situation faced by individual British subjects in Brazil, as they – no less than the Brazilians – continually tried to make sense of their new social and political surroundings, and to develop a sense of identity to match these changing contexts, while keeping their businesses solvent on a daily basis.

The Keyhole Effect

This study employs an interdisciplinary method based on the case-study approach, exploring in considerable detail social relationships 'on the ground'. In this way, the economic figures of 'informal empire' become more humanized and susceptible to critical inquiry.[6] This case-study approach works well to reveal the types of processes that were taking place as the broader and better-known international economic structures gradually developed. In this way, it is my hope to contribute to a broad historical redefinition of how Latin America's relationships to Europe were formed, defined, contested, and renegotiated over the half-century during which the newest postcolonial nations evolved their independent identities in relation to the rest of the world – a world dominated by the commercial and political networks of Great Britain.

Perhaps more importantly, this careful anthropological examination of the internal dynamics of a non-imperial British merchant community throws into relief the cultural mechanisms through which the merchants managed to survive a foreign immersion without losing the sense of British identity that kept them able to function. As such, it offers a useful counterfactual for studies of British expatriate communities elsewhere, during the early nineteenth century, when British merchant adventurers were laying the foundations for the modern-day globalized economy.[7] The same paradoxical combination of overt self-isolation with subtle adaptation to difference, with its attendant discourse of otherness and self-protective measures that often backfired in terms of health, occurred as well in the formally imperial settings of Africa and Asia. Could this mean that it was not a function of ruling-class behaviors, but rather of relatively more innocent cultural norms and their particular chemistry under expatriate circumstances?

My argument, broadly stated, is that the British community of Bahia was a construct – social, cultural, and psychological – with a specific history. The image of the community was consolidated, during the first half of the nineteenth century, in a slow process involving careful and calculated assessments as much as less-conscious conflicts and redefinitions. Its overall objective was the short-term commercial success of its members. In the service of this goal, British women were brought to Bahia, British-identified families were created and nurtured, and strong opinions were formed regarding the necessary stance toward Brazilians. British-Brazilian concubinage was accepted or condemned according to circumstance, and a keen, almost over-British, way of being characterized the behavior of the expatriates, in the process capturing the imagination of the Brazilians among whom they lived. The short-term profit emphasis pervaded the British community's decisions regarding politics (whether to support Independence) and economics (whether to invest in the illegal slave trade). This takes dependency and informal-empire theories to task, for they not infrequently assume the presence of long-range planning and conspiratorial intentionality from within the metropole. A more useful question may be whether the British merchants were representing the metropole at all – as seen from their own perspective.

The appearances of 'community' were at first staged with the conscious objective of rendering the British presence in Bahia more respectable to Brazilian eyes, thus improving the chances for successful commercial relations as well as creating a safer emotional environment for the foreigners (Chapter 5). Despite appearances, there was no inherently cohesive group of British subjects in Bahia during the first half of the nineteenth century. However, with the passing of decades and the advent of ideas about modernization, it became increasingly useful for British merchants and Brazilian elites to construct and revere the cultural superiority of the *ingleses* – the English, so that by the end of the century the high society of Rio de Janeiro consciously sought to imitate northern European upper-middle-class lifestyles.[8]

Looking from the ground up, it quickly becomes apparent that the British presence in Bahia was highly heterogeneous, and was only transformed into a recognizable community through a slow and often carefully orchestrated process of self-identification and image management. The group's principal element was the British wholesale merchant, who imported manufactured goods (mainly textiles) for sale to Brazilians, and handled most of the exports of sugar and cotton to Europe as a middleman. A handful of firms dominated the British commerce of Bahia, so that an internal social hierarchy was established. At the top were the most successful merchants and their families; then, established British professionals such as doctors and diplomats; next came the less successful wholesale merchants; and below them were the British clerks, who were usually unmarried. Outside of this structure were a small number of British retail merchants, occasional Irish working-class transients or colonists, assorted visitors and artists, and finally engineers and railroad workers late in the century. The internal dynamics of this heterogeneous group are examined in Chapter 4, and their interactions with Brazilians – especially the bonds formed between women and men – are studied in Chapters 5 and 6. Throughout the study, the emphasis is squarely upon personal processes.

This book takes an original approach. Broadly speaking, most of the economic histories of British influence in Latin America have not taken into account the personal processes related to effective self-identification that are at the heart of this study, despite the obvious necessity of this to the success of the commercial endeavor. Social histories of the British in Latin America are few and far between,[9] with almost none that speak to the early development of their urban communities over the first half of the nineteenth century. The problems associated with sexuality and gender roles are also usually ignored, although some of the most interesting recent work in the sociological, historical, and anthropological literature of the British Empire ('post-colonial') feature these themes prominently.[10]

There is minimal understanding as to how the broad economic processes of British international commercial expansion was dependant on the constant renegotiation of individual relationships and communal images in the various parts of the world where merchant communities took root and thrived. How, exactly, did this new entity – the British expatriate community of newly independent Latin America – gain weight and character over time, and become so economically successful?

Sources

Research for this study has focused on the political and the social aspects of the British presence in Brazil, particularly Bahia. At the National Archives (NA) – formerly the Public Record Office – in London, diplomatic correspondence was examined from British consuls in Bahia, including detailed analyses of the political vicissitudes of the Independence period, as well as the semi-annual reports of British shipping showing the nature and value of imports and exports up until Independence. (After 1824, the reports ceased to show the name of the consigning firm as well as the value of the cargo.) Documents generated by Bahian government officials and sent to the British consul are also preserved at the National Archives. In Brazil, the Arquivo do Estado da Bahia (AEB) yielded correspondence between the British consul and the President of Bahia and various judicial officials; records of property bought and sold by British subjects; and listings of petitioners for permanent residency and citizenship. At the Arquivo Municipal de Salvador (AMS), deeds of slave purchase were examined. Results here, however, were entirely negative for British subjects, despite overwhelming evidence that they owned domestic slaves as a matter of course, and were quite heavily involved in financing Bahia's slave trade (Chapter 2). At the Arquivo da Cúria Metropolitana de Salvador, the marriage records for the Catholic Victoria parish also revealed no recognizably British names, although the convention of de-Anglicizing names in such circumstances may have rendered invisible whatever Protestant-to-Catholic conversions that may have occurred (Chapters 3 and 4).[11]

Commercial almanacs from early in the century were found in the library of the Associação Comercial da Bahia. A rich source for social history is the archive of what is now the Igreja Episcopal Anglicana do Brasil (IEA), in Salvador, containing the original records of baptisms, marriages, and burials of the Protestant community of Bahia for the years 1836 to 1873. Despite some water damage to the parchment, enough is available to reconstruct a limited number of family trees, giving an idea of family structure, intermarriage, and demographic patterns related to age and gender. Finally, the tombstone inscriptions at Bahia's British Cemetery allow for a more personal look at how specific British individuals lived, died, and were remembered by survivors.

A comparative reading of British travel narratives from Brazil in the first half of the nineteenth century made it possible to contrast portraits of the British communities around Brazil. Many of these books also presented unusually revealing choices of appropriate subjects, and ways of phrasing comments, that made possible the psychological and cross-cultural investigations of Chapters 4, 5, and 6. One of the most important discoveries was a book written by Dr. Robert Dundas, physician to Bahia's British community for 25 years, from 1819 to 1844.[12] Although its title suggests that the book is a scientific treatise on tropical medicine, it is also a well-written and carefully thought-out analysis of the dynamics operating among the British residents of Bahia, in particular the relationship between living habits and their perceptions of the climate. Secondary works by Brazilian, British, and American authors are also used throughout the study, both for the information that they directly contain, and for what they convey about the authors' critical perspectives.

Chapter 1

British Commercial and Political Influence in Bahia

By the early nineteenth century, Portugal ruled a worldwide commercial and colonial empire whose most important asset was Brazil. In order to understand the context into which the British merchants entered upon their arrival in Bahia, it is necessary to know a few general points of the economic history of Brazil. From the early years of its existence as a Portuguese colony, Brazil provided the metropole with profits, initially through its exports of brazilwood felled by Indians, both free and enslaved. By the late sixteenth century, sugar plantations had been established in the northeastern captaincies of Bahia and Pernambuco using the labor of slaves imported from Portuguese factories and colonies in Africa. The northeastern sugar plantations provided profits to Portuguese (and, from 1624 to 1654, Dutch) overlords throughout the colonial period and well into the nineteenth century.[1]

During the eighteenth century, rich gold and diamond deposits were discovered in Minas Gerais, in the vast backlands of southeastern Brazil. This set off a southward shift in the internal economic structure of the colony. During the gold rush, slaves and capital flowed south, and the Portuguese metropole refocused its fiscalization efforts toward Minas Gerais and São Paulo, moving Brazil's administrative capital out of Bahia and into the southeastern port of Rio de Janeiro in 1763. By the 1770s, however, the gold rush had reached its point of diminishing returns. There followed a brief period during the first half of the nineteenth century when the northeastern sugar-producing regions of Bahia and Pernambuco regained the lead in productive export. By the middle of the nineteenth century, when the slave trade to Brazil was permanently ended, the lead was lost once again to southeastern coffee interests and Brazilian industrialization, both of which were increasingly based on European immigrant labor. By the time slavery was abolished in 1888, the northeastern provinces had fallen into a state of decadence that contrasted sharply to their former splendor. These processes of regional change have led to the sharp north-south disparities in development and levels of wealth which still characterize Brazil today.

This was the situation into which the British community entered in 1808, after the Portuguese emperor João VI had escaped Napoleon's invasion of Lisbon by fleeing to Rio de Janeiro under a British naval escort. He brought with him the entire imperial court and most of the royal treasury. One British observer remarked that if circumstances had been different, Bahia might well have been chosen to be the seat of empire:

> The favorable disposition of the prince-regent himself toward the city [of Bahia], was publicly expressed during his visit. Its situation, prospect, and importance, besides the beauty of the adjoining country, charmed him; he wished much to make it his residence; but political reasons, combined with the opinions of the ministry, set him down, not very contentedly, at Rio. I must confess I admire his taste.[2]

When the emperor Dom João VI arrived at Rio de Janeiro in 1808, he immediately opened the ports of Brazil to trade with all friendly nations, which in practice meant mostly Great Britain. Negotiating from a position of political strength, the British government obtained a favorable commercial treaty in 1810. Destined to become a point of seething controversy between Portuguese and British merchants throughout Brazil, the treaty allowed British manufactured goods to enter Brazil at a tariff of 15 per cent. This was one percentage point lower than that allotted to Portuguese imports, and nearly half the 28 per cent tariff rate for imports from all other foreign nations.[3]

British manufactures, mostly textiles, began to flood into the main ports of Brazil as merchants became established in wholesale trade all along the Brazilian coast. Napoleon's blockade of European continental ports intensified the process. Combined with the rapid saturation of the limited Latin American markets, British goods were sold at prices below marginal cost – a practice that in modern economic parlance is known as 'dumping' – until the blockade ended in the mid-1810s. By the 1820s, British merchant communities had become established in all of the main port cities of Brazil. In Bahia, its members would number about 120 by the mid-1840s.[4] Due to their position, the merchants wielded an influence disproportionate to their numbers. All

British subjects enjoyed the local support of privately administered British institutions sanctioned by the commercial treaty of 1810. These included a local consulate, private hospital, and Anglican place of worship. Each of these was financed by a tax levied on British commercial activity and administered by the city's local consulate.

Another important treaty concession from the Portuguese government to the British was the privilege to have lawsuits and other legal procedures involving its subjects handled through a special court of law, known as the Judge Conservator of the English Nation, instead of having to go through the local court system. The post of Judge Conservator was usually held by a native Luso-Brazilian barrister,[5] though one hand-picked by the British merchant community, who paid his salary and office expenses. The only time when a British subject could be forced to go through the local justice system was when he was caught *in flagrante delicto*, which did not often happen. The institution of Judge Conservator became one of the British privileges that most irritated the Brazilians. Tensions arising from these and other privileges gradually worsened over the decades, once the initial euphoria of independence had worn off. The British community of Bahia would soon become a target for anti-imperialist sentiment aimed at what the Brazilians perceived as a throwback to colonial days.

Commercial Activities of Bahia's British Community

The British government was well aware of the economic importance of Bahia to the Portuguese empire. The Bahia consulate was opened in 1810[6] and staffed by career diplomats through the late 1830s. The most notable of these was William Pennell (1818 to 1829), who had served at Bordeaux during the Napoleonic conflicts immediately before being posted to Bahia.[7] Due partly to this experience, Pennell would prove to be highly skillful at keeping British interests on a firm footing despite the rapid and violent political changes that plagued Bahia and Brazil throughout the early 1820s.

Great Britain had long enjoyed a peaceful and profitable relationship with Portugal and its empire,[8] and this enabled the British government to acquire information regarding the commercial potential of Bahia. Table 1 shows Portuguese–Brazilian trade data compiled from a report sent by the British consul at Lisbon to the Foreign Office in 1816.[9] The report maps out the volume of trade carried out between Portugal and each of its major colonial ports for that year, indicating Portugal's relative trade balances with the different parts of its empire. It shows clearly that Bahia was centrally important to Brazil in economic terms, and that Brazil was itself the mainstay of the Portuguese empire. In 1816, the colony was responsible for 78 per cent of Portugal's overall imports from its empire, and provided a market for nearly 72 per cent of Portugal's overall exports. Within Brazil, Bahia accounted for 29 and 26 per cent of total exports and imports from Portugal, respectively. Thus, Bahia alone generated 23 per cent of Portugal's overall imports from its worldwide empire in 1816, while consuming just under 19 per cent of its exports. Thus, the province was Portugal's leading creditor within the whole empire.

TABLE 1: Portugal's Balance Of Trade With The Main Ports Of Its Empire in 1816 [10]

Port	Value of Exports to Portugal	Value of Imports from Portugal	Portugal as Creditor(+) or Debtor (–)
Rio de Janeiro	6,444:000$000 [11] £1,530,641	7,456:000$000 £1,771,021	+ 1,412:000$000 £335,391
Bahia	**7,248:000$000 £1,721,615**	**6,823:000$000 £1,620,665**	**– 424:000$000 £100,712**
Pernambuco	6,291:000$000 £1,494,299	6,468:000$000 £1,536,342	+ 176:000$000 £41,805
Maranhão	2,986:000$000 £709,263	3,683:000$000 £874,821	+ 696:000$000 £165,320
Pará	1,398:000$000 £332,066	1,240:000$000 £294,536	+ 158:000$000 £37,529
Ceará	198:000$000 £47,030	87:000$000 £20,665	– 101:000$000 £23,990
Total for Brazil	**24,760:000$000 £5,881,235**	**25,760:000$000 £6,118,764**	**+ 1,601:000$000 £380,285**
Asia (all)	6,549:000$000 £1,555,581	8,587:000$000 £2,039,667	+ 2,038:000$000 £484,085
Islands off coast of Africa	872:000$000 £207,125	1,290:000$000 £306,413	+ 417:000$000 £99,049
Total for Portuguese Empire	**31,594:000$000 £7,504,513**	**35,922:000$000 £8,532,541**	**+ 4,327:000$000 £1,027,790**

Note: Sterling equivalencies shown for the main figures have been calculated using the 1823 exchange rate of £1 = 4$210 (4.21 milréis).[12]

While Table 1 illustrates Bahia's potential lucrativeness to British merchant interests, the reality of British success in the import-export trade of Bahia depended on individual performance of firms. By 1855, British wholesale merchants would control at least 62 per cent of Bahia's import-export trade.[13] Merchant firms were established in Bahia as early as 1810, and worked steadily through the decade to become powerful economic players in the import-export trade of the province. The data for Table 2, below, is gathered from a variety of sources, and identifies the absolute values of commercial activities in which the British merchants of Bahia were engaged from about 1810 to 1821.[14] The dip in value of British imports between 1810 and 1815 can probably be accounted for by Napoleon's blockade of European ports,

TABLE 2: British Economic Activity in Bahia, 1808–1821[15]

Year	Imports Into Bahia by British Firms	Exports From Bahia by British Firms
1808	815:047$890[16] £193,598	219:332$650[17] £52,098
1809	1,394:327$836 £331,194	1,223:085$640[18] £290,519
1810	1.775:030$480 £421,622	n/a
1815	534:088$400 £126,861	n/a
1816	1,513:205$900 £359,431	n/a
1817	1,731:098$600 £411,187	n/a
1818	2,107:357$000 £500,559	n/a
1819	1,375:119$901 £326,631	1,382:337$900 £328,346
1820	1,810:716$600 £430,098	1,923:684$000 £456,932
1821	1,783:753$700 £423,694	1,777:567$500 £422,225

during which British manufactures had to be sold at low prices in saturated markets all over South America. After 1815, the absolute value of British commercial activity again began to increase steadily. This was a trend that would continue well into mid-century, with clear implications for the social and economic status of individual merchants in Bahia, their families, and the community which they gradually built over this period of time.

Despite the almost continuous political turmoil during the period leading up to Independence, the absolute value of Bahia's imports of British manufactures climbed steadily between 1815 and 1821. If we take the year 1816 as a point of intersection of Tables 1 and 2, it appears that the imports of manufactured goods by the British merchants residing in Bahia were equivalent to 22 per cent of the total volume of goods that Bahia imported from Portugal in the same year. This is a substantial figure for a port that had been closed to commerce with nations other than Portugal, the colonial metropole, for all but the previous eight years of its history.

By taking the analysis to the level of individual firms, the distribution of wealth and power within the merchant group can be taken as a means to identify the main players of Bahia's British merchant community, and thus to illuminate its internal social organization. Table 3 shows the percentage of British trade controlled by each firm in the years immediately preceding Independence. These Board of Trade records provide company-specific information concerning the value and nature of incoming and outgoing cargo for every British shipment that put into port at Bahia during those years.

The vast majority of British imports were recorded simply as "general cargo", an expression that in practice meant manufactures and particularly textiles, according to remarks elsewhere in the consular correspondence. British imports into Bahia consisted of English cotton and woolen cloth, porcelain, glassware, flatware, saddlery, clothing, and some foodstuffs.[19] Much of what the British sold in Bahia would be considered luxury goods, although some of these items were also made available at lower grades of quality. Lower-priced imports by smaller British firms included wine, wheat, and olive oil from Spain and Gibraltar; codfish from Newfoundland; hides and dried beef from Argentina; one shipment of "natural curiosities" from Rio de Janeiro en route to Amsterdam; and in two instances, unspecified amounts of cash from London and Sierra Leone, the British colony in West Africa.[20]

TABLE 3: Proportional Share of Firms in British Commerce, Bahia, 1819–1821[21]

Name	British Imports (%)	British Exports (%)
Boothby Johnston & Co	14.3	7.2
Gilfillan Bros. & Co.	8.5	9.7
Harrison Latham & Co.	0.5	3.7
Mello Branford & Co.	5.2	5.3
Mellors & Russell	14.2	9.3
Miller Nicholson & Co.	1.4	5.2
Moir & Co.	4.9	16.8
Pringle & Astley	4.9	3.6
Ralph Brown	1.3	2.6
Schwind Schmell & Co.	0.2	0.4
Sealy Duncan & Walker	29.3	15.6
Smaller British firms and individuals	2.9	3.5

Exports shipped from Bahia on British ships mainly consisted of sugar and cotton, with an occasional load of brazilwood or foodstuffs bound for another South American port. By contrast, the handful of Portuguese merchants (Table 4, below) who used British ships for their commerce typically imported foodstuffs and exported tobacco. From this it may be inferred that British commercial and shipping activity generally served to reinforce Bahia's previous colonial role as net exporter of primary products and net importer of European manufactures.[22]

TABLE 4: Luso-Brazilian Agents Consigning Cargo on British Ships, 1819–1821[23]

Name	British Imports (%)	British Exports (%)
João Miguel Dias de Faria	0.7	1.4
Joze Antonio Ruiz Vianna	0.6	1.2
Nobre & Sobrinho	2.0	2.9
Smaller Luso-Brazilian firms and individuals	1.3	1.7

Immediately before Independence, the British merchant community was made up of about twelve large firms, along with nine or ten smaller partnerships and individuals. An indication of the uneven distribution of wealth within the community is that nearly 58 per cent of imports were controlled by the three largest import firms: Sealy Duncan & Walker, Boothby Johnston & Co., and Mellors & Russell. Sealy Duncan was an important exporter as well as an importer, and combined with Moir & Co. and Gilfillan Bros. to handle just over 42 per cent of British exports. Thus, within the merchant community a handful of firms managed the lion's share of commercial activity, and tended towards specialization in either imports or exports.

Shipping patterns varied according to the firm's financial leverage and the nature of its trade. Individual shipments tended to fluctuate in value, ranging from less than 2:000$000 (two *contos*, about £475 at the time) up to a staggering 149:350$381 (£35,475).[24] Moir & Co., with more shipments per year than any other firm, was the single largest exporter with 16.8 per cent of overall British exports, but it handled only 4.9 per cent of imports. The vast majority of Moir's ships arrived in ballast and immediately returned to England laden with sugar. In one interesting case, a single shipment worth 100:572$311 (£23,889) was consigned to Gilfillan Bros., a company that handled only 8.5 per cent of total British imports and whose shipments were usually small, showing a pattern of multiple stops in Brazilian ports on any given voyage. It is not clear why they would have concentrated so much value in a single shipment. The number of shipments for any given firm could fluctuate widely from year to year. Sealy Duncan received eight shipments in 1819 and eighteen the following year. Conditions for intercontinental trade in this pre-steamship era were precarious, with storms, shipwrecks, piracy, and enemy military operations all adding to the overall risk. The case of the *Wellington* shipwreck, off the coast of the province of Bahia, offers an illustration of these risks: its British owner managed to salvage just 1:171$220 (£278) of its cargo, on which he then was required to pay import duty.[25]

Life in Bahia: Interactions with Luso-Brazilians

To balance the risks involved in their international commercial activities, many British merchants diversified their investments. Real estate records from the early nineteenth century provide an illustration of what was done with excess capital under conditions of scarce banking facilities and uncertain political circumstances.[26] These documents show purchases of land and buildings by British individuals, as well as private loans, rental agreements, and an occasional limited partnership contract. Five substantial loans by British merchant firms to Luso-Brazilians are listed for the period, ranging from 2:188$293 (£520) to 8:600$763 (£2,043) in value.[27] It is probably safe to assume that British merchants made many other smaller loans to Luso-Brazilians without going through official channels. One interesting transaction was the establishment of a partnership between João Ferreira Guedes and the British firm Sealy Roach & Toole, who in 1811 jointly opened a fabric retail store. This venture was unusual, for in nineteenth-century Bahia the British merchants were textile wholesalers while Luso-Brazilians took care of retail, generally speaking. Because of the sharp social distinction between wholesale and retail merchants, it is rather surprising that a British firm should have been forged such an official connection to the retail market soon after its first arrival in Bahia. This was not to be the typical British mode of operation as the merchant community gradually developed a tendency to keep to itself, proud of its superior status. The merchants were to choose partners for business and marriage from among their fellow expatriates, and to hire British clerks to staff their shops.[28]

Nevertheless, a careful look at real estate transactions for the pre-independence period reinforces the idea that the successful British merchants gradually developed closer social ties with the local community. The real estate record for the earliest years of the British presence in Bahia reveals their strong preference to rent rather than buy. The first recorded rental took place when Frederick Lindeman, Bahia's first British consul, rented "houses and land in the area of Brotas" upon arriving in 1810.[29] That same year, George Sealy of Sealy Duncan Walker & Co. rented a large house in the area of Nazaré from Manoel José Vilela de Carvalho.[30] After five years, the same Carvalho also rented a house in Nazaré to Richard Latham, a partner in the firm Harrison Latham & Co. In another five years, in 1820, Latham rented another house in the Lower City, Bahia's main commercial neighborhood.[31] The recurrence of names suggests the evolution of local connections involving business interests with a degree of personal trust, which could have continued to expand until the merchant community was well-integrated into the local social fabric, should the British have found this a desirable way to proceed. What they would ultimately choose, however, was a different path – one of self-separation, isolation, and the cultivation of an uneasy attitude toward the society that enveloped them on almost every side.

Further evidence suggesting that social approximation was taking place between the British and Luso-Brazilians during the 1810s are the locally-owned businesses that used British shipping for their own import-export activity, in particular Nobre & Sobrinho, João Miguel Dias de Faria, and Joze Antonio Ruiz Vianna (Table 4). Although the majority of British shipping activity did not involve local agents, the fact that a few were consistent customers does indicate that the British were able to earn acceptance and a degree of loyalty within the local community. In the later years of the decade, as native Brazilians agitated for independence from Portugal, the Luso-Brazilian elements loyal to Portugal would become divided over the benefits and drawbacks of allowing the British to maintain their privileged position in the commerce of Bahia.

According to property transactions records (see Table 5), George Sealy was the first British merchant to actually purchase a house in Bahia, in 1816. The house was located on the peninsula of Itapagipe, an attractive promontory jutting into the Bay of All Saints, north of the main town. Not long afterwards, in the midst of the social and political upheaval engulfing Brazil as a consequence of Portugal's civil revolution of 1820, Moir & Co. became the first British company officially to sell a house in Bahia. The buyer was João Miguel Dias de Faria, one of the Luso-Brazilians who had regularly conducted business with the British (see Table 4). Between 1820 and 1824, no records of property transactions can be found for British residents. This may be one result of the intense political turmoil, uncertainty, and violence that pervaded Bahia during the four years spanning the civil revolution in Portugal and the separation of Brazil from the Portuguese Empire.

Nevertheless, this record may be misleading. It is quite possible that some British subjects simply chose not to leave a paper trail of their financial transactions. One type of property transaction that is conspicuously missing from the record of British economic activity in Bahia is that of slave purchases.[32] In this period of vigorous British abolitionist activity, all subjects of Great Britain were forbidden to own slaves after 1817, no matter where they lived in the world. And yet, in the testimonies generated by court records concerning the abortive urban slave uprising of 1835 known as the Malês rebellion,[33] several leaders of the revolt were identified as the property of British merchants residing in the Vitória neighborhood, including Mellors, Russell, and Moir. Official records clearly do not tell the full story.[34]

Other sources reveal that relations between the British and the Brazilians were unstable and changed rapidly in response to the various interventions of the British government in Brazilian affairs. A key source demonstrating the personal impact of this changing relationship is found in a manuscript letter written by Charles Fraser, an adventurous English gentleman, to Lord Castlereagh in 1812 so as to give an illuminating picture of Luso-Brazilian relations with the British around that time. Fraser came to Brazil with the first British arrivals in 1808 and made his way overland from Rio de Janeiro to Porto Seguro, on the coast of the province of Bahia, but hundreds of kilometers south of the provincial capital. There he purchased property in the most isolated place he could find, being "the only settler in the extent of 20 leagues of seacoast,"[35] and immediately began a one-man effort to civilize the local Patachó Indians. He made repeated attempts to inspire British philanthropists to support his efforts, in the belief that Brazil's relations to Great Britain could best be improved by ceasing the abolitionist crusade. He thought that resources should be directed instead to persuade the local Indian populations to provide the labor needed to develop Brazil, as the Jesuits had been trying to do until their expulsion by the Marquis of Pombal's reforms in 1759.

Fraser's high level of education and upper-class background are reflected in the fact that he was a personal friend of Foreign Secretary Lord Castlereagh. Fraser sent Castlereagh a remarkable letter, providing a well-informed assessment of the political, economic, and demographic situation of Brazil during this crucial time in its developing relationship to Great Britain.[36] In his travels, Fraser had made eloquent efforts to engage not only the Indians, but also the Luso-Brazilians, sometimes with comical results; and he was constantly amazed at the mutual ignorance that the British and the Luso-Brazilians suffered with respect to each other:

> The extreme ignorance in which the inhabitants of Brazil & of Spanish America, had been studeously kept by the old policy of their respective Governments, together with their awe of the Church & belief in its infallibility, had succeeded so well that 90 parts of 100 of the Inhabitants of Brazil are ignorant at this day that there is eve

TABLE 5: Real Property Transactions by British Subjects, 1810–1850[37]

Year	Type of Transaction	Description of Property	Owner	Transferred (sold, rented, or mortgaged) to:
1810	Lease for hire (*arrendamento*)[38]	Land and houses in Brotas	Mª Fª [Maria Francisca] da Conceição Aragão	Frederico [Frederick] **Lindeman**
1810	Lease for hire	Large house in Nazaré	Manuel Jose Vilela de Carvalho	Jorge [George] **Sealy & Co.**
1815	Lease for hire	Houses in Nazaré	Manoel José Vilela de Carvalho	Ricardo [Richard] **Latham**
1816	Sale	House in Itapagipe	Caetano José Gomes de Sta. Rita	George **Sealy**
1820	Lease for hire	House in Cidade Baixa [downtown]	Ponciana Isabel de Freitas	**Harrison Latham & Co.**
1820	Sale	House in Giquitaia	**Moir & Co.**	João Miguel Dias de Faria
1824	Sale	Lot in Victoria	Mª [Maria] da Boa Hora and others	Carlos [Charles] **Russell**
1824	Sale	Lot and ruined house in Victoria	Carlos [Charles] **Russell**	João [John] **Yonds**
1826	Sale	House on road from Victoria to Porto da Barra	Joaquina Candida de Souza	Guilherme [William] **Pennell**
1827	Mortgage	House	Guilherme [William] **Pennell**	**Sealy**
1829	Mortgage	Lot in Porto da Barra	Guilherme [William] **Pennell**	João Batista Fetal
1830	Sale	Lot in Victoria	Vicente Luís Gonçalves Ferreira	William A. **Candler**
1831	Sale	Lot in Victoria	José Francisco Lopes	Guilerme [William] **Candler**
1833	Lease for hire	Lot in Barra	Convent of São Bento	João Henrique [John Henry] **Lambert**

(continued)

TABLE 5: *Continued*

Year	Type of Transaction	Description of Property	Owner	Transferred (sold, rented, or mortgaged) to:
1834	Mortgage	House in Barra valued at 4:000$000	Manoel Gonçalves de Oliveira Vasconcelos	Frederico [Frederick] **Robilliard**
1834	Mortgage	Lot in Barra valued at 2:000$000	João Felipe [John Philip] Henning	João Henrique [John Henry] **Lambert**
1834	Lease for hire	Lot in Barra (6 braças)	Monastery of Graça	Roberto [Robert] **Paterson**
1834	Rental	House in Algibes	Joaquim José da Fonseca	Heyworth **Crabtree**
Not given (probably 1836)	Sale	House on Rua São José [downtown]	Tomasia de Souza Paraiso	João Jardiner [John **Gardiner**]
1837	Mortgage	House in Nazaré	Henrique [Henry] Samuel **Marback**	José Antonio Ferreira
1837	Sale	Lot and house on Victoria Road	Narciza **Yonds**	Joaquim Inácio da Costa
Not given (probably 1836–1839)	Sale	House in Canela	Pedro Cerqueira Lima and wife	Roberto [Robert] **Paterson**
Not given (probably 1839)	Sale	House in Canela	Roberto [Robert] **Paterson** Senior	**Irontide Napier & Co.**
1840	Sale	Land in Cachoeira	Felipe Adolfo Plessing	Henrique [Henry] **Behrens**
1840	Mortgage	Casa – São Francisco de Paula	Antônio Cosme Bahiano	**Dalglish MacNab & Co.**
1840	Sale	Ranch (*fazenda*) in Juazeiro	Jonatas **Abott** and others	João Duarte Bruno Camargo
1846	Sale	House on Rua da Faísca [downtown]	José Jesuino Alves da Silva	Tomaz Melo [possibly Thomas **Mellor**]
1847	Sale	Lot in Preguiça [downtown]	José Caetano da Costa	David **Lindgren**
1848[39]	Sale	40$000 – Lot and ruined house in Rio Vermelho	Jozé Ferreira Guimarães and wife	Thomaz [Thomas] **Mellor**

a Parliament in G. Britain [Brazilians have been] deprived entirely of the opportunities of knowledge diffused by the Press in regions more fortunate, not only by the restraints of their Govt. but by their own ignorant & illiterate condition.[40]

The usual British attitude, on the other hand, was described as a "perseverance in that blind & infatuated system of ignorance of & disregard in our Govt. for the interests, habits ... & even prejudices of the people of other Countrys [*sic*]". This, said Fraser, was damaging Great Britain's image in Brazil, and causing irreparable harm to its political interests.

Interestingly, Fraser was able to distinguish between different categories of Luso-Brazilians. As a result of what must have been a long series of thoughtful conversations with many different people, he studied their responses to British actions, and offered sympathetic explanations as to why their attitude might soon become a problem for British interests in Brazil:

> The merchants, shop-keepers & artificers of Brazil (chiefly natives of Portugal) were highly dissatisfied & exasperated against us on account of the free introduction of British manufactures & British subjects among them [while] the natives & cultivators of the soil were our friends. But [...] the late captures & interruption of the African trade, & the consequent scarcity & high price of Negroes, have caused a total change in the sentiments of the latter, & have united all descriptions of the inhabitants of Brazil in one sentiment of detestation not only of the British subjects, but have rendered the gov.t & the very name of Britain odious in the country.

The point against abolitionism was made to support Fraser's project of civilizing the Indians. It is interesting that he makes the almost Marxist-sounding distinction between urban Luso-Brazilians loyal to Portugal, who competed commercially with the privileged British merchants, and the rural Brazilian-born planter elite, who benefited from shipping and credit services provided by the British. The fact of this realization may suggest that the Foreign Office was watching for signs of an independence movement in Brazil as early as 1812. When that conflict did finally materialize in Bahia eleven years later, the "natives and cultivators of the soil" in the *recôncavo* (the sugar-growing areas around the Bay of All Saints) would indeed attract

British support, while the Portuguese-born merchants in the urban center would attack the British community in the press and try to have their privileges revoked.

A final remark by Fraser suggests that he saw signs of a sort of contest for the hearts and minds of Luso-Brazilians taking place at that moment between Great Britain and France:

> While [British abolitionist activities have alienated Luso-Brazilians,] they have in the varied proportion increased & revived their partiality for France, in so much that if by any accident a few thousand only of their troops should land in Brazil, I fear that they would be received with open arms by the mass of the people, and their country might be lost for ever to G. Britain.[41]

Fraser was looking ahead not only to the possibility of Brazil's independence, but also to the possibility that France would take advantage of anti-British sentiment to establish its own political dominance in Brazil. In the independence conflicts of 1822–23, French forces were indeed watchfully present in Brazilian ports, alongside British naval vessels; but no direct involvement or conflict appears to have occurred – in fact, a French naval officer stationed in Bahia gallantly offered protection to British subjects on board his vessel, should it be needed.[42] Nevertheless, Fraser's predictions, based as they were on his thoughtful experience and questioning of actual Luso-Brazilians, provide a counter-factual to enhance historians' understanding of the process of Brazilian independence.

In the meantime, well-to-do British residents were keenly aware of what they saw as the hardships involved in living in Bahia during this time. An anecdote from the consular records demonstrates their anxiety, and illuminates one case in particular, that of William Pennell, about whom we will hear more later on. In 1822, a petition was sent to the Foreign Office by the British merchants of Bahia, who declared that Consul Pennell's salary of £300 per year plus one-third of the total consulage tax collection – which in 1818 and 1821 yielded enough to provide Pennell with a clear bonus of 5:379$723 (£1,278) and 6:992$843 (£1,661), respectively – was insufficient to compensate for the hardships involved in fulfilling his post in a 'becoming manner'.[43] Considering that an income of 1:000$000 was sufficient to live very comfortably in Bahia, one must wonder how much of a becoming manner was considered necessary by the British community as adequate for comfort and protection, and why this was so. Something to keep in mind is that William Pennell's health had deteriorated so much after his arrival in Bahia that he was in the most extreme pain throughout the Independence period and into the late 1820s.

The record of consular correspondence and secondary sources tells the following story. Pennell arrived in Bahia in 1818, motivated by money and career. His health began to deteriorate in 1821, and by 1822 he was anxious for the presence of an Anglican chaplain. Meanwhile the independence conflicts of 1820–23 made ever increasing demands upon his skill and patience, just as his body became weakened and the illnesses added enormously to his difficulties. His doctor insisted that he return to England, but Pennell refused, believing that political circumstances made it necessary for him to remain despite the cost to himself. In fact, Pennell's skillful handling of the situation was arguably responsible for the controlled level of damage to the British community during the conflicts, as well as the ultimate positive outcome for British interests. However, on what basis can the motivations behind Pennell's actions be judged? He consistently acted in the interests of his country, but in direct violation of his own bodily needs, though his original decision to accept a posting at Bahia was connected to personal and material ambition.

It is worth pointing out the contrast between William Pennell's experience of losing his sense of a British identity while being seriously ill in a crowded city, and Charles Fraser's vigorous expressions of the intense patriotic drive he felt while living alone in the wild. For the purposes of this study, the information contained in their stories suggests that Pennell was weakened and exhausted by the constant squabbles and intrigues involved in negotiating British interests and upholding a British identity, and longed to escape the confrontation with the 'otherness' that surrounded him. By contrast, Fraser's physical and social isolation seemed to free him to focus on giving Britain the most useful service of which he considered himself capable, that of promoting harmony and mutual understanding between British subjects and Brazilians of every description, rather than turning inward and experiencing alienation from those around him. These ideas will be explored more fully in later chapters. For now, it is sufficient to point out the connection between large international political and economic processes, and the particular experiences of individuals, whose lives and subjective awareness affected and were affected by these processes.

British Political Maneuvers During the Independence Conflicts

When the ports of Brazil were opened to international trade in 1808, an intense change came about in the outlook of Brazilian-born elites. During the years 1808 to 1824, Brazil underwent the experience – without precedent in the New World – of being the seat of its own imperial metropole, after having been a closed colony for most of its history. The rapid influx of British merchants into the ports of Brazil was part and parcel of this change, as it was a British naval squadron that had made it possible for the entire court to make the transfer. The situation was so fluid that in many respects the Brazilians and British were strongly influenced by each other. These circumstances under which the independence conflicts took place in Bahia also affected individuals, and through these effects, a communal dynamic began to emerge. The British community reacted to the turmoil with varying degrees of involvement and restraint, and often went against official British policy in their actions, thus increasing internal tensions even further.

Rushing pell-mell into unfamiliar Brazilian port towns, desperately searching for markets for their merchandise, these British subjects did not know what would become of them if or when Brazil pursued its independence from Portugal. The narrative of merchant adventurer John Turnbull, for example, written in 1803 and published in 1813, made it clear that the possibility of a rich and independent Brazil beholden to Great Britain for political and economic guidance dangled before the profit-driven eyes of many merchants.[44] Parliament in London took a broad view in 1817:

> There can be no field of enterprise so magnificent in promise, so well calculated to raise sanguine hopes, so congenial to the most generous sympathies, so consistent with the best and highest interests of England as the vast continent of South America.[45]

These intoxicating possibilities seemed to be joyfully realized by 1825, when George Canning was able to declare in a letter to his friend Lord Granville, "Behold! the New World established and, if we do not throw it away, ours!"[46] There can be no question that the British government possessed an overriding intention of maintaining its hard-won economic and political foothold in Brazil, and that British merchants were prepared to reap the maximum advantages accruing to their privileged position.

However, no one knew in advance exactly how events would unfold. Would Brazil become wholly independent of Portugal? Would the political fate of Bahia match that of the rest of Brazil, or would it instead become an independent republic in its own right? Conversely, might Bahia – the only Brazilian city where Portuguese armies actually fought against independence – permanently become the last bastion of Portuguese empire in the Americas? The British consul at Bahia remained constantly aware of the many possible outcomes, and recommended to the Foreign Office an overall wait-and-see policy of neutrality toward both Brazilian and Portuguese elites. Pennell reserved just one possible scenario which in his view would require the immediate military intervention of the British navy in order to safeguard British interests – that of a social revolution.[47] As a result of this attitude, the smallest slave rebellions were watched carefully for signs of spreading to other centers, and the 1817 class-based revolutions in nearby Pernambuco were a source of great and continuing concern.[48]

The communication barriers presented by wartime tensions meant that the British consul at Bahia had not only a need to improvise policy without oversight, coordination, or support, but also a free hand to do so. British consuls stationed along the coast of South America were able to communicate among themselves ahead of the Foreign Office, advising one another as to the best course of action.[49] The obvious effect of this situation on the merchants' sense of security was the time it would take for any collective call for help to be heard and then answered. Much could happen in those four months, and independence skirmishes were not the only social crisis that Bahia faced during the first half of the nineteenth century.[50]

The fact that William Pennell was a competent diplomat who was managing to keep a cool head throughout the independence crisis did not, however, do much to alleviate the tensions and fears in the minds of individual British subjects. Ample evidence indicates that British merchants were trading with Brazilian rebels in the *recôncavo*, against Anglo-Portuguese agreements and in direct violation of the carefully thought-out policy of British neutrality. Pennell appeared quite unable either to stop them or to secure legitimacy for their actions, finally asserting to the Foreign Office that he was discontinuing the attempt.[51] One result of this was the constant denigration of British merchants in the pro-royalist newspapers of Bahia; another was the ongoing harassment experienced by individual British subjects on a daily basis.[52] Had the Portuguese succeeded in keeping Bahia as a colony, another consequence of the merchants' participation would probably have been the suspension of many of their privileges by an angry restored government, an outcome that British diplomats on both continents were at great pains to avoid. As it happened, the Brazilians won; and so by 1824, when the dust had settled, the British merchants were treated benevolently by the new government, who portrayed them as enlightened European supporters of Bahia's heroic effort for independence.[53]

Given the four-month lag in communications with the Foreign Office, the urgent pace of political events forced the British consul to improvise policy as best he could, justifying it afterwards in detailed reports. It is to Pennell's credit that, despite the tension and risks, he did not panic or attempt to make predictions regarding the outcome of each succeeding skirmish, but rather remained open and attentive to developments, never losing sight of his belief that British interests would face a serious threat only in the event of a widespread popular revolt. This he encouraged the British government to prevent, if necessary, by the use of force, revealing that the issue of social class was seen to override that of national affiliation, as far as British interests for their personal and financial security were concerned.

The independence struggle in Bahia took place in two stages. The first conflict began in 1820, when the *Cortes*, a liberal faction in Lisbon, declared a constitutional monarchy in the king's absence and against his wishes. In Brazil, this conflict changed into a different struggle between Portuguese loyalists and Brazilian nationalists, with the eventual victory of the latter. In the province of Bahia, no sooner had a constitutional government replaced the monarchists in Salvador than a nationalist revolt broke out in Cachoeira in 1822.[54] Throughout the process, not only did Pennell have to be on the alert for immediate threats to the safety of British subjects, but he also had to tread carefully around the policy of neutrality while still remaining aware of his power to influence the outcome of the overall process if he deemed it necessary. This offers a useful opportunity to reflect on how the process of Brazilian independence was indirectly shaped by the commercial and political interests of Great Britain, whose government never lost sight of how Bahia figured in the wider Brazilian and Latin American contexts.

Evidence that the British representatives operated from a broad geographical perspective is that the first sign of impending unrest came to Bahia from the British consul at Pernambuco in 1817, when that province became the first to openly revolt against Portuguese domination. Pernambuco consul John Lempriere immediately wrote a long eyewitness report and sent it out on the first British vessel to leave port, though one which happened to be bound for Bahia. Upon receiving the letter, consul Alexander Cunningham[55] immediately forwarded it to London with a cover letter stating that the spirit of revolt had not yet reached Bahia.[56] The following year Pennell replaced Cunningham at Bahia and immediately sent a report to the Foreign Office concerning the multiple rebellions taking place in Spanish America, passing along information collected by a reconnaissance mission from the United States government, and saying that the independent governments appeared to be likely to succeed.[57] Meanwhile, Cunningham was transferred on to a post as assistant consul general at Rio de Janeiro, from where he kept up a steady stream of news reports and diplomatic gossip.

It is useful to examine Bahia's struggles for independence from the British consul's point of view. The *Cortes* in Portugal declared a constitutional monarchy in 1820 and split Portuguese loyalties all over Brazil. No one knew whether the king would be persuaded to accept the new constitution, or what would happen if he rejected it. As pro-constitutionalist factions sprang up all over Brazil, skirmishes began taking place between loyalist troops and soldiers who defected to the opposing side. Pennell reported on the political situation in late 1820. His immediate reaction to this first serious threat of widespread social unrest was to recommend complete British neutrality under all circumstances with the exception of a black popular revolt:

> Any contention among the white inhabitants may lead to the employment, as instruments, of the other classes, or to the excitement of their passions, events which all consider as pregnant with incalculable evils [...] as regards the white population of this Province, the Property and Persons of His Majesty's Subjects will be respected, particularly if [...] they shall have the prudence to abstain from all political interference and shall confine themselves to their commercial and regular occupations.[58]

This was a point to which Pennell would return again and again. He firmly believed that the continuing demand for British manufactures would carry the merchant community safely through any change in government, as long as the basic social structure remained intact:

> It does not appear probable that it would enter into the system of any party to violate the friendly relations with England, and much danger can only be apprehended from the anarchy of a mob.[59]

The consul's fear of a lower-class revolt went so far as to temper his convictions regarding the need to keep Great Britain out of the line of fire:

> The presence [...] of His Majestys Ships [...] may be highly beneficial to prevent those excesses to which popular tumults might lead, even contrary to the wishes of those Leaders, by whom they are instigated.[60]

Pennell's stance on this matter probably was connected to his experiences with social upheaval in Napoleonic France. A connection is suggested in a letter he wrote to the Foreign Office in February 1821, justifying his decision to offer an immediate and enthusiastic recognition to Bahia's new Constitutionalist government:

> In the change of government which took place in France during my residence as Consul at Bordeaux, by the landing of General Bonaparte from Elba, I ... quitted Bordeaux as soon as the tri-color flag was triumphant without communicating with the new government, but I trust the circumstances by which the two cases are discriminated are sufficient to justify a [conciliatory] line of conduct on my part [...] until I shall receive from your Lordship more specific instructions.[61]

Despite Pennell's fears, no great popular revolts took place during the independence conflicts of Bahia, so we do not know whether he would have actually used British naval power to intervene. The fact remains, however, that he appeared more than willing to advise such a course of action. This in itself may represent a crucial aspect of the influence of Great Britain in the formation of Brazilian society.

By the time the conflicts in Bahia had escalated to a battle for complete independence from Portugal, British merchants were openly trading with the pro-independence faction, much to the consul's embarrassment. This created a delicate situation with the Portuguese government, which Pennell did his best to manage by arguing that such trade was legal. To support this contention, he offered a tortuous interpretation of minor articles in the commercial treaty, attempting to define the rebels as a separate nation.[62]

Tensions between the British community and the Portuguese loyalists escalated as British merchants were attacked in the newspapers for trading with the rebels, with loyalists refusing to pay debts owed to the British and urging the Portuguese government to break the treaties and revoke the group's privileges.[63] In late 1821, the Portuguese government at Lisbon alienated British merchants all over Brazil by suddenly doubling import duties on British woolens,[64] and by August 1822 even Pennell admitted that the British community strongly favored Brazilian Independence:

> The British Residents here appear very generally, almost unanimously to entertain a predilection for the Brazilian Cause, & as this feeling has not always been under the guidance of discretion, it has become sufficiently notorious to excite corresponding sentiments in the two parties. [...] I hope this predilection will not manifest itself by any Acts which may be legally or officially noticed.[65]

The pro-independence faction, known as the Conselho Interino, was based at Cachoeira, some thirty kilometers north of Bahia. Taking advantage of the tensions between the Portuguese and the British, they did much to encourage the latter's support of the revolt. Not only did the rebel provinces eagerly continue to purchase British manufactures throughout the struggles, but as the conflict came to a head, they went so far as to invite British merchants and their families to stay in Cachoeira so as to avoid any injury or loss during the planned invasion of the city.[66] When the Portuguese loyalists finally capitulated in late 1823, the Conselho Interino took control of the government and immediately began to meet British claims on property confiscated from the fleeing Portuguese.[67]

British strategies for supporting the independence of Portuguese America were subtle and fairly risky, because the British government could not afford to alienate Portugal altogether. At the same time, if Brazil or Bahia were to have remained in a colonial relationship to Portugal, Great Britain only stood to gain from the careful maintenance of its good relations with Portugal throughout the crisis. Since the situation was so filled with political ambiguities, the British perceptions of possible outcomes of the conflict, as well as their own options for responding to each outcome. They reveal not only what Great Britain actually *did* in the Independence of Brazil, but also what it *would have been willing to do* had things gone differently. This, too, deserves a place in the history of British influence in Brazil, and of Latin America in general. Once the independent government was firmly established in Brazil, however the British community found that they had other problems on their hands, as their hard-earned position of political and economic advantage created an island of foreign privilege in a country newly independent and fervently patriotic.

Chapter 2

British Merchants and the Illegal Slave Trade

Connection to Bethell

The abolition of the international slave trade over the course of the nineteenth century was largely driven by British policies and action. Brazil was the largest slave market in the Americas, but it was also a key trading partner for Great Britain. The very birth of Brazil as an independent nation had been watched over by a British midwife, in the form of a naval escort for the flight of the Portuguese court to Rio de Janeiro in 1808, and then in negotiating diplomatic recognition of Brazilian Independence in return for favorable commercial treatment and anti-slave trade concessions. Since the British merchants were mostly wholesalers catering to Brazilian elites, which is to say to the slave-holding class, they possessed a high financial stake in the illicit trade. These conflicting British objectives created a deep rift in Brazilians' perceptions of the British government, especially of the individual British merchants, who had been living in small enclaves in most major Brazilian cities since the opening of the ports in 1808. There is evidence that the British merchants were heavily involved in financing the trade, directly and indirectly, despite popular negative perceptions of their role, perceptions that sometimes led to scapegoating against individual British residents.[1]

Historical Background

In the early nineteenth century, when most regions of Latin America were engaged in establishing their own independence, Great Britain was able and eager to play a major role in reshaping the international trade policies of the fledgling countries. In exchange for diplomatic recognition of their independence, Great Britain demanded – and on many occasions obtained – treaty concessions that furthered its own commercial interests in Latin America. These had until then been thwarted by the relatively restrictive regulations regarding the colonies' trade with countries other than the mother country, although smuggling by British entrepreneurs was common before then. Along with trade concessions, British officials demanded from the new countries a commitment to end the African slave trade. In the case of the former Spanish American possessions, this was accomplished relatively easily, by the 1830s at the latest.

However, in the case of Brazil, the process of abolishing the slave trade was far more complicated, and was characterized by political and military conflicts between Brazil and Great Britain, as well as much maneuvering and frustration on both sides. Although the British government had more influence and more impact in Brazil than in Spanish America, the stakes were very high, as Brazil was then Great Britain's third largest foreign market and the British government desired to remain on good terms with both Brazil and Portugal.[2] Treaties were signed guaranteeing the trade to end by 1831, but still it continued under the noses of officials for another twenty years, and in some cases it increased dramatically in volume.

While official British policy was to apply increasing pressure on the Brazilian government to end the slave trade, in the daily practice of economic and social interactions between British subjects and Brazilians in Bahia compromises and accommodations were made that fit the changing circumstances of the various parties. The end of the slave trade came about not only because of British naval aggression, but also because the internal political and economic affairs of Brazil had changed and stabilized to a point where the abolition treaties could finally be honored and enforced by the central government.

In order to understand the intensity of British efforts to crush the transatlantic slave trade, it is necessary to examine the complicated issue of why, in 1807, the British Parliament ended the extensive and lucrative slave trading activities of British traders, and later freed its own Caribbean slaves in 1833, as part of a worldwide crusade to end the practice of transatlantic African slave trading.[3] It has been argued that abolition in the British Empire was a simpler matter than, say, in Brazil or the United States for two reasons. In the case of Great Britain, slavery was confined to the colonies rather than pervasive in the home country, and Great Britain's political system made it possible for slavery to be abolished through a simple Act of Parliament. The U.S. and Brazilian systems were more complicated.[4] Eric Williams has argued that the British went along the road of emancipation because slavery as a labor force had ceased to be profitable in the Caribbean colonies; once the trade was abolished, British sugar planters found they could not compete with the slaveholding countries, particularly Cuba and Brazil, and this resulted in the creation of a worldwide crusade against the slave trade.[5] Other historians have argued that humanitarian movements in England were primarily responsible for the powerful anti-slavery drive and the force with which emancipation was carried out, through popular movements, diplomatic channels and military force;[6] and that they succeeded in spite of economic interests operating in favor of allowing cheaper slave-grown sugar to enter Great Britain's ports later in the century.[7]

Regardless of the underlying motivating factors, the British government's commitment to end the slave trade was clear. How this effort played out in Brazil was a slow, at times theatrical, and tortuous process. In the words of historian Leslie Bethell:

> Few Brazilians accepted at face value the humanitarian basis of Britain's anti-slave trade campaign; its purpose, they firmly believed, was first, to ruin Brazilian agriculture to the advantage of British West Indian interests and, second, to break Brazil's links with Africa in order to facilitate British expansion there and the subsequent development of the African continent as an economic rival of Brazil.[8]

Bahia was a major slave importer throughout the time of the conflict, especially because the first half of the nineteenth century represented a window of prosperity between the decline of gold deposits in Minas Gerais (1790s) and the rise of coffee interests in São Paulo and Rio de Janeiro (1840s). For this brief period, Bahia regained its pre-eminence as a sugar producer, making it both a focus for the slave trade and a center for British commercial interests. This was also the period when the conflicts over Brazilian Independence made British actions and policies carry substantial weight with local officials. Thus, it is useful to understand how the British anti-traffic conflicts manifested themselves in Bahia, whose British merchants ultimately depended upon the health of the local slave-based economy to ensure the viability of their own commercial interests. Later in the century, Bahia's British community would lose much of its political and social influence as a result of the unpopular policies of its government, and of the decline in wealth that resulted for the community's best customers, the local elites.

Diplomatic Recognition and Anti-Slave Trade Concessions

In 1822, Canning wrote to Wellington, "It is needless to observe that … recognition [of Brazil] can only be purchased by a frank surrender of the slave trade."[9] The first important agreement signed in Brazil was the Treaty of Friendship and Alliance between Great Britain and Portugal, signed at Rio de Janeiro on 19 February 1810. The Portuguese royal family was beholden to England for the assistance of the British squadron in its escape from Lisbon to Brazil. This, along with England's growing interest in the suppression of the slave trade, led to the inclusion in the 1810 treaty of Article X, in which Portugal agreed to the general principle of the gradual abolition of the transatlantic traffic and to its restriction in Africa to the Portuguese colonies. Later, difficulties over the enforcement of the treaty and protests of injustice by Brazilians led to the signing on 21 January 1815, at the Congress of Vienna, of a Convention between Great Britain and Portugal by the terms of which Great Britain established a fund of £300,000 to provide for the claims of illegal detention of Portuguese ships captured on the suspicion of being engaged in illicit slave-trading. On the following day, another treaty was signed which prohibited the slave trade north of the equator and provided for consideration of the total abolition of the traffic at some point in the future.

The Luso-Brazilian emperor Pedro I did make efforts to enforce the earlier treaty and end the slave trade. He limited the number of slaves brought from Africa to a figure determined by the tonnage and accommodation capacity of the ships, forbade the branding of Africans, required sanitary measures and the presence of a physician on every ship, and established standards for food and water. He even established a financial reward for shipments in which the number of deaths in the transatlantic trip did not exceed a certain proportion of those on board. Whatever the effect of these efforts at regulation, the slave trade continued to increase, and the traffic south of the equator with Portuguese colonies was still open.[10]

Soon, however, Brazil's desire to obtain Britain's diplomatic recognition of its independence led to the signing of a new treaty in Rio de

Janeiro in 1826 that further restricted the African slave trade. It was passed by the British parliament in 1827. The target date for the final abolition of the Brazilian slave trade was set for 13 March, 1830. The treaty provided for the slave trade to be treated as piracy after three years, but in the meantime allowed it to continue south of the Equator. It did not permit slave ships north of the line to be seized except when slaves were actually on board, even though the vessel might be fully equipped for, and known to be engaged in, the slave trade.[11]

Meanwhile, British subjects and British vessels were entirely forbidden to engage in the trade. British and Portuguese warships were given the right to detain and search any merchant vessels of the two nations suspected of carrying illicitly acquired slaves, but only the ships on which slaves were actually found could be brought for trial before the special tribunals established for this purpose. Two such tribunals, or Mixed Commissions, were instituted, one on the coast of Africa and the other in Brazil.[12] Captured ships were sold at auction, and their cargoes were either confiscated or returned to Africa, usually Sierra Leone. This compromise solution would change over time as the British became increasingly belligerent in their efforts to crush the illicit traffic.

The treaty of 1826 had the effect of doubling slave prices in Brazil, and led to much animosity against the British on the part of Brazilian slave traders and all those whose livelihoods depended upon the continuation of the traffic. It has been argued that the slave trade continued to increase throughout the 1820s, despite treaty sanctions, because of the great demand for slaves and the consequent profits, in the order of five hundred per cent, available to those who illegally brought in Africans to be sold on the block.[13]

The main causes for the continuation of the illegal trade were the strong conviction that slavery and the slave trade were essential to the Brazilian economy; resentment against British interference in the internal affairs of the Brazilian Empire; the unpopularity of the steps which the Brazilian government had taken, voluntarily or otherwise, to suppress the trade; and, most importantly, the continuing demand for slaves in the Brazilian market.[14] In effect, British authorities were well aware that Brazilian slave traders were unlikely to stop their activities on account of the new treaties, for the very obstacles and sanctions these created also served to raise the prices of slaves in Brazil, thus increasing the potential profits available to illicit traders to the point where it was nearly impossible to suppress the traffic. Nevertheless, there were liberal factions within the Brazilian government that supported the ending of the slave trade and expressed increasing frustration with the tenacity of slavery's hold on Brazil.

Once the trade became illegal by treaty, the liberal central government instituted strong measures to enforce the new legislation. The regulations for the execution of the law of 7 November, 1831, promulgated on 12 April, 1832, provided that all ships entering or leaving Brazilian ports had to be thoroughly inspected by police, and any slaves found on board would be seized and their traffickers imprisoned after trial. The British consul in Rio de Janeiro was sufficiently impressed by these efforts to report that 23 slaves out of 40 recently landed near Rio had been seized by Brazilian authorities, "proof of the feeling which now exists amongst the better class of Brazilians against the abominable traffic".[15] Meanwhile, in Bahia, a newspaper notice announced that heavy penalties would be faced by anyone who continued to be involved in the slave trade.[16]

During the first three years after the trade became illegal, the overall number of slaves brought into Brazil was considerably reduced. Many scholars agree that this was due to the excessive imports during the years leading up to 1830, which saturated the market;[17] but it soon picked up again (see Table 6). After the trade became illegal, it expanded to recover much of its former volume and even its respectability. By the late 1830s, it was even dangerous for authorities to try to intervene in the traffic: "Magistrates and officers who carried out their duty might be assassinated or removed from their commands".[18] As the situation became increasingly dire, British authorities decided to tighten up the sanctions and passed the Palmerston Bill in 1839, authorizing British warships to seize slave ships registered in Portugal and sailing under the Portuguese flag.[19] This reduced the number of slaves imported, but as it considerably raised the price of those who did arrive, the overall effect on the illicit trade was not strong enough. The unilateral Aberdeen Act of 1845 had more teeth in it, and provided for the outright seizure of Brazilian ships on suspicion of involvement in the traffic. The Aberdeen Act was a key factor in suppressing the Brazilian slave trade at last, though it also coincided with the strengthening of Brazilian institutions as the last internal revolts were put down.

Brazilians objected stridently to the Aberdeen Act, holding that by international law, no state could exercise jurisdiction over the property

TABLE 6: Slaves imported into Brazil, 1791–1855 (in thousands)[20]

	Imported into Brazil, South of Bahia	Imported into Bahia	Imported into Brazil, North of Bahia
1791–1795	47.6	34.3	43.1
1796–1800	45.1	36.2	27.4
1801–1805	50.1	36.3	31.5
1806–1810	58.3	39.1	26.1
1811–1815	78.7	36.4	24.3
1816–1820	95.7	34.3	58.3
1821–1825	120.1	23.7	37.4
1826–1830	176.1	47.9	26.2
1831–1835	57.8	16.7	19.2
1836–1840	202.8	15.8	22.0
1841–1845	90.8	21.1	9.0
1846–1850	208.9	45.0	3.6
1851–1855	3.3	1.9	0.9

or persons inside the territory of another state, that the ships of a state are considered to be part of its territory, and that the right to seize and search on the high seas was a belligerent right only.[21] However, the British justified the Act, maintaining that since the two countries had agreed to treat the slave trade as piracy, any subject of either country guilty of such crime was "placed within the reach of other laws than those of his own country".[22] Whatever the justification, however, the Act appears to have had its desired effect: "On April 27, 1852, England notified Brazil of her permanent withdrawal of British warships from Brazilian waters on condition that there was no resumption of the slave trade".[23]

Brazilian historian Luís Henrique Dias Tavares has argued that while it is tempting to accept the interpretation that increasing British pressure was the main factor in ending Brazil's slave trade at mid-century, it would be a better idea to examine the reasons why Brazil itself was better able by then to put an end to its own trade.[24] British efforts had gone on for over fifteen years with little effect on the volume of the trade; but in the four short years following the anti-traffic law passed by the Brazilian legislature in November of 1850, the Brazilian navy and judicial system were able effectively to suppress the trade on its own coast.[25] He argues that this happened because a conservative, balanced internal solution had been found for the problem of continuing the slave trade. First, it finally became clear that the end of the trade did not necessarily mean the end of all slavery; and secondly, what he calls "anti-traffic elements" had been growing in strength and reducing resistance to anti-traffic activity. These elements were: slave revolts (particularly the abortive Malês uprising of 1835), the increasing use of steam power on the sugar mills (*engenhos*), the decline of the sugar economy, and the rise of coffee with its immigrant-friendly structures and objectives, which did not harmonize with the continued use of slave labor. Both factors were at work: the British naval forces were making it increasingly risky for slave traders to operate (raising the costs of insurance, among other things);[26] but at the same time, the Brazilian government was in a better position to cooperate with the anti-slave trade efforts than it had been before, having mostly emerged from the political and economic turmoil of the early nineteenth century.

The Slave Trade in Bahia

Bahia, a major slave-trading port, received a significant proportion of the slaves illegally imported into Brazil. From 1800 to 1850, approximately 316,300 enslaved Africans landed at Bahia. Out of this total, 98,600 arrived after 1830, when the trade was outlawed. Imports to Bahia alone made up 18.4 per cent of Brazil's total slave imports for the years 1800–1850, and 14 per cent of imports for 1830–1850.[27] This was so even when coffee was rapidly becoming a major crop in the southeastern regions of the country, and slave shipments to Rio de Janeiro were reaching very high numbers.

In 1831, the liberal Francisco José de Montezuma claimed that the trade was carried on so openly at Bahia that even the names of the dealers were publicly reported as a matter of course.[28] The British consul at Bahia in 1827, William Pennell, reported to George Canning at the Foreign Office that the abolition treaty would be regarded by Brazilian governments as "a dictation of a superior authority from which it is lawful to escape, rather than as a compact which they are bound to enforce", adding that it was the popular conviction of Brazilians that the British government had bribed and intimidated the government to adopt what was essentially a British agenda.[29]

The British diplomatic representatives at Bahia were often hard pressed to keep up their duty of denouncing slave landings, and to protect British subjects who were attacked or otherwise harassed in the process of carrying out British abolitionist policy. In 1818, when the trade was only illegal north of the equator, the captain and crew of a British cruiser had observed a Portuguese ship taking on slaves in the area of Popo, Africa, and heard the crew boast that they would make it to Bahia with the cargo. Upon their arrival, British Consul Cunningham wrote to Lord Castlereagh:

> Concerning a Portuguese slave ship called the *Cisne*, which having been detected while in the act of smuggling slaves on shore upon the coast near the mouth of this Harbor, not only to evade the customary duties upon them, but also to get rid of those negroes who upon landing would have been recognized as being the natives of that part of the Coast of Africa which is prohibited from carrying on that Commerce, was embargoed by order of [Bahia's] Governor, the Conde de Palma, [creating] considerable commotion among the Portuguese Merchants of this City, and becoming a topic of general conversation. A report was made to me stating that [the British cruiser's captain] and several of the crew had publicly declared that they saw the *Cisne* take on the slaves.[30]

Reports of increasing violence by Portuguese traders in fending off British seizures also appear in the diplomatic correspondence, as in this letter from 1819:

> A report prevailed for some days in this City that a Portugueze Vessell had landed Slaves on this Coast, and had afterwards been scuttled; that she had been captured North of the Line, on the Coast of Africa, by an English ship of War and that the English Seamen put in charge had been murdered. [...] I [requested an investigation by Brazilian authorities but] found it difficult to procure authentic details, from a general apprehension that personal Injury might result to the Informants.[31]

The diplomatic correspondence for Bahia suggests a relationship between the international incidents of slave-ship captures by British naval forces on the one hand, and increasing animosity or ill-will of local Brazilians towards British subjects living in Bahia on the other:

> HM Sloop *Morgiana* arrived in this Port the 21st May bringing with him as Prize the Portuguese Schooner *Emilia* of Bahia, captured on the coast of Africa with about four hundred slaves. This occurrence has tended to revive prejudices & irritations connected with former Captures of Portuguese Ships ... [Sailors must not enter into] discussions under the influence of irritated feelings calculated to disturb the harmony of existing friendly relations, the preservation of which your Lordship's Instructions so strongly in force as an essential part of the Consular Duties.[32]

This pattern would continue and worsen as the century wore on, with violent skirmishes and attacks between Brazilian and British sailors

becoming more and more common.

As early as 1812, Charles Fraser, an English gentleman who traveled throughout Brazil learning about customs and mores, had reported that, while the importation of British manufactures had turned the urban elite of Brazil's society against the British, the aggressive anti-slave-trade activity had managed to turn all parts of society against them, including the landed elites who earlier had favored the British innovations to trade.[33] In the mid 1820s, a wave of violent crimes against individual British merchants and ship captains in Bahia took place, and was deemed serious enough for the merchant community to decide to issue a collective written complaint to the president of the province.[34] Several of the crimes had been committed by uniformed soldiers, a circumstance that understandably alarmed the community of British merchants resident there. By 1829, the consul had linked such violence – and its implicit official condonement – to the prevalence of openly anti-British sentiment:

> [A] most atrocious attempt at assassination [was] perpetrated yesterday evening by a soldier of the 20th Battalion on the person of Mr. Richard Nicholson, a very respectable British Merchant established in this City and on that of his two nephews all of whom were most severely wounded. [...] It is not for the first time that complaints have been made to me on the insolence with which the soldiers of this garrison behave to Foreigners and to British Subjects in particular in the streets without the slightest provocation, and I have myself been frequently an eyewitness to it.[35]

The consul was also often called upon to demand redress for insults unprovoked attacks on British vessels in port or near the harbor.[36]

In some of these cases, the Brazilian soldiers and sailors were probably acting out of a sense of outraged sovereignty. British abolitionist pressures were increasing, while British manufactures still enjoyed their preferential import tariffs, a relic of the British navy's assistance in transporting the entire Portuguese royal court to Rio de Janeiro during the Napoleonic invasion. Furthermore, the institution of Judge Conservator was still in place, a special court acknowledging the extra-territorial rights of British subjects. The diplomatic correspondence does not specifically state that the anti-British sentiment was tied to Britain's increasing pressure to abolish the slave trade, but this almost certainly was the case, and the general perception of the British as being pushy, privileged, and insolent probably added to the aggravation and led to attacks on local British residents by disgruntled patriots. Ironically, such scapegoating was misplaced: as will be seen, the health of British commerce in Bahia itself depended in no small part upon the continuation of its slave trade. In the meantime, the daily lives of British subjects in Bahia were none too comfortable:

> Mr. J. Buckley, a British Merchant established in this City, and residing in my immediate neighbourhood [was] robbed last night at about ten o'clock on the highway near the Fort S. Pedro, by four [...] soldiers. [...] There is not the slightest doubt to me from actual observation that plans have been formed to rob the inhabitants of this part of the town ... there can be no longer any doubt on the subject and unless speedy and effectual measures are taken, great depredations and even loss of lives ... must ensue. [I ask you to] quiet the apprehensions of the inhabitants of this part of the town, a great part of whom are British subjects, and fully rely on your Lordship's protection.[37]

A few months later, in December 1829, soldiers attacked a British merchant in his home, wounding three men with their bayonets. In his letter to the consul, the merchant expressed outrage at the escalating level of violence against British residents of the foreign enclave in the relatively isolated Victoria neighborhood.[38] With 13 March, 1830 being the date for abolishing the trade as agreed by treaty, the evidence suggests mounting tension on the part of legitimate (i.e. non-marginal) elements of Bahian society against the British as a group, rather than random criminal activity. A couple of years later, when the consul's own official messenger was attacked and ridiculed by soldiers, his outrage was so great and his demands for redress so strident that he nearly transformed the event into an international incident.[39] Problems of aggression against British residents and visitors would continue throughout the century.

As anti-British sentiment in Bahia became something of a lightning rod for local anti-abolitionist feeling, it was also used by Brazilians for their own ends. The following anonymous letter was sent to Consul Parkinson in 1832 to denounce a local slave trader:

> The schooner Thereza, leaving tomorrow for the Mina Coast under Portuguese flag, is actually Brazilian, belongs to Manoel Cardoso dos Santos, and is going to pick up African slaves to bring to Bahia, as he has done in Havana. [You] must immediately notify the Provincial Government to search and unload the schooner, where you will find hidden inside a textiles box a Cauldron, irons and other accoutrements for [the slave trade].[40]

Parkinson acted quickly on the anonymous request and forwarded the note to the President of Bahia urging him to take action. Since the British were being blamed for unpopular anti-slavery activities, it should come as no surprise that Brazilians took advantage of the situation for their own benefit.

By September 1836, the British commissioners at Rio de Janeiro wrote that "at no period has [the trade] perhaps been ever carried on with greater activity and daring".[41] In the late 1840s, when the Aberdeen Act was being put into action, the frenzy of slave traders was such that Consul Porter wrote a report on the profitability of slave trading in Bahia:

> I beg leave to call your Lordship's attention to the Brazilian yacht "Andorinha" of 80 tons burthen, which vessel has made eight successful voyages to and from the coast of Africa, having actually landed 3,392 slaves at this port, receiving the usual freight of 120 reis per head, amounting to £40,704 sterling, calculated at the present rate of exchange of 24d. per milrei ... Her first cost, including everything necessary for the voyage, may have been about £2,000. The parties interested in the vessel admit that, after deducting all expenses, she has left a clear profit of more than 800 per cent.[42]

Understandably, British efforts to end the slave trade by force aroused strong discontent in Bahia. An article appearing in a local newspaper in 1849 condemned British abolitionist tactics on several counts:

that the slaves seized by the British were taken to Sierra Leone presumably to be liberated, but the most able-bodied among them were invariably pressed into service in the British armed forces; that on many occasions slave ships captured near Bahia were simply turned around and sent to Sierra Leone without the opportunity to replenish their supplies, increasing the suffering and mortality of those on board; that the violent means of capture injured many of the slaves on board, since British sailors were rewarded per African head captured, whether alive or dead; and that such facts were not generally reported in the British newspapers.[43] Even the British foreign secretary noticed that there was "a certain enmity against Great Britain in Brazil arising out of British efforts to suppress the Slave Trade ... [the Aberdeen Act] rankles not only as regards the Slave Trade, but it hurts their pride, because they think they have been insulted; it is an Act that has offended their nationality".[44]

The Aberdeen Act empowered the British navy to search and seize Brazilian and Portuguese ships on an unprecedented scale. Together with a renewed commitment by the Brazilian government to end the slave trade, the number of slaves imported into Brazil fell dramatically in 1851. The trade did not end altogether, as the yellow fever epidemic that swept Bahia in the mid-1850s reduced the size of the slave population and led to a temporary revival of the trade.[45] The last consular letter in the state archives of Bahia that mentions slave shipments dates from 1856.[46] In that same year, British traveler Edward Wilberforce published a narrative recounting a conversation with a tavern-keeper in Braganza, near Rio de Janeiro:

We had some conversation together, in the course of which, after touching on various topics, we got to the Slave-trade, on which subject he grew vehement, and, taking up the last number of a Brazilian paper, showed us an article wherein the English were stigmatized as robbers, pirates, cut-throats, and what not, because the Harpy had taken a vessel which the Brazilians obstinately chose to consider a legal trader. The hotel-keeper shouted out 'Pirates, Pirates, Ingleze!' [*sic*] nor did we contradict him, as it saved a 'world of voice' to agree."[47]

About a decade later, the diplomatic fiasco that became known as the 'Christie Affair', in which a British diplomat refused to apologize for the seizure of a legitimate Brazilian vessel,[48] so incensed Brazilians that the renowned nineteenth-century Brazilian poet Fagundes Varella wrote an entire volume of scathingly critical verses about the British to express his outrage at their insulting rapaciousness towards a nation that had "drenched in waves, in rivers of gold their ungrateful country".[49]

British Merchants' Interests in the Slave Trade

The popular Brazilian perception of Great Britain's violent abolitionism, however, masked a more sinister reality. Brazilian anger against British actions damaged the Brazilian government's willingness to cooperate in ending the trade, and resulted in daily harassment of individual British subjects. An examination of the economic role of British merchant enclaves (in this case that of Bahia) in the international slave trade, especially after it became illegal, shows that their continued prosperity relied heavily upon the existence of the slave trade. There were two main reasons for this: the credit system used by the British merchants depended on the regular flow of slave trade profits, and the actual manufactured goods sold by the British were needed for the slave trade.

Before the abolitionist movement began, the British slave trade was high-volume and heavily financed through sophisticated mechanisms. When the anti-slavery movement gained steam around the turn of the nineteenth century, "the Londoner was as much alarmed as his confederate at Liverpool",[50] for while the merchants of Liverpool owned and outfitted ships that carried manufactures to Africa and slaves to the West Indies, the London commission agent handled the complex financing required by the trade. Planters needed long credits to purchase slaves, while merchants needed quick cash remittances in order to buy cargoes to send to Africa. This generated commissions, interest, and speculation on a scale that led to a credit crisis in London by the closing years of the eighteenth century, with a chain of bankruptcies that would continue well into the nineteenth century. The trade was known to be crucial to the health of major financial interests in London: during a debate on parliamentary resolutions respecting the slave trade, an alderman said, "If it [the slave trade] were abolished altogether, he was persuaded it would render the city of London one scene of bankruptcy and ruin".[51]

Given these conditions, it would have been surprising if the vast commercial and financial networks set up over centuries in London and

Liverpool to support and sustain the international slave trade had suddenly vanished or been completely transformed,[52] just at the moment when Great Britain was finally gaining access to the new Brazilian market, where slavery was the mainstay of economy and society. Financial investors in London and Liverpool did not only provide capital and manufactures for the trade: they built and outfitted ships, so the British ironworks industry was engaged in making and selling trade-related paraphernalia such as cauldrons and leg and neck irons, well into the years after abolitionism became official government policy.[53] Far from trying to make a modest profit on selling consumer goods to Brazilians on a small scale, it made sense for the British merchants entering Brazil to capitalize on their access to Brazil's major import, slaves.

In the opening years of the nineteenth century, as British merchants traveled to the major cities of Brazil and established their trading communities, they retained ties with home firms in London, Liverpool and other English cities, acting as their local agents. In an era before international banking, this system of multinational enterprise allowed for the establishment of sophisticated credit and payment arrangements. The slave trade to Brazil was not entirely illegal before 1830, and although British subjects had been officially forbidden to own slaves since 1807, they could and did take part in the traffic. British merchants were active in Brazil between 1822 and 1830 and testified before the Select Committee of 1831–32 that they had provided English manufactures to be used in the trade from Bahia, Pernambuco, Maranhão and Pará.[54] These manufactured goods were exchanged for slaves in Africa, which were then brought to Brazil. The exact pattern of trading changed somewhat over time: throughout the 1820s, Brazilian sugar, tobacco, and *cachaça* (sugarcane spirit) were still valuable commodities in the slave trade, while by the 1840s the demand for English guns, gunpowder and textiles had eclipsed the traditional Brazilian agricultural goods in the trade. Toward mid-century, as coffee became an increasingly important Brazilian export, the profits from selling slaves were used to buy coffee, which was to be exported to the United States. Indeed, American observer Daniel Kidder was able to report in 1845:

> It has not been generally known that notwithstanding the opposition of the English nation to the slave trade, and her vigorous efforts to suppress it, yet that the strong bulwark of that traffic has been the English capital, by aid of which it has been carried on.[55]

A persuasive case explaining the participation of British merchants in the slave trade – a trade the British government had effectively forced Brazil to declare illegal – is made by Dias Tavares.[56] He argues that not only did the British sustain the slave trade as it had existed when they arrived in Brazil, but they also bolstered it after it became illegal through the nature of their financial investments. By the late 1830s the Portuguese slave traders were able to continue purchasing and out-fitting new ships that were fast enough to outrun the British anti-slaving squadrons, ships which (not coincidentally) were manufactured in Great Britain and the United States. The lull in slave imports during the early 1830s was reversed later in the decade and increased up until 1850, in large part because British activity in providing long-term credit allowed new players to enter the market even as barriers to entry became higher due to the technological sophistication that was necessary for illegal operations.[57]

Economic historian David Eltis provides a brief discussion of the role of British enterprise in supporting the slave trade to Brazil during the first half of the nineteenth century. British merchants in Brazil provided goods on credit of up to twenty-four months.[58] Significantly, he suggests that the British merchants probably tended to take up an equity position in the slave-trade enterprise by accepting slaves in payment for goods, in grave violation of British law. Eltis' documentary research shows that "it was certainly common in Rio de Janeiro for British houses to advance merchandise in the knowledge that the chief security for payment was the successful exchange of that merchandise for slaves on the African coast".[59] Furthermore, the necessities of the slave trade led to innovative financing practices, such as a futures market that developed as dealers contracted to deliver slaves at fixed prices before fitting out an expedition.[60] In 1850, Consul Robert Hesketh, who had lived in Brazil from 1808 to 1847 including three years in Bahia, affirmed before the Select Committee in London that all Brazilian commerce obeyed the command of British capital; all British manufactured goods were sold on credit; all of their buyers were con-nected to the slave trade; and he calculated the total amount of British capital invested in Brazil at five million pounds, at least one-half of which was diverted to the slave traffic.[61]

The main slave traders of Bahia were prominent members of local society, with Cerqueira Lima and André Pinto da Silveira most often mentioned. There is no doubt that they had strong links with the major

British firms in Bahia. One document in support of slave dealer Manoel Francisco Lopes, of the ship *Guyana*, was signed by a number of prominent British merchants, including Charles Lane, Michael M. Roocker, Alexander Paterson (British doctor), John Elliot, George Mumford, Edwards Hols & Co., Richard Latham, J. Whateley (British consul), S. S. Davenport, James Napier, J. B. Forster, Gerekens, W. Hughes, Edward Jones, James Stewart, J. J. Astley and John Sharpe. The *Guyana* left Liverpool in service (*fretado*) to slave dealers in Bahia, where it was loaded with slave-trade merchandise such as colorful cotton textiles and glass beads. This slave-trading cargo was loaded by Manoel Francisco Lopes, José Maria Ferreira, Joaquim Pinto de Menezes Campos, and João da Costa Júnior & Co., all well-known slave traders. Furthermore, the cargo was consigned to two slave dealers in Africa, Joaquim Pinto de Menezes Campos and Domingos José Martins.[62] Another example of the ongoing close financial relationship existing between British merchants and Portuguese/Brazilian slave traders is the fact that in his will, slave dealer Francisco Lopes Guimarães of Bahia requested that his heirs continue to invest the profits from their business in the London firm Forster & Brothers.[63]

How could this behavior on the part of British merchants have been justified? An attempt to defend their role appears in the following letter written in 1845 by Rio's British merchants to Mr. Hesketh, the British chargé d'affaires in Rio, in response to complaints about their activities:

> Any one who has the least idea of business, will at once perceive the utter impropriety of any merchant requiring of another who proposes to him a mercantile transaction, what he intends to do with the goods he buys or wishes to order.[64]

This 'don't ask, don't tell' defense is not quite acceptable; it is clear that the British merchants knew where their merchandise was going, and what would have to happen for them to receive payment for it – i.e. the slave expedition must be successful.

The integrity of British abolitionist policy toward Brazil was compromised by the actual commercial interests of the British merchant community.[65] Knowing the financial investment of Bahia's British merchants in the slave trade, it is difficult to avoid the element of hypocrisy in the following passage, sent by Consul Parkinson to the President of Bahia in 1833 on the subject of a rumored slave shipment received in Bahia:

I shall consider myself much obliged by your Excellency's [...] communication of such information as may enable me to satisfy the British Government that the authorities of Bahia are sincere and zealous in carrying into effect the philanthropic intentions of the Supreme Government.[66]

Parkinson is here referring to the obligation of the *Brazilian* government to stop the slave trade – at a time when the British merchants themselves had a strong interest in continuing the trade as long as possible.

Meanwhile, and somewhat ironically, British naval forces continued to pursue and attack Brazilian slave vessels. In one case, a slave ship was captured and brought right into the Bahia harbor, causing a problem:

The Brazilian Polacca *Bella Miguelina* having been captured with a cargo of slaves on board by HM Sloop *Grecian*, and anchored in this Port in consequence of a want of water and provisions [...] at about half past nine o'clock on the same evening, the said Polacca was attacked by a large party of armed men, in two country barques, who attempted to board her; but were beaten off after considerable resistance, having wounded the officer in charge, and two seamen. Such a glaring act of violence and piracy, committed under the very batteries of the Imperial Forts and vessels of War, calls for your Excellency's most active interference....[67]

What sort of British profits may have been bound up in the success of the *Bella Miguelina*'s voyage? Even the consul's own firm may have invested in the enterprise. Here is a second example of a British consul's efforts to denounce slave trading in Bahia:

Already during this month in addition to the *Felicidade*, a large brig, just out from this port, perfectly fitted for the slave trade, which [was] captured by HBM's Steam Vessel *Sharpshooter*, it appears that on the 1st Inst. the *Liberdade,* a yacht, landed on Ilha dos Frades, within view of the forts of Bahia, upwards of six hundred human beings now consigned to slavery, and on the 3rd Inst. another vessel, supposed to be named *Bridgtown*, is reported also to have landed three hundred negroes in this bay.[68]

The archives feature several such letters denouncing slave disembarkations taking place in the light of day, pleading with the President of Bahia to put a stop to them.[69] The element of hypocrisy present in such requests must not have escaped either the Brazilian or the British authorities involved. On the other hand, perhaps the situational circum-stances made it impossible for the consul to do anything other than protect the British interests, even when those of the British merchants contradicted those of the British government, in the matter of abolishing the slave trade.

There was an understanding on the part of prominent Brazilians that the British merchants had an interest in continuing the slave trade. How, then, could this be reconciled with the anti-British sentiment, with individual British merchants being attacked in the streets by Brazilian soldiers, and, much to the consul's embarrassment, British soldiers in port constantly involved in skirmishes with Brazilian sailors? Lower class Brazilians were most likely to be involved in such outbursts. Witness the following letter, from 1821, in which Consul Pennell attempts to demand redress from the President for some ill-treatment received by British sailors on an anti-slaving mission:

> It has been my uniform endeavor to promote that spirit amongst my countrymen which ought to exist between friendly, and allied Nations, & which endeavor I am persuaded, their Excellencies the Governors reciprocate. But I regret to remark that this spirit has not marked the treatment which the Morgiana received in this Harbor from the lower ranks of Society.[70]

There was a complex interplay of at least two factors operating on either side of the Brazilian–British relationship: the British govern-ment's interest in abolishing the trade, versus the British merchants' interest in keeping it alive; and on the other hand, the Brazilian elites' complicity with the merchants' financial interests, versus the non-elite Brazilians' perception of the British as alien, meddlesome, privileged, and threatening to the best interests of their country.

Anglo-African Subjects in Bahia

There remains one extremely interesting category of conflicts among British interests in Bahia. These were the situations that arose when a black British subject got into trouble and had to appeal to the consul. In several instances, Africans of British nationality were sold into slavery by Brazilians, or otherwise insulted, and appealed to the British Consul at Bahia for protection. One of these cases is worth quoting at length, as it describes the trajectory of one British-African man from being a member of the crew of a British anti-slave cruiser to becoming a slave himself:

> The Brig *Volcano do Sul* in 1819 was captured […] on the coast of Africa for being engaged in the illicit Slave Trade … an English Officer and four White and four Black Sailors were put on board the said Brig for the purpose of taking her to Sierra Leone. [A few days later] part of the Crew of the *Volcano do Sul* that had been left on board (one of whom was Francisco Xavier a Mullatto and Master) rose and murdered the five White men and two Black men; and the other two Black men were allowed to remain on board with the Slaves … the Brig arrived on the coast of Brazil when the whole of the Slaves were smuggled on shore, and with them the two English Black Sailors, and all were indiscriminately disposed of and sent into the interior of the country; one of these English Black Sailors called Quashee Sam made his escape in 1821, and returned to his native country in HBM's ship *Morgiana*, the other named John or Quanini Quambo has also lately escaped and is now at my residence in this City ready to give his evidence … this man is extremely anxious to return to Africa, and […] I have to solicit that a Passport may be granted to him for this purpose.[71]

The resilience and resourcefulness shown by the two British Africans is remarkable. They managed to escape being killed on board the *Volcano do Sul*; then, after being sold into slavery, survived for two and five years (respectively) working on plantations in the interior, probably learning Portuguese in the process; managed to escape and safely make their way back to the capital city; and then somehow persuaded two British officials to take up their cause and return them to Africa. Considering the level of privileges enjoyed by white British residents of Bahia at that time, and their connections to the slave trade, it is a rather ironic circumstance that some of their fellow British subjects were reduced to being slaves themselves.

Another such case occurred in 1851, long after the slave trade had been made illegal, and indeed after the bulk of the trade had been successfully repressed. Four British subjects were kidnapped in Gallinas on the Guinea Coast of west Africa and brought to Bahia, where they were sold into slavery. One served there as a cook for two years, before being sent to Rio de Janeiro and resold. The consul writes:

Two of the [four] British subjects alluded to, John Tobin and David Johnson, are still in slavery; and I am directed by HM's Envoy at the Court of Rio de Janeiro, not only to bring the whole facts of this case to the knowledge of your Excellency, but also to require the immediate liberation from bondage of the said John Tobin and David Johnson, and to call for the punishment of those persons who are implicated in this infamous transaction.[72]

Minute details are given in the letter, including the names of the shipmasters who kidnapped and sold the men, the name and address of the Bahian man who purchased the cook, and implicitly the whereabouts of the two British subjects who still remained in slavery. One may assume that the two other British subjects managed to make their escape, and perhaps provided the details conveyed in the consul's letter. One difference between this case and the previous one is that here the consul depended on the President to free the men, while in the former case the slaves had already escaped and placed themselves under the protection of the British crown.

Although not every black Englishman who set foot in Bahia was sold into slavery, embarrassment could and did occur, requiring official intervention. Take this letter sent by the captain of an anti-slaving cruiser in port at Bahia to the British Consul in 1821:

One of my chief men yesterday, when employed by me on His Majesty's Service ... was forcibly dragged to Prison and his Krees [arms] taken from him ... this man altho' a native of Africa is by the Lords of the Admiralty rated a Petty Officer in this Ship, and in justice to this most useful class of Men I must protest against their being in any way maltreated in the Port of a friendly Power [...] outrages of this nature against the subjects of His Britannic Majesty while actually carrying into execution the Laws of Portugal, cannot fail to be visited with the displeasure of their own Sovereign.[73]

In a subsequent letter, the captain admits to having learned that "the laws of this Country prohibit such Arms from being born in the streets by persons of his description".[74] Here is a black British officer, professionally engaged in stopping the slave trade, who is attacked by Brazilian soldiers in the streets of Bahia on account of being black and bearing arms in public. One of the most interesting aspects of the captain's attitude toward this case is that he apparently saw his anti-slaving mission as carrying out the laws of Brazil, rather than a policy of Great Britain that most Brazilians found obnoxious and threatening; and he seemed perplexed at the unfriendly reception he received from the locals. To top it off, the captain was ultimately reprimanded by the consul for the indecorous behavior of the British soldiers sent to fetch the African officer from his predicament: "You will [...] prevent the recurrence of any circumstance on the Part of your Officers calculated to excite or justify unfriendly feelings".[75] The British consul often walked a fine line in Bahia, mediating between the need to maintain the dignity and privileges of the British community and the equally pressing need to avoid overt conflicts with the local authorities.

Slave Ownership Among British Residents of Bahia

Another approach towards examining the issues of race and slavery operating within Bahia's British community in the early nineteenth century is to observe the relationship that individual British subjects had toward individual slaves, rather than toward slavery as an abstract idea. British subjects around the world were expected by their government to refrain from owning or trafficking in slaves since the early years of the abolitionist movement, and were formally prohibited from it by the Brougham Law of 1843.[76] At the Arquivo Municipal da Cidade de Salvador, where most records pertaining to the buying and selling of slaves are preserved, not a single instance of a slave having been purchased by anyone with an English name could be found, let alone any prominent British merchant of the time.[77]

Nevertheless, some members of the British community certainly did own slaves, probably on a domestic basis. The main evidence for this is from the published testimonies collected during the trial of the leaders of the abortive urban slave uprising of 25 January, 1835, which was known as the Malês (Muslim) revolt, and has been extensively studied by Bahian historian João José Reis.[78] Had this urban uprising not been aborted at the last hour by a freed Nagô woman who informed her master, it might well have developed into the greatest urban slave rebellion of the nineteenth century. As it was, the authorities descended upon sixty or so leaders at their meeting-place at a house in the center of town before dawn, fighting broke out and continued in the streets, and eventually ended with 57 casualties, according to official reports: fifty Africans, five soldiers, and two civilians.[79] The rebellion was distinguished by the fact that most if not all of the participants were Muslims, and had a level of cohesiveness among themselves that was unusual for slaves in Bahia, given the wide variety of African backgrounds represented there. The rebels were headed in the direction of Victoria district, the main residential street for wealthy British residents, when they were detained at Forte São Pedro and ultimately forced to turn back. According to the official records of the trial, no fewer than six of the fifteen leaders belonged to British merchants: Frederic Robilliard, William Benne, Dr. Dundas (the community's British doctor), Melors Russell, and Moir of Moir & Co.[80] Several of the testimonies refer to clandestine meetings held by the rebel leaders on the property of a British merchant named Abraham:

> [Among the] leaders of the Clubs who met at Englishman Abraham's house [were] the following Nagôs: Diogo, Daniel, Jaimes and João, slaves belonging to Abraham and leaders of the Club, went out [on the night of the rebellion] and returned the following morning with blood still on their trousers. [...] Pedro, a slave of Dr. Dundas, was shot in the leg and was a leader of the Club.[81]

Other British subjects are mentioned in the testimonies as well:

> [This court] demands the imprisonment of the defendants, Diogo, Jaimes, Daniel, and João, all Nagôs, African slaves of Englishman Abraham; Nogeno, João do Carrinho, Joãozinho Moleque, Pedro, [and] Miguel, all Nagôs, slaves of Joseph Mellors; Nicobé, Dassalu, Gustad, all Nagôs, slaves of Englishman Stuart ... Thomas [and] Carlos, Nagôs, slaves of Frederic Robilliard; Antônio, Nagô, slave of Englishman James Ridy; Paulo and Thomas, slaves of Englishman Weiss [...] João [and] Carlos Vica, slaves of Englishman [illegible]; Luiz, Nagô, slave of [William] Benne; Pedro, slave of Dr. Dundas.[82]

The interesting fact that such a disproportionate number of the leaders of the slave rebellion belonged to the British merchants did not escape the attention of local Brazilians, who had a number of different interpretations for the fact. Historian Pierre Verger uncovered a contemporary report by the French consul at Bahia, in which he explains how the British were viewed as not exerting sufficient control over their slaves, perhaps even inciting them to revolt.[83] The report ironically points out that Mr. Cerqueira Lima, a major slave dealer also resident in the Victoria neighborhood, had not had a single slave involved in the revolt.[84]

Why would a British merchant in Bahia own slaves in the first place, why would he necessarily have trouble disciplining them, and why would anyone believe he would attempt to incite them to revolt? An answer to the first question may be found in the words of Robert Hesketh, British consul at Rio de Janeiro, who admitted in 1840 that he owned three slaves as domestic servants, giving as his reason that, "in this country of slave labour, no provisions can be had, no articles of dress made, no dwellings repaired, nor any hired conveyance, or porterage made use of, without employing slaves".[85] As for the second and third questions, it is possible to speculate that the disproportionate number of British-owned slaves among the leaders of the Malês rebellion could have resulted from the fact that so many of them belonged to the Nagô nation; their concentration in the relatively isolated Victoria district; the time and opportunity to meet regularly at Abraham's; and less likely, the possible exposure to information about British anti-slave trade interests, if such conversations were conducted in a language understood by the slaves. This would perhaps have increased the slaves' hope for an end to slavery, and inspired rebellious thoughts.

In any case, the British merchants of Bahia owned multiple slaves as a matter of course, against their country's own laws, customs, and policy.[86] In Rio de Janeiro, as late as 1841 British merchants not only owned and auctioned slaves (for instance, Cannell Southam & Co., and A. Lawrie & Co.), but also punished them physically with great cruelty. Some of the atrocities inflicted by British subjects upon their illegally-owned African slaves included whippings, zinc masks, adjustable finger rings, neck and arm irons, chains, and handcuffs.[87]

The voice in the wilderness came from British merchant George Pilkington, who published a pamphlet in 1841 urging his fellow country-men to free their household slaves and take on hired labor instead. His factual statements, together with his persuasive arguments based on marginal utility analysis and offered in a straightforward dialectic style, described the full situation:

> We both agree that slave-hunters are thieves and murderers. Why then should any of you, in the slightest degree, contribute to keep that market open, by which alone such thieves and murderers are tempted to perpetrate their bloody crimes? [...] The housekeeper

who has from one to six slaves, startling at this proposition, says: I must have servants; and, if I did not purchase them, another would. If another would, then have you left his want unsatisfied, that he may tempt the trader to send for as many as you have thus snatched out of his hands, to procure which two must be murdered for every one delivered. [...] I am now asked: should we then leave this Empire, merely because we must neither buy nor hire slaves? I answer: No, – but you should count the cost of remaining; you carefully calculate all expenses of profit and loss, doubtless not omitting the expense of servants. For this, I suppose, you charge the interest of money advanced for slave servants and messengers, who, when closing accounts, are sold as bales of goods, and the proceeds placed to credit. I say, if your speculation be unprofitable without thus saving the difference between the expense of such slaves, and the wages unjustly withheld from them, it is, most decidedly, not worth the leaving your country and friends to undertake. But, if your reasonable profits be sufficient to enable you to hire free men, and none can be procured; then send for English servants; also, for carters and carts [instead of relying on the more usual hand-carried sedan chair for daily transportation]. The former may be indented for a term of years.[88]

Pilkington seemed truly determined to appeal to the common business sense of his compatriots. But then he went on to make a sensitive analysis of the brutalizing effect that decades of slave-holding had worked upon the British psyche in early nineteenth-century Brazil:

If, then, british [*sic*] principles be your pride; do these justify you in being slave-owners? – No, – no, – in direct opposition to English principle, you hold men in bondage; and, having breathed the miasma of slavery, subscribe to the opinion that these, your unoffending fellow immortals, [*sic*] should be kept in a state of ignorance. 'How else (said one to me, who spoke the general opinion) can the minority hold the majority in subjection, unless we keep their minds in a state of brutism?' [...] for all confess the Creole slave manifests the worst disposition; the African three or four years imported, the better; and the new Negro, the best. Thus does both theory and practice belie the assertion that they are brought here to be christianized [*sic*] and civilized.[89]

He then returns to the business-sense vein of argumentation, ending his presentation by demonstrating that the marginal utility to the merchant of that small differential between the cost of slave versus hired labor cannot possibly be comparable to the utility value of the merchant's immortal soul, for surely he would be brought to damning account in heaven for such criminally conscious misdeeds.[90] Since the trade was brought to a final end within ten years of the publication of Pilkington's pamphlet, however, the merchants were probably able to attend to the states of their immortal souls without too much loss of utility in the meantime.

Effects of Slave Revolts on Bahianos' Perceptions of the Illicit Trade

Whether fomented by the local British merchants or not, the Malês revolt in Bahia succeeded where British policy had failed: Brazilians began to take stock of the racial situation in Bahia, where blacks outnumbered whites in a disproportion that increased every day as long as the illegal trade flourished. As a result of this renewed awareness of these demographic dangers, not only were the leaders of the rebellion severely punished (executed by firing squad; sentences of up to six hundred lashes; life imprisonment with forced labor; deportations), but large numbers of free blacks were deported to Africa and many others "returned to Africa spontaneously to escape the climate of terror imposed on the African community. [...] Manumitted Africans could no longer freely rent houses, organize *batuques* [drumming parties], participate in candomblés, or be Muslims".[91] Bethell cites a speech by the President of Bahia to the Bahia legislative assembly in early 1835 reminding them of the increasing dangers to social harmony resulting from the continued importation of Africans.[92] After all, the white minority of Bahia had shrunk with the flight of the Portuguese after Independence to less than a quarter of the total population.[93] Nevertheless, not even this fear of a violent black revolt dampened the illegal slave trade for long – in Rio de Janeiro, less than two years later, British authorities were reporting that the trade had never been carried on "with greater activity and daring".[94] It would be nearly two more decades before the combination of intensified British naval confrontations and a newly stable Brazilian central government managed to bring an end to the illegal trade at last.

Finally, the story of British involvement in the slave trade of Bahia is a good illustration of how a set of values – capitalism and anti-slavery – that appear to go together in a broad context, in fact are seen to eat at and destroy one another when viewed in a specific historical and local context. The capitalist British merchants were in Bahia to make a profit; one of the most profitable enterprises there and then was the slave trade; and so, in the short run, it made perfect sense that British capital would go to support the slave trade, legal or not. This compromise cost the British community much of its moral superiority, as judged by its own cultural standards; and it cost something in local political influence, if the diplomatic correspondence is any guide; but it more than made up for these losses in the form of gains in economic advantage.

Chapter 3

Public and Private Lives of the British Community

The occupations and ambitions of the British merchants who lived in Bahia gradually changed over the course of the early nineteenth century, and so did the nature and influence of the community that they created around themselves. From 1808 through the 1810s, the British presence in most of the ports consisted of bachelor merchants, perhaps junior partners, who set themselves up in Brazil as quickly as possible in order to sell the excess wares that were being blocked from continental ports under Napoleon's blockade. Speed was essential, and the development of social relationships with locals was not a priority. Later, as supply and demand for British textiles and luxury goods stabilized and began to grow, the emphasis of British business expanded to encompass shipping of Brazil's primary exports alongside the indirect financial involvement in the slave trade discussed in the previous chapter.

The public face of the British community underwent changes as the century progressed. By the 1840s and 1850s, Great Britain's abolitionist policies had made the British more and more unpopular in Bahia. Many of their legal privileges were withdrawn, while the impending end of the slave trade rendered Bahian sugar less attractive as an investment, in comparison to coffee and manufacturing in Rio de Janeiro and São Paulo. By the latter half of the nineteenth century, the best-capitalized British merchants were turning their eyes toward the newly developing financial markets of São Paulo, and attrition from Bahia's British merchant community increased.[1] Later in the century, the new British arrivals tended to be tradesmen rather than merchants – such as watchmakers, machinists, or engineers working on the new railroads.[2] The merchant families who opted to stay eventually intermarried with Brazilians and the strict boundaries of the community gradually dissolved. Today, virtually nothing remains of the British presence in Bahia, apart from traces left in place names, idiomatic expressions, and a vague nostalgia among some *Bahianos* for the nineteenth century, the century of the *ingleses.*

The British community was numerically small in relation to the economic and political influence it exerted, and probably reached a maximum of 120 to 150 members by mid-century.[3] A petition from 1819 was signed with the names of fourteen British merchant firms, but by 1828 a different petition was signed by 23 firms, which shows that the number of firms had increased by sixty per cent in ten years.[4] However, by 1859 the number of firms had again fallen to 24, almost the same as in 1828.[5] This probably reflects the waxing and waning of British commercial interests in Bahia, according to the political and other vicissitudes of the early nineteenth century in Brazil.

Attitude and Adjustment

The two constant factors in the outlook of British merchants in Bahia were their preoccupations with cultural identity and personal financial gain. These took different forms as the political and economic context gradually shifted around them. At first it made no difference to business whether the British presented a semblance of 'community' to their Brazilian clients, but by mid-century this had become a fundamental aspect of their continuing success and security. The evidence suggests that this process did not happen by itself, but was to some extent a deliberate strategy of the British merchants for ensuring personal and commercial survival on several levels. A review of British attitudes towards Bahia through those decades illustrates this well.

In 1803, before the opening of the ports, a British merchant named John Turnbull briefly visited Bahia during a trip around the world. He expressed great excitement about the resources that Brazil could offer Britain in the war against Napoleon, not only as an outlet for merchandise, but also as a base for ship-building operations and the production of agricultural and other essential supplies such as rice. In Turnbull's view, the war on the Continent and the recent loss of the American colonies increased Brazil's importance to British interests.[6] Turnbull saw Brazil as a country bursting with potential, bound to become independent, and, considering Portugal's precarious situation at the time, more or less up for grabs. Especially interesting is his conviction that the merest nudge from the British government was all that would be needed to persuade the Brazilians to begin producing whatever was required by British markets.[7] Additionally, he urged his readers to consider how the growing Spanish and French influence in Brazil might yet ruin all of these possibilities: "Some further circumstances occurred to convince me, that a clandestine intercourse, very prejudicial to the interest of Great Britain in time of war, is maintained between the Spaniards and the Portuguese". And when he asked a band of local musicians to perform *God Save the King*, he and his group were treated instead to *La Marseillaise*, much to his annoyance.[8]

Turnbull's concluding statement about Brazil tells of the intensity of interest that may have been growing in the minds of many British merchants at that time:

> Brazil must, in every respect, be considered as a new country. We must sow before we can expect to reap. The maturer wisdom of [Great Britain], our greater knowledge of the nature of commerce and cultivation, must suggest the means to the Portuguese inhabitants and government; and the community of interest will insure us their cordial co-operation. No country under heaven … is better suited [in resources and location] than Brazil, both to render itself and allies great and rich.[9]

When Brazilian ports were opened to British imports at favorable duty rates five years after Turnbull's visit, the same frenzied excitement seemed to dominate the thinking of British merchants, who rushed in to take advantage of this new market as a way to overcome the hardship imposed by Napoleon's continental blockade. An account which covers the 1810s is that of John Luccock, a cloth merchant from Leeds who went to Rio de Janeiro in 1808 for exactly those reasons. He describes how British manufactured goods were unloaded, willy-nilly, into a port with inadequate facilities; so that the boxes of merchandise ended up splayed across the adjacent beaches, where breakage, spoilage and theft took their toll.[10]

Luccock's story, which was published shortly after his return to Britain, is illuminating. He had agreed to remain in Brazil for a maximum of ten years, until 1818, which he did; but he was able to bring over his wife and children in 1812. He died just eight years after returning home, at age 53, believing that his health had been ruined in Brazil. Historian Olga Pantaleão has described Luccock's experience as typical of most of the *ingleses* during this early period.[11] Luccock, however, was married, and had had his family as well a British manservant near him for most of that time.[12] In the earliest years of the British presence in Brazil, most merchants went to Latin America as bachelors to seek their fortunes and establish themselves professionally, intending (like Luccock) to return to Britain as soon as possible. However, many stayed on, and so the various British communities began to grow.

W. P. Robertson, writing in 1843 about his experiences as a merchant in South America in the previous decades, referred to "the highly irregular living of unmarried Englishmen, during the first years of their settlement at Buenos Ayres". He explained that this situation "gradually gave way to the softening and humanizing influence of female society; so that in 1818 or 1819 we had sobered down to a very well conducted community".[13]

Before the steamship and telegraph, which were only introduced in the 1850s and 1870s respectively, communications usually took two months to travel each way between Brazil and Britain. Under these circumstances, the isolation experienced by the British community of Bahia was quite real. Its members had to rely upon their own resources to maintain a sense of identity and cohesion, and to signal the separateness of that identity to the surrounding host society. The first problem in this respect was to establish its physical presence and social legitimacy. Large, luxurious homes were purchased or built in a very beautiful area just outside of the main town, which was called Corredor da Victoria, or Vitória in the modern spelling. The name does not refer to Queen Victoria, but to the mile-long road connecting the Forte de São Pedro, on Campo Grande, to the Igreja da Vitória, one of Salvador's oldest churches. Vitória remains, to this day, one of the best neighborhoods in Bahia.

Many British merchants acquired property throughout Victoria, in the main town, and in the interior of the state. Records at the Arquivo do Estado da Bahia show numerous real-estate purchases by British subjects throughout the early nineteenth century. Table 5 lists real estate properties bought and sold by individuals known to be British. Some, like those in Cachoeira or Juazeiro, were in distant rural areas. The record shows that for the early part of the century, British subjects bought and rented – rather than sold or leased out – property, showing a process of settlement and growth that would reverse itself later in the century. Although prices are not listed for sales or rentals, two mortgage transactions suggest that British subjects were willing to make substantial investments in real estate (two and four contos, 2:000$000 and 4:000$000, respectively). Such investments may have served to strengthen British merchants' ties to the Brazilian community, while enhancing their influence in the local economy.

Identity and Respectability

The next problem was to establish the respectability and especially the trustworthiness, in the eyes of a fervently Catholic population, of a foreign group made up mostly of Protestants. In 1812, the gentlemanly explorer Charles Fraser wrote to Lord Castlereagh from Porto Seguro, in the southern part of the province of Bahia, about the alarming ideas that the Brazilians whom he had met entertained with respect to the British:

> .... *a Nation of Foreigners & Heretics* whom the[...] Infallible Mother Church had uniformly taught them to regard with that peculiar degree of horror & detestation with which we contemplate the Inhabitants of the Infernal Regions.[14]

The same issue came up in a narrative written by the British merchant Henry Koster, who had grown up in Portugal and also was interested in the Brazilian point of view. In 1816 he published the following comments about the British merchants of Pernambuco, among whom he had lived for several years:

> Without any outward appearance of religion, how are we to expect that the people of Brazil are to regard us as any thing better than what we were represented to them as being in former times? – as pagans, animals, and horses – *pagoens, bichos,* and *cavallos,* this is literally true.[15]

Koster's interests were obviously economic. A bad image is bad for business, and in a religious country, any outward appearance of religion will be better than none at all, even if the religion in question were itself despised by the locals. Throughout Brazil, the British at first had had to bury their dead in unconsecrated ground. In Bahia, only in 1813 was permission granted for a small Protestant cemetery to be built off the Ladeira da Barra, a scenic spot overlooking the bay, just beyond the Victoria road. A British hospital was opened in 1815, and was housed under the same roof as a Protestant chapel for several decades.[16] The

Brazilian emperor's permission for non-Catholic services, however, included certain conditions: the building had to resemble a normal house, and no form of proselytizing was allowed.

By 1845, roughly half of the British community regularly attended Anglican church services, in a building large enough to accommodate a hundred.[17] By 1853, a yellow fever epidemic had forced the British hospital to relocate to the peninsula of Bonfim. At about the same time, the Anglican chapel came to be housed in a handsome classical building on Campo Grande, which was then a large military practice field located where the Victoria road meets the Fort of São Pedro on the edge of the old town.

Koster's recommended strategy for respectability appears to have paid off. A modern Bahian historian, Thales de Azevedo, wrote a newspaper article in 1993 about the need to preserve the British cemetery. He lamented the demolition (in 1975) of the British chapel on Campo Grande, which he described as "the most significant marker of the British presence among us, the beautiful old St. George's Church ... one of the city's most valuable monuments". Azevedo pointed to the British as having made an important contribution to the civilization of Bahia. But the visible presence of national institutions normally associated with private life not only enabled the British businessmen to appear respectable to Brazilians: at the same time it served to remind them of their own identity *as* different, reifying their separateness in a manner almost perversely positive.

A few stumbling blocks remained. Until about 1823 there was no Anglican clergyman in Bahia, so a degree of improvisation was necessary for the enactment of community rituals. The British consuls were equal to the task and began to solemnize the community's marriages, in a spirit of plucky self-reliance in isolation. One of the consuls even compared himself to a commander of a British ship of war on the high seas.[18] Along with the existence of the British burial ground, chapel, and hospital, such marriages were a fundamental means for recreating the respectable British middle-class family on Bahian soil. However, when the British consul William Pennell decided in 1823 to check and make certain that he had the legal authority to perform these marriages, he was sharply rebuked by George Canning, who replied that only a religious official, whether British or Brazilian, could legally preside over the marriages of British subjects in Brazil.[19] He was unmoved by Pennell's protests that Catholic priests in Bahia would never

consent to perform a marriage between Protestants, and insisted that
Pennell cease the practice at once.

The sudden realization that all of the marriages of British subjects
that had taken place in Bahia were invalid (to say nothing of the funeral
ceremonies) precipitated a crisis of legitimacy for the community, at
least for its uppermost members. For example, both Boothby and
Johnston, of the firm Boothby Johnston, the second most important
British firm in Bahia at that time,[20] had been married in Bahia by
William Pennell. As he put it,

> Mr. Boothby is desirous to do whatever is necessary to give a legal
> sanction to his Marriage. Mr. Hardman & Mr. Johnston (two
> Merchants now resident in the Brazils, who were married by me)
> will I am persuaded from my personal knowledge of their character,
> be desirous to pursue the same honourable conduct.[21]

The word "character" in this context seems to function as a key term
linking private to public respectability, hence also to social position
within the business hierarchy. Pennell went on to explain that several
children had already been born from these unions, and urgently asked
Canning to decide whether a second marriage ceremony in, say,
Scotland might "be sufficient in these cases, to make the offspring
already born, legitimate; or whether the defect can be cured by any
other remedy." One can see how the softening influence of family life
really depended upon important rigidities, essential for sustaining self-
respect – self-image – in the highest strata of this micro-society.

This tangled situation displays the intimate connections between the
most personal and the most impersonal areas of life, with the business
arena uneasily located somewhere in between. There is something
absurd about a distant government official holding the power to legitimate or destroy the personal worth of a man in the privacy of his nuptial
bed thousands of miles away. Nevertheless, it was precisely the sacrifices
necessary for sustaining such boundaries that kept the expatriate
community aware of who they really were, no matter how exotic the
situation might happen to be. Pennell's careful phrasing almost seems to
suggest that Johnston and Hardman were not quite as keen as Boothby
to enact a second wedding in Scotland, but if necessary Pennell would
take it upon himself to persuade them. "Character," legitimacy, law,
personal and collective respectability, and the survival of the
community as such – the survival, in effect, of British business concerns

in Brazil, as carried out by these particular people – were all inter-connected in ways that were fairly well understood.

Demography, Intermarriage, and Family Life

As the various members of the British families married among themselves and occasionally with Brazilians, the community grew both in size and stature throughout the first half of the nineteenth century. The most useful archival source for demographic and family history is to be found at the British chapel of Bahia, in a series of parchment books recording the baptisms, marriages, and burials of British and other Protestant residents from 1836 to 1873. The marriage records in particular have suffered water damage so that the data is incomplete; but nevertheless it is possible to reconstruct a qualitative picture of family and community life from these records.[22]

Cross-referencing names from all available sources (residency and naturalization applications, merchant signatures from official petitions, gravestone inscriptions, and secondary literature) with the baptism records allows for a rough calculation of fertility. Between 1836 and 1863, 62 children were born to known British subjects, out of which approximately sixty per cent were female. The twelve family trees which it has been possible to reconstruct show that each mother had an average of five children, and about one out of every ten infants died before reaching the age of five.

In that same period, 42 known members of the British community died and were buried in the British cemetery. Here the gender demographics are reversed, as two-thirds of these were male and one-third female.[23] There were deaths in every age range, one-eighth occurring after the age of seventy; the oldest, Mr. Charles Roberts, was ninety when he died, in the year 1850. The record shows an occasional female death in prime childbearing years. Three suicides are recorded, two of them of young men who were working as clerks in British firms.

Intermarriage with Brazilians was limited, particularly during the first half of the century. The archives of the Catholic Cúria Metro-politana de Salvador do not yield a single British name in its marriage records for the Victoria parish for the first half of the nineteenth century, although this may be due in part to the practice of translating English names into Portuguese on Brazilian documents – Michael Rooks was changed to Miguel Rochas, for example.[24] The surviving British chapel records show only two instances of a British man marrying a Brazilian woman: Andrew Comber married Maria Emilia Freitas in 1835, and Silvanus Earp wed Maria Amália de Sá Bittencourt in 1850. The Combers went on to have four children, one of whom, Charles William, grew up to marry Eleanor, the daughter of British merchant Joseph Porter, in 1864. This suggests that the Comber family aligned itself more closely with the British side than the Brazilian. In 1867 Joseph Porter's son, Eleanor's brother, married Hannah Helena, the daughter of Johnson Bielby (of Johnson Bielby & Company), whose own sister Maria Eliza had married the merchant Francis White Mackay in 1855 when he was still a clerk. That series of marriages brought together the Bielby, Mackay, Porter, and Comber merchant families in just three generations. Another series created close kinship ties among the prominent families Schwind, Benn, and Dutton in less than twenty-six years.

The small size of the merchant group renders such patterns difficult to explain, except in terms of a group of people who saw themselves as separate from the local community, and made a concerted effort to remain that way, raising their children with the expectation that they would not marry out. Still, British–Brazilian intermarriage may have occurred more frequently than these sources show. The British vice-consul James Wetherell noted in the 1840s that, "when some of the Brazilian [women] are married with foreigners, particularly Englishmen, [their married name] has a curious effect, e.g.: – "Donna Maria Gusmaô [sic] Eulalia de Silva e Jones".[25]

The community's child-raising practices were similar to those of British expatriate communities elsewhere, in that those who could afford to send their children to boarding schools in Britain often did so. Of those who remained, some probably had private tutors due to social reasons and the absence of a British school. Nevertheless, several of the children who were educated in Britain returned as adults to live in Bahia. Daughters, in particular, may have preferred to live in Bahia rather than return permanently to Britain. James Wetherell commented on the much higher prestige that young English ladies enjoyed within the expatriate community, compared to what they might expect in the home country.

> Foreign ladies, from their scarcity, are treated with considerable deference, and I think enjoy themselves much, although during a portion of the day-time they are left to their own resources. They

meet with much attention, and I do not wonder at their wishing to return after having been at home. In England they have not that same undivided attention paid them, but abroad they can be little *queens* if they like.[26]

However, the records also demonstrate that many British children who were born in Bahia did not remain, or return, to marry there. The probate inventory of the wealthy doctor John Ligertwood Paterson shows that in 1882, when he died, all of his heirs were in England, though two of his children had been born in Bahia.[27] Meanwhile, none of the four children born in Bahia to Dr. Alexander Paterson (who probably was John's brother) seems to have married there, so he too must have sent them to be educated in Britain. When British merchant George Mumford died in 1862, his probate inventory made reference to his longtime companion Maria Constança Ebbe and their eight children, five of whom were being educated in Europe at that moment.[28] On the whole, this pattern of social integration as a separate community within the local society resembles that followed by the British communities of Buenos Aires, Santiago, and Nova Lima during the nineteenth century.[29] Over successive generations, however, the Brazilianization of the community would be inevitable, though some British identity markers would persist for decades.[30]

Life in the British Enclave

The British merchants' households probably were large and bustling, with children, slaves, family, and associates dropping by for visits, as well as frequent outings to vacation homes. The American missionary Daniel Kidder mentioned in his narrative from 1845 that the English chaplain in Bahia, Rev. Parker, had a family home in Victoria and also a summer residence in Rio Vermelho, on the sea coast a few miles beyond the entrance to the bay.[31] Many of the British may have had such homes as a mark of status. Dr. Robert Dundas, who attended the British community for 25 years as medical superintendent of the British Hospital at Bahia, tells of a family struck with typhus while on holiday at their seaside property in São Lázaro. The household was said to consist of "Mr R.," his wife, his brother-in-law, an English housekeeper, and five black servants (who were probably slaves);[32] so in this household, three adults were served by a staff of six.

An example from the diplomatic correspondence shows that Consul William Pennell, who was probably the best-documented British resident of early nineteenth century Bahia, had brought with him two daughters – one of whom was old enough to escort Maria Graham around town during her visit in 1821[33] – and two nephews, who worked in merchant firms and also held jobs at the consulate.[34] Pennell's wife is never mentioned, so it is likely that he was a widower, and that his daughters (with or without an English housekeeper) would have had the responsibility for running the home, supervising the slaves,[35] managing the entertainment duties associated with the consul's position, and caring for him during his illnesses in a tense time of delicate political maneuvers associated with the political independence of Brazil.[36]

Most of the British merchants tended to establish their residences along the Victoria road.[37] This road follows a gradual descent from the edge of town, along an elevated ridge about 180 meters high overlooking the bay, sloping gently around the land's edge, and arriving at the sheltered beach of Porto da Barra. Along its upper reach, most of Bahia's British and other foreign merchants lived in mansions that consistently were described by visitors as being large, elegant, spacious, well-built, and tastefully decorated.[38] Perched along the summit of the ridge, these homes commanded stunning bay views that were repeatedly admired by the authors of travel narratives.

As it happens, the probate inventory of Dr. John Paterson allows for the re-creation of the full interior of one such British home, though from the latter half of the century. The inventory was compiled by the British consul, who appears to have walked through each room, taking down a list of the contents of each. Paterson had a large library, which doubled as a consulting room, on the first floor. Next to it, a drawing-room entrance containing a sofa and large cupboard led into the large drawing-room itself, furnished with a large table and eleven chairs, two sofas, eight upholstered chairs, and assorted small tables. After this came the sitting room, which was somewhat smaller; and then a stairway lobby with two cupboards containing fancy glassware. In addition there was a small, simply furnished, bedroom and an impressively furnished master bedroom. Paterson's personal items included a large collection of linen clothing (23 pairs of trousers, 54 collars, etc.) and a medallion representing his membership in the Brazilian Order of the Rose. The inventory ends with a "Ground Floor" category covering the dining room and ground floor rooms. Paterson's estate also had five hens, a duck, three horses, a cow and a calf; so the rural feeling of a Brazilian country property intermingled with the elegance of this Victorian gentleman's residence.[39]

The area of Victoria was generally said to possess the most pleasant of views, the purest air quality, and the deepest sense of peace to be found in the city of Bahia. Its British homes possessed extensive grounds, cultivated into gardens whose lush tropical vegetation contributed to an overall atmosphere of freshness, color, and fragrance that delighted those who visited it. John Candler commented on the "rich views of land and ocean" visible from the merchants' homes.[40] Maria Graham expressed great pleasure over a *soirée* in the garden house or gazebo of Consul Pennell, which "literally overhang[s] the bay. [Behind it] flowers and fruits mingle their sweets even down to the water's edge".[41] The British community's longtime doctor, Robert Dundas, declared of Victoria that "nothing more beautiful than this suburb can well be imagined".[42] Daniel Kidder was all but overwhelmed by "the finest gardens that Bahia affords, the most enchanting walks, and the most ample shade [...] the best houses, the best air, the best water, and the best society".[43] This American missionary remarked that whereas in Rio de Janeiro, each section of town had something to commend it, in Bahia the best of everything was united in Victoria, so it was a natural choice for any foreigner's residence. "He who looks for any one spot that combines more of external beauty", enthused Kidder, "will roam long and widely over the face of the earth".[44] The British homes were described by James Wetherell as being built of stone, with porticoes and large flights of steps, tiled roof, and exterior walls plastered with stucco, "washed either white or some pale colour, producing, if in the country, a beautiful contrast to the surrounding green foliage".[45]

Among themselves, the community maintained an active social life. This included evening entertainments in the open air, and dances held in open-windowed salons. "Small dancing parties frequently take place", wrote Wetherell, "and when all the windows and doors are open it is really not so warm as an English drawing room".[46] The general atmosphere in the Victoria neighborhood was very pleasant. Dr. Dundas explained that "unlike what occurs in other hot regions, the delightful serenity and coolness of tropical moonlight may be enjoyed with perfect impunity, the mind being undisturbed by those visions of fever and malaria which float before the imagination in less favoured climates".[47] This interaction between impressions – the imagination, *imaginário*, that the British brought with them to Brazil – and actual physical conditions, recurs constantly in the story of British life in Bahia, though this was not always a health-producing interaction. Sometimes their ideas created a collective subjective reality that did not correspond to the actual physical conditions around them, and this could cause severe emotional and physical strain. Dundas did report that the British body could not healthily sustain a residence of more than five to seven years in Bahia, and noted that the problem was especially severe for females. The implications of this are explored more fully in the following chapter.

British Merchants at Work

While most British merchants preferred to live just outside of the main town, their workplaces (known as 'counting-houses') were generally located on or around Rua da Praia, in the busy lower city. This street ran the length of what was then a very narrow patch of land between the port on one side, and a steep hill ascending to the upper city on the other.[48] In addition to commercial buildings, the custom-house (*alfândega*) and enormous warehouses were located there. Kidder's experience of the Rua da Praia was that "the buildings are old, although generally of a cheerful exterior [...] the street is very narrow, uneven, and wretchedly paved".[49]

Visitors to Bahia almost invariably commented on the crowds, dirt, and noise of Rua da Praia, and contrasted it with the beauty of the city viewed from the sea and the relative calm and pleasantness of the upper town. James Prior, a British naval officer who visited Bahia in 1813, expressed his relief at the moment of moving out of the range of the Praia stench: "Here the chest freely expanded, and we could be said to breathe once more without fear".[50] Maria Graham, the 36-year-old wife of a naval captain who stopped at Bahia with him in late 1821 and later became governess to the children of Brazilian emperor Pedro II, wrote this lively description of Rua da Praia:

> It is extremely narrow, yet all the working artificers bring their benches and tools into the street... Along the walls are fruit-sellers, venders of sausages, black-puddings, fried fish, oil and sugar cakes, negroes plaiting hats or mats [...] dogs, pigs, and poultry [...] and as the gutter runs in the middle of the street, every thing is thrown there from the different stalls, as well as from the windows.[51]

Each day, British merchants commuted on foot from the heights of Victoria to the noise, bustle, sights, and smells of Praia and back again. The haven-like quality of their homes, praised by experienced travelers, must have been substantially enhanced by this sharp daily contrast between home and workplace. At the same time, the necessity of physically experiencing this daily attack on his sensibilities gradually inured the longtime resident to the shock experienced by the new arrival. This is one aspect of the process of psychological change undergone by members of Bahia's British community as they adjusted to their tropical home, and it is of special interest because it so encapsulates both the separateness and the connectedness of British residents to the Brazilian reality in which they were immersed.

Even the commute itself represented a mixing of the exotic and the ordinary. Almost every travel narrative gave considerable space to describing the *cadeira*, a sort of palanquin taxi consisting of a chair suspended from a wooden frame and usually carried at a diagonal angle on the shoulders of two barefoot black servants. The hilly topography of Bahia, combined with the disrepair of its streets, rendered wheeled vehicles impractical; exotic or not, the *cadeira* was usually accepted as a matter of course by British visitors.[52] From their perspective, it added considerably to the local color:

> You meet with captains of ships, English and American sailors, fashionable ladies, bishops and fat priests, passengers from emigrant ships, the old and the young, the lame and the blind, all riding about in these cadeiras.[53]

In addition to the visual carnival of color and movement, the widespread use of *cadeiras* created an auditory experience that added to the exoticism. In Wetherell's words:

> A person fresh from England, and the bustle and noise of an English town, will be much surprised at the *quiet* of Bahia. The absence of vehicles [...] the want of horses, the nearly noiseless tread of the unshoed black population [...] give it thus the appearance of a deserted city, as if something had happened to the inhabitants.[54]

It was not only the widespread use, practical advantages, and entertainment value of the *cadeira* that made it part of the daily integration of British merchants and their families into the local society. Status considerations probably played a part in the decision not only to hire *cadeiras*, but even to own one – and the slaves to carry it. Most evidence suggests that the British walked far more often than was socially acceptable, or even physically healthy.[55] Nevertheless, they kept private *cadeiras* and slaves to carry them. Dr. Dundas mentions a woman, "Mrs. D., wife of a British merchant, returning home in her cadeira – a sort of palanquin peculiar to Bahia".[56] The probate inventory of John Andrews, dated 1862, listed five slaves including "Nei, African, about 40 years of age, *cadeira* carrier".[57] How might this have been justifiable, in terms of the anti-slavery stance fundamentally required for a proper British identity during the early nineteenth century?

American missionary Daniel Kidder unwittingly revealed the analogy which probably served to rationalize slave ownership in the status-conscious minds of British merchants: "To keep a cadeira or two, and negroes to bear them, is as necessary for a family in Bahia, as the keeping of carriages and horses elsewhere".[58] Kidder observed, without the slightest irony, that the livery of the unshod carriers and the expense of the curtains and ornaments of the *cadeira* served to denote the rank and style maintained by the family.

Kidder, who elsewhere in his book praised efforts to end slavery in Brazil, was able here to draw a direct analogy between a black man and a horse, not only as a source of labor power, but principally as a material possession conferring status upon its owner.[59] Kidder was unlike the average British merchant in that he had long personal experience of slaves and slavery in the southern United States. But under the circumstances, the rationalization did seem to offer a fairly straightforward way for an otherwise liberal-minded British businessman to make the conceptual shift necessary to become a slave-owner in Bahia. The question of slave ownership, then, is a theme pertaining to the material circumstances as well as the psychological adaptation of the British merchant community in Bahia.

Habit and Appearance

In imagining the daily activities of the British merchant community, it is necessary to have an image of how they looked. The main aspect of personal appearance usually is the wearer's apparel. How did they dress? How did they look against the background of early nineteenth-century Bahia? What impression did this make on outside observers? Because of its social and economic connotations, clothing may be read as a text or code, telling the story of the wearer's social role in the context of a physical and social environment with all its historical specificities.

Clothing is an obvious vehicle for expressing group affiliation and/or identity in general, thus serving the function of immediately including or excluding others from the group. Partly for that reason, details of dress are often carefully recorded in historical sources. Also, clothes affect the wearer's health, as the body is freed or constrained in systematic, gender-specific ways over long periods of time. In the particular situation of the British community of Bahia, the need to signal identity apparently outweighed by far the need for physical comfort. Thus, it provides another way to examine the situation of the isolated British expatriates. Trying to live in a physical-social environment very different from their own, and where their very difference was a key factor keeping them together, these individuals were preserving their ability to cope as a group while preventing each individual from adapting too closely to Bahia.

John Luccock, the cloth merchant from Leeds who worked in Rio de Janeiro during the 1810s, made a point of comparing British and Brazilian clothing styles. He pointed out that his Brazilian buyers did not favor the dark, drab colors worn by British men of their class. Luccock's note was intended as a market recommendation. He rejected several bales of fabric sent by his supplier, for this reason:

> [These are] too gloomy for people who laugh at themselves. Let us have no drabs – we have no Quakers here. We want no dismal colours suitable for an English November. [...] We live in a lively climate, and with people who love to laugh.[60]

Obviously, in the saturated markets of Bahia and Rio de Janeiro during the 1810s, merchants' concerns had to be on the side of understanding Brazilian tastes so that these could be catered to. Luccock's tone even suggests that he was not unsympathetic to the Brazilian predilection for liveliness in dress and demeanor. But the issue of different tastes in clothing may gradually have taken on a more important function for the British community – that of establishing their own superior status vis-à-vis Brazilians of their own class and above

Traces of this may be found in later narratives. By 1856, Wetherell, far from appreciating the liveliness represented by the bright colors worn by Brazilian men, described them in a deprecatory way:

The Brazilians, the men, when they appear in public, are very showy in their dress, quite French in their fashions, and as far as possible removed from the quiet of an English taste.[61]

But Wetherell also thought that Brazilian men ought not to wear dark clothes, either:

A full suit of black is the proper dress for ceremonious visiting, &c., – an absurd custom in a tropical climate, and a relic of Portuguese barbarism.[62]

The first criticism appears to blame cultural differences, but the second suggests that no correct solution was possible. Brazilians' departure from the discreet British taste was a mark of inferiority, but dark clothing was obviously ridiculous in a hot climate when worn by the showy Brazilians, regardless of the formal social circumstances.

According to Wetherell, the fashion sense of elite Brazilian men veered from the offensive to the absurd. He saw their styles in terms of extremes: too brightly decorated, too dark and oppressive, too overdone in public, and too slovenly in private:

Upon returning to his house, a Brazilian will remove everything but his shirt and drawers ... putting on a dressing-gown, and thrusting his bare feet into tamancas (wooden shoes) he will remain in this undress.[63]

Wetherell found this custom of private undress bordering on the contemptible, particularly as it contrasted so sharply with what to him was an excess of self-decoration in public. His remarks were meant for an audience of elite British readers, who would know that a respectable person would behave as if on display even in the privacy of his own home.

On this point, Maria Graham provided corresponding evidence for women, though she visited Bahia twenty years before Wetherell. Acutely aware of the function of fashion as social insignia, she noticed and recorded details of women's clothing very carefully during her visits. She also interpreted her observations in revealing ways. On a Friday morning in October of 1821, the daughter of Consul Pennell took her on a round of morning visits at the houses of her Brazilian acquaintances. Graham was appalled by what they saw:

When they appeared, I could scarcely believe that one half were gentlewomen. As they wear neither stay nor bodice, the figure becomes almost indecently slovenly, after very early youth; and this is the more disgusting, as they are very thinly clad, wear no neck-handkerchiefs, and scarcely any sleeves.[64]

Her subsequent discovery that these same Brazilian gentlewomen were perfectly capable of presenting themselves in full European formal style did faze Graham somewhat, but not for long. At a ball given by the British consul three days after her round of visits, she admitted having

great difficulty in recognising the slatterns of the other morning. The senhoras were all dressed after the French fashion: corset, fichu, garniture, all was proper, and even elegant, and there was a great display of jewels.[65]

But, alas, the Brazilians lacked *grace*. Since they did not *habitually* wear the corset and other restrictive garments, they could not move naturally in them. Therefore,

[O]ur English ladies, though quite of the second rate of even colonial gentility […] bore away the prize of beauty and grace; for after all, the clothes, however elegant, that are not worn habitually, can only embarrass and cramp the native movements […] 'she who would *act* a gentlewoman in public, must *be* one in private life.'[66]

Unlike Wetherell, she does not criticize the French showiness of Brazilian women's formal dress, but that is probably because British women also followed French styles and did not mind being showy. Bright clothing was all right for women, but only as long as it was displayed with the proper deportment; and here it was that Brazilian women failed to make the grade, as far as Graham was concerned. As it happens, Wetherell noted the very same flaw in Brazilian men:

When thus 'got up,' they have a stiff and awkward appearance, easily to be accounted for; they are quite unaccustomed to the finery – 'ease before elegance.'[67]

These remarks suggest a British attitude toward Brazilians that had to do with much more than superficial appearance. After all, clothes are just merchandise, and can be bought for money as any merchant knows. The real superiority of the British taste lay in the meta-garment, the *habit*, of wearing restrictive and over-layered clothes in every circumstance. In a way, both Wetherell and Graham believed that the true British attitude was to be demonstrated by this very refusal to accommodate the foreignness of the surrounding climate. To change one's clothing styles for something more suitable to the circumstances would amount to giving up the real essence of a British appearance: elegance and grace. These were seen to flow exclusively from the daily habit of wearing the clothes that one would be wearing if one were in Britain, which is in a sense to say that Britain is where one properly ought to be, and where one will certainly return as soon as possible.

In the service of this idealized non-surrender of their bodies, British men wore layered clothing and walked everywhere in the sun. Dundas pointed out the dangers of the excessive perspiration that resulted from such habits, but the merchants apparently would not listen.[68] Meanwhile, each day, British women had to remain at home while wearing layered dresses over tight corsets, in the absence of any other social pressure to do so.[69] Clearly, the physical discomfort endured by British men and women every day, and their free hand in criticizing the customs of Brazilian elites, were just two sides of the same coin. It was one more artificial barrier between the community and its environment. It was, in fact, a way in which they simultaneously affirmed and denied the obvious – that traditional British habits constituted inappropriate behavior in the Brazilian (or at least the Bahian) context.

According to Dr. Dundas, British women became physically ill in Bahia at a higher rate than British men. He found this noticeable enough to treat it a separate section of his book, which he entitled "European Females in Tropical Climates":

> This unexpected result must, I apprehend, be accounted for by the more indolent habits and mode of life of the former, favoured, if not altogether induced, by the languour inseparable from high temperature, sanctioned by the prevailing customs in most tropical climates, where household occupations are not attended to as in Europe, where fashion or custom precludes the enjoyment of active exercise abroad, and where even mental exertion is to some extent laborious.[70]

Dundas appears to be making a reference to slavery, as well as to British women's habits of daily living:

Notwithstanding [...] the more regular and temperate habits of the female, and her exemption from many of the ordinary sources of tropical disease, as exposure to the sun, atmospheric vicissitudes, over-fatigue, &c., yet are these advantages more than counter-balanced by the inactivity and indolence almost necessarily connected with her position.[71]

Thus Dundas implies that private lifestyle choices were the real culprit behind the illnesses that were so commonly suffered by Europeans in Bahia. Since most of those Europeans happened to be British, it seems likely that those choices had a lot to do with maintaining the psychological protection of their clearly demarcated identities, even at the cost of the physical safety of their bodies. The men need not have exposed themselves to sun or over-fatigue; they could have used a *cadeira*, and adopted the local custom of taking an afternoon nap. The women did not have a choice. Dundas admits that they had to remain at home, indolent and inactive, in order to express their proper role as respectable high-status wives *in both cultural languages*. It is likely that the local elites could tolerate the spectacle of British men walking around in the sun more easily than that of a British woman living an active life outside of the confines of their houses, let alone of the enclave itself.

Elite Brazilian women were required to stay at home almost all of the time, but they were able to wear light, loose clothing. This the British women could not do; Maria Graham's comments on the in-decency of Brazilian women's house clothes makes this clear. Wearing tight garments all day long, kept "almost necessarily" at home, and unable to pursue the physical, mental and social activities which presumably would have kept them at least as healthy as the men, it is no wonder that the British women got sick. In essence, they were paying in their bodies the price of keeping up the behavioral demands of both British and Brazilian society. A cultural discourse interrelating nationality, class, hygiene, climate, and health thus operated to keep the British self-consciously separate from Bahia, its environment, and its people.

Chapter 4

Mind, Body, and Perception: Health and the British Expatriate

Dr. Robert Dundas noticed that British men and women frequently experienced severe physical and emotional illnesses while living in Bahia, and worked for decades to try and understand the reasons why. One systematic aspect of the phenomenon, he wrote, was the new arrival's overwhelming elation with the beauty of the place; how this enthusiasm gradually mellowed to a general satisfaction characterized by good health for a few years, if good personal habits were maintained; and then, suddenly, came a sharp downslide into a state of physical malaise and emotional distress. In the section of his book entitled "First Symptoms of Break-Up", Dundas described how his countrymen would endure in this depressed state for months, even years,

> complaining of mental and bodily fatigue on slight exertion – their air languid, the feelings below par, the countenance sallow, the eye dull and with a slight tinge of yellow, the pulse weak and easily accelerated, the appetite modified, the lips slightly clammy, the bowels irregular, the urine commonly scanty and turbid, the testes pendulous, with a peculiar sense of uneasiness, irregular distribution of animal heat, profuse perspiration from trifling causes, moral or physical, and a morbid sensibility to the slightest atmospheric vicissitudes.[1]

Because Dundas included moral (emotional) circumstances as well as physical influences in his analysis, the conclusions related in his book reveal something about the community's subjective experience. Dundas observed that for the first seven or eight years of the expatriate's tropical residence, the urine was markedly acid; "this state, under the influence of climate, gradually changes"; and finally, as the subject fell ill, it became neutral, or even alkaline.[2] He interpreted the suddenness of the onset of illness to mean that "the economy [had been] profoundly charged with the elements of disease".[3] In other words, Dundas concluded that something about the physical and moral environment of Bahia was a time bomb for Europeans: no matter how healthy they seemed, their metabolism slowly and invisibly became contaminated, and sooner or later many would succumb to ill health, fevers, internal disorders, and finally death. In his "endeavours to solve the difficult problem of the period at which a tropical residence can no longer be borne with impunity", Dundas assumed that there was something inevitable about their lack of resistance.[4] Although he was interested in emotional effects of the illness, he did not really look at the probable emotional causes, the collective subjective environment in which the British were embedded.

In addition to the physical stresses endured by the British community in Bahia, evidence of constant emotional anxiety during the tense years surrounding the process of Brazil's Independence from Portugal may be found in the diplomatic correspondence of Consul William Pennell.[5] A possible indication of the spiritual (emotional) state of the British community at that time was the financial value which they placed on the presence of an Anglican clergyman, for whom the merchants insisted (over Foreign Office objections[6]) on offering and advertising a salary of 2:500$000 (£600), two and a half times what they were offering for the post of British surgeon at the community's private hospital. When a decision was being reached in the early 1820s about appointing someone to the post, the discussion reached an emotional level unusual for the normally dry consular correspondence. In an 1820 letter concerning the importance of posting a British chaplain and surgeon to Bahia, Pennell remarks:

> [I] have heard intelligent Foreigners (even of the Catholic Religion) speak with approbation of that peculiarity in British Commerce by which such an interest is shown ... to the morals, the health, and the misfortunes of British Subjects in a foreign clime, & as tending to elevate the character of British Merchants beyond that point to which an undivided attention to mere profit & loss would have carried it.[7]

When Pennell had been engaged in salary negotiations upon arriving in Bahia some years earlier, he had firmly believed that money could compensate for personal hardship. He wrote in 1818: "[I was informed] that the Income was such as to render it advisable to risk the ill effects of climate, and the many other inconveniences attending a residence in this Country".[8] Despite its natural beauty, Bahia was widely viewed as a hardship post. A petition signed by nearly all of the British merchants in 1819, in which they urged the Foreign Office not to reduce Pennell's share in the consular fund, cited some of the sacrifices required in living at Bahia:

> We do not think [the consular emoluments] in any respect, too large, when a due consideration is bestowed on the excessive prices paid for every article of subsistence, the nature of the climate, and other circumstances besides the expense necessarily incurred to support, in a becoming manner, the respectability of the Consular Office.[9]

Pennell himself had stated earlier that the elevated salary was a prime motivation for him to exchange his post at Bordeaux for Bahia, and was outraged when at first the raise did not materialize.[10] After spending a few years in Bahia, however, Pennell appeared to have found that something more was required to sustain emotional health under the circumstances. The letter he wrote in 1822, requesting a clergy-man, contained the following statement:

> The Mercantile Society is benefited by the presence of men of liberal education – their observations and researches may aid the progress of knowledge, may suggest improvement, in our own Institutions (or what would be better) *teach us to prefer them to all change* – a preference, which it might be presumed would not arise from the blindness of prejudice, but from the perspicacity of cultivated minds.[11]

This is a puzzling statement. The circular reasoning concerning the role of a liberal education is not typical of Pennell's crisp prose. He seems to be expressing a yearning for something to force him and other British expatriates to remain always the same, to protect them from a change that was arising in response to the foreignness of their surroundings. But why? Loss of identification with the homeland seemed to be Pennell's chief fear for the character of British subjects abroad, a danger that he and a committee of merchants hoped would be assuaged and made more manageable by the presence of authoritative British figures, in particular a spiritual leader.

It seems very likely that the British clergyman's expected role was indeed to keep the British community closed off as much as possible.

The testimony of American traveler Thomas Ewbank, concerning his impression of an 1856 service at the British Chapel in Rio de Janeiro, gives this idea some weight:

> The prayer-book handed me was one of those issued 'by authority,' polluted with royal mandates, enjoining upon its owner what he is to believe and whom he is to pray for ... accompanied with a profusion of damnatory clauses, enough to make a savage shudder. It tells every one who doubts its dicta 'without doubt he shall perish everlastingly.'[12]

This form of worship irritated Ewbank enough for him to snap, "I would not stay a week in heaven with the red bigots that conceived it, or the intriguing ones that perpetuate it".[13] It is very likely that the same prayer-books were used by the British congregation at Bahia, at its mid-century height.

The British chaplain exhorted his congregation to stick to its creed. The British doctor looked to medical explanations for the malaise he observed. The British diplomat seemed more drawn to concerns of character and national identity for describing the danger, even though he himself was very ill at the time. In all these cases, a problem of physical and psychological dimensions was perceived to be systemically present in Bahia's British community throughout the early nineteenth century, and the problem was considered to be endangering the success of the British merchant enterprise overall.

Pressures, Counter-Pressures, Mental and Physical Health

The British community of Bahia was composed, first and foremost, of wholesale merchants; theirs were the interests reflected in the trade treaties negotiated with Brazil.[14] All other members may be viewed as satellites to these central players. As such, the group's primary interest, as well as the dominant characteristic of its daily activity, was business: buying, selling, signing contracts, transporting and warehousing goods, extending credit, collecting debts, supervising employees, and so on. Economists tell us that success in these activities largely depends on the agent's ability to maintain a realistic sense of inner confidence regarding the immediate future, that is, on having a critical level of certainty that the situation will remain stable enough for contracts of all types to be upheld. It is probably fair to assume that such confidence was painfully lacking for the British merchants of Bahia, at least between 1808 and 1824. The ups and downs may be empirically trackable: as the insurance industry exists to sell improved certainty for financially risky situations, insurance prices may be viewed as an accurate, quantifiable measure of fluctuations in the insurer's level of future uncertainty at a given time with respect to a given outcome. Unfortunately, there are presently no studies of British insurance prices for independence-era Latin America with this perspective.[15] Nevertheless, it is not unreasonable to suggest that some tension would have been experienced by the merchant who needed to keep his firm profitable under volatile conditions, especially when these were compounded by the relatively unreliable means of transportation and communication of the time. Furthermore, as the slave trade gradually foundered on the shoals of British militant abolitionism, the British merchants of Bahia, whose capital was indirectly tied up in the success of individual slave shipments, probably would have had an increasingly hard time identifying their private interests with those of their sovereign government. All of this, combined with the increasing British reluctance to fully connect with the local society, caused further stress in that it restricted legitimate access to useful sources of support.[16]

The same political forces that opened up the window of opportunity for British merchants to establish themselves in Bahia also made their position there complex and unpredictable during the first decade and a half. To recall the discussion in Chapter 1 regarding the consul's lack of control over the merchants' arms smuggling activities, one might ask why these merchants made the decision to actively choose a side in a conflict for which in fact they had every interest in remaining neutral. Barring advance knowledge of the outcome, their behavior was not quite rational. Was the short-term profit motive such an overriding force in the businessman's mind that he could not see the danger? Or did a Turnbull-ish enthusiasm for an independent, British-friendly Brazil, spiced with a Byronesque sense of adventure and excitement in exposing themselves to danger in support of an heroic cause, lead many of these British men and women to act in ways that only increased the amount of danger and uncertainty they faced? Bahia was the main place in Brazil where the independence tensions were more than a battle of nerves. Real violence broke out in the streets. The anticipation of widespread social conflict was strong enough for the Foreign Office to arrange for a British naval vessel to be stationed on the Brazilian coast, with orders to evacuate British persons and property if necessary.

This was the main reason why Maria Graham happened to be in Brazil during 1821 to 1824; her husband was the captain of such a ship. One of the things that Graham noticed during her stay was the way in which different segments of the British population in Brazil were acting on different principles of positioning. While neutrality was the official line, she saw that in Bahia, the naval officers were covertly supporting Portuguese loyalists.[17] Consul Pennell was unable to persuade a British naval officer to promise protection to a high-ranking Bahian official in case mob violence was to break out.[18] Given his professionalism and experience, Pennell probably would not have made such a request if it were not in the longer-term interests of British policy; however, he carried virtually no authority with the captain, who insisted on neutrality. This probably intensified the overall atmosphere of no one being quite in control of the situation, with stakes very high in terms of political privilege, property, and life.

The material situation of the merchant community during the early nineteenth century differed substantially from what it would be after 1850 in another respect: isolation from the homeland was far greater in the early years. Regular steamship service between Bahia and Europe, and the first transatlantic telegraph cable, were only established in 1851 and 1874, respectively. These technological advances fundamentally changed the relationship between Brazil and the rest of the world. Before, communications from Bahia to Europe took about two months to reach their destinations, depending on the vicissitudes of weather, political circumstances on the seas and at ports of call, and the routing convenience of the trader or officer commanding the ship, among other things.[19] Afterwards, communications were much faster, drawing closer the planners and executors of British policy towards Brazil and other parts of the world, reducing opportunities for local improvisation and flexible response.[20]

Another source of materially-based stress would have been the constant fear of street violence. Maria Graham reports in her straightforward style:

 The police here is in a wretched state. The use of the dagger is so frequent, that the secret murders generally average two hundred yearly, between the upper and lower towns.[21]

The wretched state did not show much improvement throughout the early nineteenth century.

Finally, the health situation cannot be ignored as a material factor of stress. Even if Dundas's eventual conclusions about the toxicity of Bahia's climate were wrong, the constant belief in the mind of each British person that his or her body was slowly being poisoned by foreign contaminants present in the air, water, and soil would eventually take its toll upon the sturdiest man or woman. Furthermore, the actual illnesses to which one or one's family and acquaintances fell prey must be taken into account. Many a British subject was rushed home to Europe in critical condition, including Consul Lindemann's wife, Consul Pennell, and Dr. Dundas himself. Even Maria Graham became sick during her few days in Bahia. Many British women, men, and children died in Bahia as a result of illness.[22]

It is the psychological effect of this constant, background fear of illness and disintegration that is of greatest interest here. The British merchants cared greatly about their health; it just happened that given their reasons for being in the tropics, these merchants had to engage in an unsettling optimization calculus, whereby health risks were weighed against profit opportunities as each increased over time. Dundas was quite conscious of this. In a key section of his book, he describes his self-appointed professional mandate:

> To assist the practitioner in arriving, under circumstances of doubt, at a sound opinion on one of the most serious and embarrassing, as well as one of the most frequent questions submitted to his judgment in all tropical countries: viz., the period beyond which a longer residence cannot safely be permitted to the European. As this decision will frequently involve not only the health, but the future career and fortunes of the individual, the bearing and importance of the question will at once be comprehended by all tropical residents, professional and non-professional.[23]

The irony, in the particular case of Bahia, was that the climate was in fact fundamentally healthy. Judging from a close reading of Dundas' own observations, most of the differential in ill health experienced by the British in Bahia (as compared to affluent Brazilians) was directly connected to their insistence on clinging to particular living habits known to be pernicious in the professional opinion of Dundas himself.

Thus the British appear to have generated much of the pestilence they perceived in their environment by insisting on overruling the most modern medical advice, as well as going entirely against the grain of local knowledge. Why they did this had a great deal to do with their style of identifying national with personal identity, then sustaining it in a context where nearly all familiar boundaries, and ways of marking them, were absent.

Dr. Robert Dundas, who was appointed to head the British Hospital at Bahia in 1819 and spent the next 25 years in that capacity, wrote a scientific treatise explaining the situation at the end of his sojourn. The book – entitled *Sketches of Brazil, including New Views on Tropical and European Fever* – dealt almost exclusively with Dundas' experiences and observations of Bahia and its residents during the first half of the nineteenth century. Most remarkably, until now this work has remained unused as a source for the social history of the British presence in Brazil. As such, it is valuable for two distinct purposes: first, the factual reporting of physical conditions prevalent in Bahia and the overall health of its British and Brazilian residents; and second, the style in which Dundas interpreted and explained the observed phenomena, and what this can tell us about the efforts of a highly educated, socially well-connected, British professional to make sense of his experiences in early nineteenth-century Bahia. A second useful source are the collected notes of British vice-consul James Wetherell, edited and published posthumously by his friends in 1860 and entitled *Stray Notes from Bahia: Being Extracts from Letters, &c., During a Residence of Fifteen Years*. Wetherell lived in Bahia from 1843 to 1857, which means that he arrived on the scene the year after Dundas left it. Wetherell was then twenty-one years old, and seems to have been constantly fascinated by his surroundings. His notes provide useful support and illustration for many of the arguments set forth by Dr. Dundas, as well as others suggested by this historian.

The defining feature of Bahia's British community during the early half of the nineteenth century was its separateness from the surrounding society. This was expressed physically in the geographical location of its residential enclave, psychologically through a medical discourse of health and climate, and socially in the restriction of acceptable relationships with Brazilians and with British subjects of a lower class than their own. The overall subjective experience of Bahia for the average British resident changed with the length of his or her stay. Dundas noted how Bahia intoxicated the European's spirit, enveloping him in an intensely pleasurable experience during the first few years. However, he maintained that an extended stay was likely to injure the body's constitution beyond recovery, not only physically but also mentally. The main question in the doctor's mind was to determine the precise point of diminishing marginal returns to health, as it were; and upon reflecting on the evidence he observed in Bahia, Dundas concluded that "a European in the prime of life, and free from any especial tendency to disease, will resist the deleterious influence of the tropics for a period varying from five to seven years, according to circumstances".[24]

In his book, he describes a mixture of healthy and unhealthy factors in the British experience of Bahia. In the end, Dundas considered Bahia to present a set of interesting exceptions to the situation of British merchant communities elsewhere in the tropics. According to him, it should not have been a healthy place at all, but it was. Dundas submits his study as a guide for British tropical-medicine doctors and other professionals whose duties required a sophisticated understanding of how setting, climate, and social dynamics could affect the health of expatriate individuals, both during and after their time abroad. Bahia, in his opinion, provided an ideal case study, which may mean that his analysis of this particular British merchant community can be helpful as a control group for comparison to those in other parts of the world during this period.

According to Dundas, the city of Bahia presented a superabundance of factors that would normally be expected to lead to enormous levels of epidemic disease and general insalubrity.[25] The streets were ill-paved and usually had an open gutter running down the center, through which flowed the town's raw sewage. Also, "when once out of order, the streets seem[ed] never to be repaired, but left to become, in process of time, almost impassible".[26] Houses had no water closets, and were crowded and poorly ventilated. Throughout the first half of the nineteenth century, all water supplies had to be transported on the heads of black servants or slaves.[27] There was no provision for the collection of trash, and the dead were buried inside churches and city limits. Finally, in every season, heavy rains inundated the lower city, soaking it with the "filth and offal" of the upper city.[28]

One result of this was a vast accumulation of refuse in the middle of public thoroughfares such as the Conceição da Praia by the port, where "there are heaps, or rather mounds, of decaying animal and vegetable matters, fermenting under the powerful rays of a tropical sun, disengaging every kind of noisome effluvia, and often of such an offensive character as to impress the sense of taste scarcely less powerfully than that of smell".[29]

Nevertheless, despite all of the dangerously insalubrious characteristics of Bahia, no powerful disease had ever ravaged the town. "Every species of endemic or epidemic malady – yellow fever, cholera, influenza, typhus, and dysentery"[30] had passed over this particular tropic port. Dundas credits this to the evenness of the temperature (hardly ever below 22 celsius in winter, or above 28 celsius in summer, the daily fluctuation being about six degrees)[31] and the constant gentle sea breeze enjoyed by its residents. Bahia's "freedom from atmospheric vicissitudes" was superior to any other place he knew. This was especially true with respect to the area in which most of the British merchants made their homes. Without question, the Victoria neighborhood was in the healthiest part of town. Since most of Dr. Dundas' patients (and he himself) probably lived there, it is richly treated in his book. He repeats the lush and pleasing description relayed by most visitors to that neighborhood, quantifying details such as the height of the road running along the ridge above the bay (some two hundred meters).

Dundas also discusses what he viewed as the Victoria's delicate balance of micro-environmental factors upon the health of its residents. Because it was a mile south of town and at a higher altitude, the area was exposed to strong humid trade winds, as distinct from the gentle constant breeze that pervaded the more sheltered main town. Or, more accurately, it became exposed to such winds after the sheltering Graça Wood, some 800 meters upwind of Victoria, was cut down in 1822. This happened because the city had been blockaded by pro-independence factions and troops of the Portuguese general Madeira occupied Victoria as a defense outpost. Madeira then ordered that Graça Wood be completely clear-cut in order to keep the rebels from advancing under its cover. As a long-term result of this political stratagem, "the strong sea-breeze being no longer broken by the woody screen, intermittent fevers have been of much more frequent occurrence in the Victoria".[32]

Varying references to the 'air' of Bahia illustrate the contradictory ways in which the British regarded the climate that constantly surrounded and affected them. Dundas managed to see Bahia as simultaneously

super-healthy and super-pestilent by crediting the former circumstance
to the Bahia's unique *breeze* – healthy air moving into the city,
implicitly from the outside, the beyond, the not-Bahia:

> [If not for] the influence of a NEVER-FAILING BREEZE [...]
> Bahia, inundated with the most offensive and noxious animal and
> vegetable exhalations, with a total neglect of cleanliness, and absence of
> those police and sanitary regulations so essential to the public health in
> other countries, would prove a very Golgotha, modified, however, no
> doubt, by the habits, constitution, and temperament of the people.[33]

Although temperatures and precipitation are measured and pronounced consistently pleasant in his book, still the climate is variously
referred to as too hot, too breezy, too humid for the health of a native of
Britain, who must take care not to over-expose himself to it. The nights
were always cool, and Dundas reassuringly stated that bedroom windows could be left open as long as one was careful to avoid direct
exposure to the dangerous breeze. Mosquitoes were not to be feared, as
they did not carry disease; and the "hot, suffocating winds of other
tropical climates" were unknown.

The views of the young vice-consul James Wetherell were something of an exception to the norm. Like Dundas, he noticed that "[t]he
elasticity of the atmosphere, combined with the peculiar situation of the
city has the effect of producing a very equal temperature",[34] but when
describing the open-windowed balls of Victoria, he remarked upon the
delightful absence of a different kind of heat and suffocation, that of
indoor English parlors: "There is nothing to fear from close and heated
rooms, you are dancing in pure fresh air".[35] Wetherell's remark seems
to assume that his British reader at home would harbor a fear of prolonged
containment in enclosed and stuffy spaces; but Dundas, writing for the
expatriates themselves, could not stress too strongly the importance of
avoiding open-air perspiration and of the need to keep a physical barrier
between oneself and the ocean breeze. Yet, while perspiration was said
to be dangerous, even life-threatening, he spoke of moderate open-air
exercise as necessary to health, an idea not shared by the Brazilian
elites, who did not walk anywhere they could take a *cadeira*, and
particularly avoided the noonday sun.[36]

Wetherell seemed to have a much more direct style of experiencing
his surroundings, and didn't usually let culturally preconceived structures of meaning to shape his reaction for him. On the subject of local

food items, he begins by noting in passing that many of them "sound strange to English ears, and are stranger still to English tastes, so prejudiced as we are in such things",[37] but belies this immediately with a long and vivid description of *carne seca, caruarú, vatapá, mocotó, feijoada*, all traditional dishes of Bahia, and which he seemed to know well; sometimes he enjoyed them, sometimes not. Elsewhere he stated apologetically that he could not bring himself to eat cooked snails, and so was unable to describe these to his readers.[38]

The foolhardiness of the British expatriate who insisted on being out in the sun at noon in the tropics, while everyone else stayed indoors, has become something of a stock image. Bahia was no exception. Dundas believed that the custom was anything but harmless.

> Those whose duties frequently lead them from the lower to the upper city, often suffer from [intermittent or continued] fever, without other apparent cause than the sudden transition from the warm but equal temperature of the lower city, to a strong, cool, and humid sea-breeze, which they encounter while bathed in perspiration and exhausted by the labour of ascending a considerable eminence.[39]

The subtitle of Dundas' book, *Remarks on a Premature Decay of the System Incident to Europeans on their Return from Hot Climates*, refers to what he considered to be his key contribution to tropical medicine: even those Europeans who appeared to have adapted well to life in Bahia often fell deathly ill upon returning to Europe. To explain this, Dundas suggested the following theory: Bahia's heat and humidity caused Europeans to perspire excessively much of the time. This sweating first dehydrated the body, and then began to take over the excretion process, which in turn reduced kidney function. When the individual then returned to a cold climate, "the renal system is suddenly called on to resume its long dormant function; but it is too late", the kidneys have permanently atrophied, and horrendous sufferings of the digestive and circulatory system (gout) would result.[40] Dundas had done a postmortem study of nine individuals who had resided in Bahia for a period of sixteen to nineteen years and then returned to Britain, dying shortly thereafter. He found that five of them had suffered atrophy in both kidneys.

Oddly, he did not diagnose the problem to be simple dehydration due to insufficient intake of water, which additionally would have accounted for most of the symptoms of breakdown listed earlier. The question here is more subtle than this. Why did the British merchant, privately so critical of the local climate, insist on exposing himself to weather that even his Brazilian counterpart considered unhealthy? Wetherell suggested simply that "It is only characteristic of his own self-opinion – 'Pooh! pooh! sun can do me no harm – until he finds himself laid up with fever".[41] The merchants must have had a psychological need that was being met by this otherwise destructive behavior. Many visitors contrasted the stench (air) of Praia with the perfumed freshness (air) of Victoria. What sort of perceptions caused the British businessman to go out of his way to expose himself to the stench, while protecting himself from the perfume?

This signaled the underlying psychological strain of maintaining a separate and superior 'Britishness.' The merchant would mind the foreign climate, but in his own way. Viewed in this light, the contradictory references to Bahia's weather are not incoherent, for their purpose was to subtly remind the British community that they were there to work, not to live; it was thus that they were at once able to take the climate, yet unable to take it. In other words, the problem to them was about how to make a profit overseas, while preventing the experience from affecting them permanently in any way. Dundas' prescription of a maximum stay of five to seven years in the tropics did seem to settle this matter elegantly, sidestepping the contradictory elements and providing a sort of algebraic solution to what was to him merely an environmental equation.

But bodies and minds, physical and the emotional environments, are intermixed. It was not only the perceived environmental toxins, nor only the lack of proper fluid intake or excessive sun exposure, that could destroy the merchant's body and mind in a situation of cultural immersion. On a more personal level, it may be important to consider the isolation felt by people who were so cut off from their families and friends in the homeland. James Wetherell, who actively enjoyed living in Bahia, gave a moving account of this ever-present feeling when he wrote of the night sky:

> Bright as the sky is by day, brighter far is it by night, when – 'Blue the sky/ Spreads like an ocean hung on high/ Bespangled with those isles of light/ So wildly, spiritually bright' […] So varied is the starry scene from that presented by the Northern Hemisphere, that *that* more than anything else, gives one forcibly the idea of the immense distance of one's 'northern home.'[42]

Nevertheless, the community's physical sufferings were very real. A manuscript report of Consul Pennell's medical condition, written by Dr. Dundas himself in 1826, gives a keen illustration of this.

> In the summer of 1821 the debilitating effects of a tropical climate were first manifested in [William Pennell's] constitution, by great derangement of the digestive functions, followed by spontaneous hernia of the right side, on which occasion I urgently recommended a voyage to Europe, which was not, however, acceded to, though its necessity was, in a few months, but too fully established, by progressive debility, and the supervention of dropsy of the testicle, for which a surgical operation was resorted to – Mr. Pennell was, moreover, subject to periodical attacks of gout, which, as his general health declined, gradually became more irregular and uncertain.[43]

Pennell was praised by Dundas in the book he later wrote precisely on account of his "studious and abstemious habits".[44] But his illnesses obviously could not be blamed only upon the tropical climate. The consul's duties after 1821 placed him under intense stress, given his responsibilities and the deteriorating political situation. It may be possible to generalize his situation to the merchants, whose living habits left much to be desired in terms of health, and who were facing increasingly serious problems in their own businesses. What must now be questioned is the extent to which such illnesses were a function of their *responses* to Bahia's climate and environment, rather than of the physical or even social environment itself.

Living Habits, Class, and Identity

Besides the general physical environment and people's individual characteristics, factors affecting health include personal habits of diet (including water and alcohol consumption), sleep and exercise, and – especially in the nineteenth century – clothing. Dundas recognized this: his study suggested that the habits of Bahia's British community could do with improvement. Ideally, he wrote, the merchant should take a conveyance home from work, instead of walking. Once home, a twenty-minute rest is necessary. Dinner should be eaten before 5:30 pm, and should consist of nothing more than one type of meat and one well-cooked vegetable, served with stale bread. The recommended intake of alcohol with dinner is three or four glasses of French wine (preferably claret) and one or two glasses of fortified wine immediately after the meal. The evening should then be spent resting, or in calm conversation with an intelligent friend. Bedtime should be around 10:30 pm.[45]

This seems to suggest that Dundas thought the British merchants ate and drank too much, exhausting themselves in arguments as much as in exercise. But he explained this behavior by its significance as a marker of class identity. He noted that businessmen usually maintained excessive and unhealthy eating and drinking habits as a mark of social position, and when these were carried to the tropics, it seriously exacerbated the danger of illness. In a passage entitled "Pernicious Influence of Habits of Life in Certain Ranks in England", Dundas acknowledged that matters of physical health were connected to concerns of class identity and cohesion. The typical merchant in Britain, after working hard all day and walking home two or three miles "probably impressed with the importance of exercise to the preservation of health", usually would have a heavy and luxurious dinner, including strong wines and brandies. Afterwards, in the close heated rooms mentioned also by Wetherell, the merchant would exhaust himself with the discussion of local and general politics. He would then suffer through "feverish nights, disturbed sleep, and nervous exhaustion on the ensuing day". Dundas points out that these physiological excesses were especially dangerous to those who had recently returned from the tropics, for these persons tended immediately to "fall under the control of the social customs incident to that rank of society to which they belong".[46]

This sort of thing was certainly happening in the British community of Bahia, and it did not escape Wetherell's notice. He wrote this short description: "The living of foreigners is what would be termed *hard* – heavy late dinners with large quantities of wine or beer, supposed to be necessary to support the body under the trying effects of the climate".[47] The mocking tone suggests that their real reason was probably of a less respectable nature. Dundas, too, mentions dismissively a similar argument by merchants in Britain that "the climate of England demands a stronger or more stimulating wine" than the light claret the doctor recommended for good health. This idea, he wrote, was "among certain popular fallacies, originating in prejudice rather than in reason".[48] Obviously the merchants in Bahia were rationalizing a class-marking behavior by reference to the existence of an external environmental threat to the entire group. Whether the rigors of the climate were Northern or Southern made no difference to the rationalization, despite their opposite characteristics. It is likely that the idea behind the heavy eating and drinking was that it enhanced the ability of each person to bear the difference in setting by exaggerating what on a deeper level kept him the same. It came down to maintaining daily personal habits. If these made him physically ill in the tropics at a much higher rate than in the homeland, at least his sanity – his sense of psychological boundaries – would have been preserved.

Writing long before Wetherell, Maria Graham had noticed that her compatriots in Bahia were prone to a certain form of nationalistic expression. She described with sarcasm "the gentlemen of the English club, who meet once a month, to eat a very good dinner, and drink an immoderate quantity of wine for the honour of their country".[49] Her remark supports the idea that the maintenance of particular living habits, even if irrational in terms of physical health, was necessary to safeguard the psychological security or identity of each member of the British group.

Internal Dynamics and Subjective Dissonance

Returning to the early years of the British presence in Brazil, we may recall that the merchants had a very short-term profit orientation due to the wartime frenzy in Europe and the political uncertainties in Brazil. There is evidence that the British merchants were constantly burdened by fear of the immediate consequences of failing at the wholesale business – the loss of class that would result if he were forced to become a retailer. John Mawe's narrative description of Rio de Janeiro in 1812 made this clear:

> These gentlemen had calculated upon doing business only in the large way they had set apart their hours for horse-exercise, and for going to their country seats. [...] The idea of vending by retail was a bitter which destroyed all their pleasing anticipation of doing business in style: they came out as merchants, and could not stoop to be shopkeepers: and many of them, rather than yield to that degradation, sent goods to auctions. Others with more prudence accommodated themselves to circumstances, and were not offended at being asked for a pair of boots or a hat.[50]

This feeling of class insecurity persisted as an organizing principle for the British merchant's interpretations of his experiences in Bahia. As the community grew, most British families lived in or around the

Victoria neighborhood, and tended either to socialize in one another's homes, or to make brief expeditions by horseback or carriage to out-lying areas. Maria Graham noted in 1822 that "the English are [...] hospitable and sociable among each other. They often dine together: the ladies love music and dancing, and some of the men gamble as much as the Portuguese".[51] John Candler, who visited Bahia in 1852 and stayed with a British merchant and his young wife, later described the community's usual daily schedule:

> In the daytime, and till four o'clock in the afternoon, they super-intend their business in the city; after which they return to their country abodes to dine, and claim the evening for study, rest, and recreation. The usual time for taking an airing is immediately after dinner, before the sun sets, or later in the evening when it is moonlight. At this part of the day equipages are to be observed on all the roads, with ladies and gentlemen on horseback, and afford a pleasing and animating sight.[52]

This postcard sketch suggests a lively socialization among equals, along the lines of the country-squire ideal that Mawe identified as a key expectation of British merchants who came to Brazil seeking their fortunes during the early nineteenth century. Viewed in this way, these men, women, and children appeared to have the lives of characters from contemporary author Jane Austen's novels, as transposed to the tropics.

Indeed the British society of Bahia was said to be more congenial and welcoming than that of most places in Brazil. James Henderson, an Englishman who made an unsuccessful bid for a diplomatic position at Rio de Janeiro and later became British consul general in Bogotá, Colombia, claimed in 1821 that:

> Bahia is considered by the English merchants a more agreeable place of residence than any of the maritime towns of the Brazil, and a more social intercourse has existed among themselves than at some of the other places.[53]

Besides the daily promenades, "visits of friendship" also took place in the evenings.[54] Rounds of social dinners given in honor of a new visitor were often described in travel narratives. Apart from entertain-ment in private homes, an occasional cultural event was available to the British in Bahia. These included the opera and theater companies touring from Europe which performed at the Theatro São Joao.[55] The occasional cricket match on the military practice field of Campo Grande, between the Victoria and the main town, probably helped to serve the needs of the community to congregate in a culturally specific social activity.[56]

Besides walking in the sun, two popular forms of exercise mentioned in many narratives were horseback riding in the surrounding countryside, and the *fête champêtre* or picnic on the seashore. In this Romantic period, British girls and young women in Bahia apparently had considerable freedom to enjoy their situation. One woman's afternoon revels landed her in Dr. Dundas' office by the following day:

> Mrs. D., wife of a British merchant, lately arrived from Europe, in the prime of life, and married but a few months, had been out at a *fête champêtre* on the sea coast. She danced, and perspired, freely; and after the excitement of the day, was exposed to the cool sea breeze of the country, while returning home in her cadeira.[57]

Dundas mentions the nearby village of São Lázaro as being a "favourite evening ride of the British and other foreign residents".[58] Maria Graham enjoyed riding around the banks of Tororó lake. Most writers of travel narratives make reference to riding in the country, out to the village of Rio Vermelho or some other point along the shore. The surviving record of title deeds and probate inventories shows that British merchants often owned homes in such areas. This interest in horseback riding probably served a group-identity function in that it was an immediately recognizable marker of class as well as of nationality, and involved a group movement away from the Brazilian space, out towards the more neutral – and perhaps less unfamiliar – realm of 'nature'.

All this activity would seem to demonstrate that the British were basically content and unified in their separation from local society. However, a closer examination of the sources shows that this was not entirely the case. Even within this tiny group, internal stratification was a powerful force. The clearest instance of this concerned the employment of British clerks by merchant firms throughout the period. They were deliberately isolated by the society of well-heeled expatriate merchants. William Scully noted in 1866:

> The situation of the young Englishmen, sent out as clerks to the many English mercantile houses in Brazil, becomes most deplorable. Placed by their employers in a house with one or two negroes to attend them, and rigidly shut out from the society of their compatriots,

by that snobbishness of English intercourse abroad (nowhere greater than in Brazil), which makes the tinker of kettles dread contaminating association with the tinker of saucepans, these, in many cases, gentlemanly young men, too often take refuge from the dreary monotony of their existence, and from their feelings of isolation in a foreign land, in all the excitement of immorality and dissipation.[59]

Indeed, of the three suicides recorded in the burial records of Bahia's British Chapel, two were young men, and the only one whose profession was recorded was a clerk. The entry reads: "January 27, 1847. William Henry Chapman, age 25. Clerk in house of Messrs. Lyon & Benn Merchants. Shot himself with a fowling piece, while in a state of insanity, as appeared from his letter".[60] Chapman's experience seems to bear out the pattern of isolation, dissipation, and breakdown reported by William Scully (and Dundas) then examined by Gilberto Freyre, who connected the insanity with syphilis and the suicide with its associated stigma.[61] The combination of intense and ongoing stresses particular to the situation of the British in Bahia also should be noted, exacerbated by permanent social rejection by their compatriots as well as by respectable Brazilians,[62] and suggest that this was probably enough to drive at least one young man to suicide.

But something more is happening in this passage. As editor of the *Anglo-Brazilian Times*,[63] Scully had ample opportunity to observe and criticize what he reported to be a pernicious exaggeration of social distinctions among the different classes of British persons living in Brazil. A close reading of the passage, however, provides a very interesting insight into his own mode of perception. In particular, his sidelong insertion of the words "in many cases gentlemanly" seems to reveal the very semi-conscious class exclusivity that he was trying to point to in the other merchants: in a statement condemning the evils of social snobbery, Scully's chief concern was for the higher-class members of the clerk population. Even worse, his way of ridiculing social pettiness was to introduce a working-class image, that of the tinker. In other words, Scully was saying that it is patently ridiculous to distinguish between a tinker of kettles and a tinker of saucepans, yet noble and compassionate to remember that some office clerks are more gentlemanly than others.

The idea that a sense of class pervaded the British merchants' perceptions of those around them also helps to explain a puzzling occurrence described in Maria Graham's narrative of her brief visit to Bahia. She and her young guide, Consul Pennell's daughter, made an extended round of visits to the gentlewomen of Bahia early one morning, even though they knew that it was not the Brazilian custom to visit or be visited before noon.[64] When they found the Brazilian ladies completely unprepared to receive them properly, instead of apologizing and returning at a more convenient time, Graham obviously enjoyed the spectacle, and later framed her narrative of it to put down the local elites in caustic terms. After viewing the spectacle of a household hurriedly being put into order for their visit,[65] the two women saw nothing wrong in staying just long enough to get a good look around before proceeding to the next house. Only two homes are described as presentable: one belonged to a judge, and the other to a naval captain, the profession of Maria Graham's own husband. In her narrative, Graham indulged in a reaction of disgust: to the houses, the interior decoration, her hostesses' personal appearance, and even their topics of conversation. "To say the truth, their manner of talking on the latter subject [disease] is as disgusting as their dress, that is, in a morning: I am told they are different after dinner". Given her self-conscious expertise on matters of class-appropriate behavior, however, it seems obvious that both she and the consul's daughter either considered themselves to be above the local norms of correct deportment, or were oblivious to their loss of status in the eyes of the Brazilians who had to endure their rudeness.[66]

But Graham's disdain went deeper than her disregard for Brazilian ladies. Her surprise upon subsequently seeing them in formal European fashion at a ball given in her honor by Consul Pennell was discussed in the previous chapter. She grudgingly admitted that they were able to present themselves appropriately, but immediately put them down again for lacking naturalness of movement in their corseted finery, judging that "our English ladies, though quite of the second rate of even colonial gentility ... bore away the prize of beauty and grace".[67] The competitive, hierarchical outlook she showed towards the Brazilians extended also to her own English associates, while her expression of superiority assumed the complicity and approval *of her reader.* She, too, may have been grasping for a sense of her own identity and class position when immersed in unfamiliar social circumstances, as a sort of default reaction.

Earlier, we saw that William Pennell desired the presence of a liberally educated spiritual leader to prevent the merchants from becoming somehow less British, and subtly undermined the ideals of liberal education itself. The journalist William Scully, self-appointed gadfly to the British communities of Brazil, was considerably (though quite unconsciously) hypocritical in his tirade against British snobbery.[68] Impoverished gentlewoman Maria Graham, eager to establish the superiority of British refinement with respect to Bahian high society, knowingly committed serious social offenses against her Brazilian hostesses, ridiculed in print the money-mindedness of every British man she met there, and ended by putting the entire British community – in fact all British expatriates everywhere – beneath herself socially.[69] Why did such well-educated men and women, individually of considerable integrity,[70] entangle themselves in such paradoxes when it came to a question of securing their personal identity under expatriate circumstances?

An insight into the double binds inherent in the situation may be glimpsed through a very close reading of William Pennell's letter (see page 83). A certain back-and-forth rhythm is discernible in his style. Essentially, Pennell states that the fossilization of his own institutions is preferable to their improvement; halfway realizes the bigotry of such a position; and through the expression "it might be presumed", more or less pleads to be allowed to justify himself by the same values he has violated. There is an uneasiness in the letter's tone. In essence, the passage openly claims that British expatriate merchants in general needed to be guided by liberally educated men, such as, naturally, Pennell himself and his illustrious correspondent; and this recalls Maria Graham's conspiratorial tone. The argument Pennell was offering appealed to class allegiance more than to reason, and it was awkward but effective. Why else must the justification have been "presumed", and why did he assume that his presumption would be accepted? His use of the word "us" is inappropriate from almost every angle, too, suggesting that Pennell was having trouble articulating his correct affiliation under the circumstances. It would seem that Pennell, Graham, and Scully were suffering from something that might be called a blindness of cultivated minds.

It has been well noted by some British philosophers, artists, and intellectuals, that class consciousness exercised to a minute degree has been a quintessential characteristic of British social organization. The following three examples may credibly illustrate this general point. To begin with Adam Smith's *Theory of Moral Sentiments,* first published in 1759:

Though it is in order to supply the necessities and conveniences of the body, that the advantages of external fortune are originally recommended to us, yet we cannot live long in the world without perceiving that the respect of our equals, our credit and rank in the society we live in, depend very much upon the degree in which we possess, or are supposed to possess, those advantages. The desire of becoming the proper objects of this respect, of deserving and obtaining this credit and rank among our equals, is, perhaps, the strongest of all our desires, and our anxiety to obtain the advantages of fortune is accordingly much more excited and irritated by this desire, than by that of supplying all the necessities and conveniences of the body, which are always very easily supplied.[71]

Evelyn Waugh presented a related idea in 1956, when he made the following observation about English society:

Dons [...] speak of 'upper, middle, and lower classes'. Socialists speak of 'capitalists, bourgeois, intellectuals, workers'. But these simple categories do not apply in England. Here there is very little horizontal stratification [...] There is instead precedence, a single wholly imaginary line (a Platonic idea) extending from Windsor to Wormwood Scrubs, of separate individuals each justly and precisely graded. In the matter of talking together, eating together, sleeping together, this mysterious line makes little difference, but every Englishman is sharply aware of its existence, and this awareness often spices these associations very pleasantly.[72]

In a very different but no less incisive manner, British dramatist Keith Johnstone discovered in the 1960s that realistic scenes could be improvised on the spur of the moment even by non-actors, so long as they were trained to recognize their already fully developed "status skills" and then put these to creative use, spontaneously shifting identities and status relationships among themselves on stage in ways that functioned dramatically to arouse the interest of the audience. In 1979 Johnstone set out his ideas in a book. By 1992 *Impro* had gone through nine re-prints, and remains a best-seller in the field today. A concluding passage contains the following: "I don't myself see that an educated man in this culture necessarily has to understand the second law of thermo-dynamics, but he certainly should understand that we are pecking-order animals and that this affects the tiniest details of our behaviour".[73]

The British expatriate James Wetherell gave away just such an orientation with respect to Bahia, when he complained in the 1850s that:

The character of the Brazilians appears to me to be *selfish*. There are no high exclusive ranks of society – wherever you go amongst them you find that all descriptions of persons are admitted upon the same footing of "hail fellow well met." At evening parties there are persons visiting amongst some of the first people, who at home would be scouted from respectable society. The Brazilians in affairs of common life do not seem to have any object to attain. They have no higher station to look forward to generally speaking than the one they occupy.[74]

If the merchants believed, even on a semi-conscious level, that to be properly British was to be keenly sensitive to mutually exclusive gradations of class and to act accordingly, the British community of early nineteenth-century Bahia would have found itself in a rather neurotic situation. Determined to see itself as superior and yet unable to manipulate the complex social codes of its host society,[75] the group's sense of security in Bahia would have depended upon the mutual construction of its Britishness.[76] But then, the most readily available and effective expression of that Britishness within the community would have been for its own members perpetually to be distancing and defining one another as fundamentally separate along finer and finer gradients. With this mindset, the community's cohesion would have been fatally linked to its own corrosion. The reproduction of class-conscious social structures from the homeland, miniaturized within a tiny expatriate community and concentrated to the point of toxicity, may have been what Scully wished to convey when he denounced "that snobbishness of English intercourse abroad, nowhere greater than in Brazil".[77]

When the inherent internal contradictions of their situation are taken into account, it should come as no surprise that after a few years' residence in Bahia, the average British man or woman would have been "profoundly ... charged with the elements of disease, awaiting but the slightest touch from any disturbing moral or physical agency to determine an explosion".[78] Dundas believed that the pathology was located in the physical climate of Bahia. The fact that even he could have chosen to ignore his awareness of the merchants' unhealthy habits, and present instead a scientific argument blaming Bahia's climate for the British illnesses and inability to cope, is perhaps the best evidence that the true poisons lurked within the *psychological* climate of the British community itself. Ironically, the very inflexibility that so damaged the health of individual merchants is probably the same thing that made it possible for this and other British merchant communities to retain their particular identity and survive as institutions for so long, in so many different parts of the world.

Healthy Eyes: The Aesthetic Perspective

Although one cannot claim to understand with certainty the inner psychological states of a group of historical actors, it is clear that the British residents of Bahia fell sick often, even though the climate was physically not conducive to disease and the newly arrived British person usually felt enraptured by the beauty and feeling of the place: "Every tropical sojourner [fully admits that] years of subsequent exhaustion can never entirely efface the recollection of the buoyancy of spirits, unclouded mind, and exquisite appreciation of mere animal existence, which [...] characterize the first years of a tropical life".[79] Dundas' diagnosis that this euphoria was simply a mechanical effect of the tropical sunlight, and would give way to a complete physical and mental breakdown within five to seven years,[80] naturalized a process that was not at all inevitable, as many merchants died only after fifty to seventy years' residence in Bahia.[81] Dundas himself remained there for a quarter of a century. The more affluent Brazilians stayed out of the sun as much as possible. James Wetherell, who remarked upon the hard living of his countrymen in Bahia and laughed at their insistence on exposing themselves to the sun, did not comment much upon illnesses in his detailed writings. This could be taken to mean that he stayed healthy as a result of paying attention to his living habits, and was free from fearing 'climate' in the abstract. Unfortunately, he died of an accident at age 36, so the long-term effects of this more reasonable tropical sojourn on his physical health will never be known.

The question remains as to why Dundas interpreted the evidence before his own eyes in a way that blamed everything on mechanistic processes such as subtle toxins in the air and water, and the brain-addling effects of the sun, instead of highlighting the merchants' identity challenges and its links to their insistence upon class-bound living habits. Possibly it is the very need to acquire and retain control over an unfamiliar and unpredictable situation that can lead to the distress observed in this chapter. It is worth examining as closely as possible the experience of British people who seem to have responded well to Bahia, over a period greater than five to seven years, without breaking down and without shutting themselves away. Arguably they shared an outlook of flexibility and openness to their situation, and were less preoccupied with redefining it in idiosyncratic terms or being in control of the outcome than with simply observing what was going on around them, remaining effective in the moment, and permitting themselves to be changed by external influences if it so happened.[82]

To begin with an early example, when Brazilian ports were flooded with British merchandise in 1812, John Mawe commented upon the aversion felt by most British merchants at the idea of being forced to go into retail trade, rather than wholesale. He made a point of noting that while this situation drove many wholesalers to send their goods to auction and give up altogether:

> [o]thers with more prudence accommodated themselves to circumstances, and were not offended at being asked for a pair of boots or a hat. These persons reaped all the advantages of the trade, as they got their price by selling to those whose necessities prompted them to purchase, and were ever ready to sell by the package when opportunity offered.[83]

It is likely that the more flexible merchants would have best been able to recover their fortunes eventually and revert to the country-squire manner of life they preferred, once the economic and political situation had become more stable and the other merchants had given up or been eliminated by "circumstances".

Also illuminating is the consistent style of experience present in the writings of James Wetherell, whose inquiring, appreciative gaze played upon Bahia for a period of fifteen years. He paid attention to the conversation of shopkeepers and slaves; was often invited into Brazilian homes, weddings, and festivities; and gave his full attention to whatever caught his interest, be it a seashell, cockroach, sunset, or the personal habits of his Brazilian and British associates. He wrote in a lively style almost entirely free from the self-interest, suspicion, condescension and even malice that characterized many of the narratives by other contemporary observers of the same scenes. Wetherell thought it was very funny that the British merchants insisted on walking in the sun, eating and drinking too much, and going to absurd lengths to pretend to engage in entertainments associated with the English upper class.

> I have heard of some few people, great sportsmen of course, sadly incommoding themselves by going shooting 'up the country'. I believe there are snipe to be had but they have to be eaten almost when and where they are shot. It must be a much more luxurious mode of shooting to tempt me. Swamps in a hot climate terribly cool one's *ardour*. Fever and ague specters are apt to haunt one too vividly for such sport.[84]

Wetherell's way of seeing was carefully educated, refined, and *aesthetic*. This is what enabled him to breathe in everything around him, taste it, understand it, put it into words, and then breathe it out again without fearing the irrevocable loss of self in engulfing otherness that so preoccupied his compatriots. Many of his brief notes show a real sense of 'framing' the experience in terms that made it visibly beautiful, striking, amusing, moving, and so on, without actually stating it to be such:

> I saw a charming picture the other evening at the Piedade Church fiesta. A monk (an Italian, dressed in dark-brown robes) leaning over a balcony, firing off a sky-rocket. He was holding it at arm's length, and had a face with a long beard, like the saints' in some of the paintings of the old masters. As the rocket shot up into space, his face was upturned watching its course, and the shower of sparks which fell cast a strong light upon his countenance. The subject would form a very effective *bit* of painting.[85]

> A great portion of the ceremony no one seems to understand except the priests near the altar. In fact, how can it be expected for the people to be serious when the "*solemnity*" invariably commences with an overture to an opera, played by an excellent band in the singing gallery.[86]

Wetherell usually restricted himself to stating facts, but in such a vivid manner that his private experience was implied and very effectively conveyed. Here is how he handles the event of witnessing the punishment of slaves:

> Palmatoria, a piece of wood about three quarters of an inch thick, the upper part being rounded – being a disc with a handle. It is used to punish blacks, and particularly by striking them on the hand. From its size, the strokes must be more painful than those from a ruler, which, in our school-boy days, we occasionally received.[87]

The brutalizing effects of slavery are subtly conveyed in a description of a large boar tied by its feet to a pole and carried in this position: "The blacks do not seem at all careful of the *feelings* of animals. They use them brutally".[88] Neither did the less obvious aspects of such violence escape his attention: "Runaway blacks, when brought back, have, as a punishment, a ring of iron fastened round the neck... this badge is considered a great disgrace, for when out their acquaintances jeer at them".[89]

He listened closely to the conversations of slaves, and they appear to have responded to his attention:

> The blacks, when they meet one another, reiterate, like the Persians, the same word of salutation several times, and as in that language the phrases 'Selamat,' (I congratulate you on your safety), and 'Teijibeen,' (I hope you are well): so the Negro blacks use 'Ogirai,' (Good Morning), and 'Occuginio,' (I hope you have risen in health)." [90]

> Several of the blacks here are, I believe, Mahommedans, and some of them write (what I presume is Arabic) very elegantly. Such an accomplishment, however, sometimes causes the practisers 'to come to grief,' for the Brazilians, like all other ignorant people, are very frightened about what they cannot understand. One black will sometimes write a message to another, or write his prayers, and the moment the police find out the man is in possession of such writing, they cry out plots and assassinations, rising of slaves and murders; and the poor black fellows are imprisoned and perhaps banished the country, the greatest crime proved against them being these *mystical* characters. I have in my possession a book of prayers, given me by one of my own servants; it is carefully written in black and red letters, the latter apparently forming the commencement of the sentences. [91]

There can hardly be a more effective way of expressing the inhumanity of slavery than such quiet descriptions from personal experience.[92] This is not to say that Wetherell was free of contemporary racial preconceptions:

> It is a curious circumstance that the minds of the blacks should for so many ages have remained in a stationary condition, and although political and local circumstances may have greatly operated to retard the development of their condition, yet it seems much more natural that this state of darkness should proceed more from physical causes.[93]

When Wetherell died at age 36, his notes were discovered among his possessions. These were arranged, edited, and published in London by his friends, who inserted an introduction and eulogy that gives an insight into his character. "His life had been a chequered one: of late years clouded by family misfortunes; but, from his first starting in a mercantile career, his buoyancy of spirits and amiability of character rendered him a general favourite".[94] It goes on to describe Wetherell's mediocre diplomatic career, which culminated in the post of Vice Consul at Paraíba, "almost the lowest stepping-stone". Soon after leaving England for Paraíba in 1858, his mother, "to whom he was most tenderly attached, died; and for the first time in his life, his spirits seemed completely broken". At that point, he showed his mettle: instead of returning to his home and friends, or shutting himself into his duties at Paraíba, he "took a trip to Pernambuco, and also into the interior, to rouse himself, and all thought he would gradually regain his elasticity". Instead, he fell down a flight of stairs in his house and died of a concussion. This was very unfortunate. The fact, however, is that unlike most of the other British merchants, Wetherell was not bound to his homeland as a psychological point of reference, though his ode to Bahia's night sky revealed his awareness of being far from home. In his attitude we may find a clue as to how he was able to enjoy himself so much in a completely foreign setting, engaging and writing about topics ranging from insects to foods to curious local customs, laughing at the eccentricities of his compatriots, staying healthy, and being generally happy there for fifteen years.

Although Wetherell counted upon the sympathetic understanding of his friends and readers, his style failed to suggest any real desire of identifying himself as higher or intrinsically better than most other people around him. In his notes, Wetherell showed a style similar to those of Fraser, Koster, and perhaps Dundas, in that he did not try to place himself in some fixed position vis-à-vis the social world surrounding him; he only openly engaged, enjoyed, and understood well enough to convey with good-humored precision what he saw. His outsider status, as a well-educated young man, who had taken up the diplomatic career more out of intellectual curiosity than personal ambition, probably contributed to his ability to interact in fruitful ways with whomever and whatever he found himself facing.

The effect of his attitude on the Bahianos around him is likely to have been similar to what was felt by the Brazilian ambassador Miguel Paranhos do Rio Branco, who discovered Wetherell's book in a small shop in Wales in the late 1950s, and subsequently arranged for a commemorative translation to be published in Brazil:

> One could almost say that [James Wetherell] fell in love with the city where he lived for fifteen years; for only one who truly loves a place can so closely understand its life, noticing the small details that usually are overlooked by most foreign visitors, and nearly always describing everything with absolute self-assurance. [...] He integrated himself, body and soul, into the life of Bahia.[95]

It is by no means clear that Wetherell was in fact in love with Bahia. For all we know, he would have been every bit as interested in Paraíba and Pernambuco, or anywhere in the world that his travels might have taken him, had he lived longer. Certainly Wetherell's friends in England credited him with an inquiring spirit and a sense of wonder to balance his critical eye. What Paranhos' interpretation does show, however, is that the openness that Wetherell brought to his encounters tended to establish an overall sense of direct experience and common goodwill, which in turn would have encouraged further openness and fruitful exchange. Stumbling across the little book in a secondhand shop over a century later, the diplomat Paranhos, feeling – like Wetherell – far from home, tells of how he was affected by his words:

> Under the grey skies of Wales, the notes of the vice-consul [...] brought back to me a taste of the warmth of Salvador [...] with my British colleague, I stroll along each of its streets and hills, go into every church, taste acarajés and vatapá, and seek to enjoy everything ... the city is so fortunate as to offer.[96]

This immediacy of experience, which Wetherell was able to convey by avoiding the superimposition of his own interpretation upon what he observed, touched a responsive chord in Paranhos and others who have since read the book. It generated a feeling of communal understanding, rather than the difference and 'otherness' one might have expected from so contrasting a pair of men.

Considerations on the Position of British Women

Although most of the evidence for women's attitudes and behaviors is indirect, it can be argued that their position demanded a Wetherell-like flexibility, for their daily material home-making duties placed them on the front lines between the British and the Brazilians, so to speak, and they constantly had to mediate between the two societies. Taken together with their early nineteenth-century separateness from the business concerns of their husbands and fathers, this gave them a natural sideline-observer status with its attendant benefits. As a result, many of them creatively managed their situations so as to secure themselves greater status and better treatment than would have been available to them in the homeland (see Chapter 6).

Possibly the best documented example of how differential gender roles allowed British women greater flexibility than British men in the context of an early nineteenth-century expatriate community in Latin America comes from Argentina. W. P. Robertson and J. P. Robertson published in 1843 a series of letters written during their trading sojourn to South America. In one letter, W. P. waxed eloquent over the marvelous success of his hostesses, the Postlethwaites, at their home in Corrientes:

> Mrs. Postlethwaite and her daughters were of so accommodating and lively a disposition, that they adapted themselves with wonderful tact and facility to the habits, feelings, and customs of the people among whom they resided; and with whom, as a natural consequence, they soon became great favourites.[97]

These women's willingness to engage the local society did nothing at all to harm their Englishness. On the contrary, Robertson had started this letter exclaiming over how much he "was pleased now to see what a truly comfortable and *English* home they had established in so unknown and remote a quarter of the globe".[98] If, like class, comfort was also an idea carrying uniquely English overtones, i.e., the coziness of home as a place intimately combining physical and emotional ease,[99] then the Postlethwaites may have been making a choice to express their Britishness by overruling class-conscious considerations of personal superiority in favor of making their home a place where a sense of camaraderie predominated toward each and every guest. They themselves reaped the best rewards of this approach, and in the process, perhaps promoted British business enterprise in Corrientes beyond what an isolationist style would have been able to achieve.

Many British subjects were unable to achieve the level of immediate engagement in Bahia that Wetherell, Fraser, and Koster showed in interpreting their experiences. Unable or unwilling to relinquish the self-imposed barriers that separated them from the surrounding environment, they clung to habits of perception and behavior that worked to destabilize their health and happiness. On a wider scale, the impact of such choices made itself felt in the overall shape that British enterprise took in Brazil. Most British individuals who came into contact with Brazilian society, we will see, interacted with it on different levels of intimacy and formality, and re-interpreted themselves and each other as a process of mutual influence unfolded over the early decades of the nineteenth century.

Chapter 5

Brazilians and the British: Images and Reflections

Compared to other cities in Brazil during the first half of the nineteenth century, Bahia had a social environment that was conducive to broad interaction and mutual influence. As one writer declared of Bahia, "The society of this city is considered superior to that of Rio de Janeiro, and the families appear to maintain a more social intercourse with strangers".[1] The British came to Brazil primarily for commercial purposes. No matter how much they desired to keep themselves socially separate from the local Brazilians, the nature of their business caused them to be in constant contact with the locals, much as the women's work required interacting with local providers of household goods and services.

Judging from published narratives of the period, most British residents in Brazil preferred to remain invested in preconceived notions which in turn buttressed their determination to keep apart, thus sustaining the distance that prevented deeper acquaintance. Superficial facts could easily be made to fit the existing theory on both sides, and a sense of safety eventually arose from the predictability of readymade judgments, even though these were not really based on any consistent effort to know the other. British authors of narratives about Brazil were keenly observant of class-specific behaviors on the part of Brazilians, and often gave considerable attention to the manners and appearance of Brazilian women as a category unto themselves. These observations were limited by several factors, including the reluctance of Brazilians to allow themselves to be observed in certain circumstances. Where facts were scarce, imagination filled in the gaps; and so, by comparing these narratives one against the other, and also to secondary sources, they may reveal at least as much about the observers as about the observed. Common British perceptions of Brazilians were mostly unrefined and negative, so the few writers who wished to investigate the facts presented their readers with detailed evidence, fruit of long observation.[2]

Writers such as Dundas, Walsh, and Scully made an effort to give Brazilians a fair review, and included both negative and positive points. Nevertheless, they were ultimately unable to overcome the traditional prejudices entirely.

British Views of Brazilians

When referring to Brazilians, British writers usually meant white Brazilians. Only Dundas and Walsh made any effort to understand the life and manners of the working classes. The British saw themselves as uniformly superior to the Brazilians in practically every way. Physical descriptions sometimes focused on hygiene which, like clothing, carries social as well as physical connotations. Wetherell and Graham criticized Brazilian men and women, respectively, for what was perceived as a lack of personal cleanliness. Not only does a Brazilian take off most of his clothes when he goes home, says Wetherell, but he will sometimes change his shirt for a soiled one because he feels more comfortable that way.[3] Graham, with her penchant for detail, relates of the Brazilian gentlewoman's undress:

> In this hot climate, it is unpleasant to see dark cottons and stuffs, without any white linen, near the skin. Hair black, ill combed, and dishevelled, or knotted unbecomingly [...] the whole person having an unwashed appearance [...] who is there that can bear so total a disguise as filth and untidiness spread over a woman?[4]

Earlier she complained that the Brazilian women were not wearing enough to be decent, without reference to their private-space comfort in hot weather; but here she refers to the climate in order to criticize even the color of their thin clothing. The passage also seems to imply that the darkness of the women's hair, like that of their clothes, was somehow unclean.

Graham is mostly concerned with hygiene/appearance, particularly the presence of physical details signifying class. To her, white linen next to the skin looked clean, and was therefore elegant in hot weather, even in multiple layers; but to be "thinly clad" was disgusting, regardless of climate, custom, or privacy of setting. The Brazilian elites looked "unwashed" and that was that, in spite of the fact that they bathed at least as often as their foreign visitors.[5] Thus British perceptions worked to prove that Brazilians were awkward in public settings and dirty in their private time; and all this somehow associated the climate of Bahia with the backwardness of its elite, naturalizing what was no more than a value-laden interpretation of superficial differences.

Being wholesale merchants, the British were viewed by elite Brazilians as socially superior to retail merchants, who in this period were mostly Portuguese or French;[6] but they were still definitely viewed as inferior by the upper-class Brazilians themselves because of the association with commerce.

Two quotes demonstrate the equivocation. The first is from William Scully, editor of the *Anglo-Brazilian Times* and generally well-disposed towards the locals:

> The Brazilian gentlemen are remarkable for temperance and frugality, and for natural talent may compete with any other nation, but so much cannot be said of their industry. Some yield themselves up to the charms of literature and science, but most of the upper class are content with a monotonous daily round of existence, made up of many naps during the day, gapes over the balconies in the afternoon, and a réunion in the evening, with an occasional visit to the opera. In truth, the warm and mild climate predisposes to indolence, and the youth, after having passed through the ordinary course of a college education, or having loitered a few years with a private tutor, enters into public offices, or, sinking into domestic insignificance, fritters away his life in indolence, or in the endless frivolities of street perambulation.[7]

Scully's observations ignore fact that the British upper classes, like their Brazilian counterparts, also lived leisurely lives. Like other expatriate British merchants, he considered his own class to be at the very least on a par with the highest society of Brazil, and his own middle-class ideas about industry and thriftiness were the norm against which the Brazilian elites were to be measured and judged. That behavior which Scully called "indolence" he easily attributed to the climate, a catch-all justification which in this case may have masked a set of beliefs about race.[8] Scully's narrative was carefully crafted to give an overall positive impression of Brazil and the Brazilians. Nevertheless, it is clear that he viewed his own middle-class standards as absolute, and saw no problem in judging the Brazilian upper classes for not meeting them.[9]

On the other hand, Dr. Robert Dundas, a liberal professional who was not himself involved in commerce and moved with ease among different classes in both Britain and Brazil, wrote in his own narrative that "the higher classes in all countries pretty closely approximate".[10] The comment was not complimentary, as he quotes a satirical poem about London society to drive home his point:

To rise at noon, sit slip-shod and undressed,
To read the news, or fiddle, as seems best,
Till half the world comes rattling at his door,
To fill the dull vacuity till four;
And, just when evening turns the blue vault grey,
To spend two hours in dressing for the day;
To make the sun a bauble without use;
Quite to forget, or deem it worth no thought,
Who bids him shine, or if he shine or not.[11]

This sounds much like Scully's disgusted description of the Brazilian upper classes; but here, climate is no excuse. Scully, as a well-off British resident of Rio de Janeiro, seemed to have a vested interest in reassuring himself and his associates of their social superiority. This may have been a way of compensating for their lack of personal political power, or it may have been a cultural characteristic that British merchants tended to carry with them wherever they went.

Scully's compatriot and contemporary W. P. Robertson criticized the ignorantly superior attitude of many British merchants abroad. Robertson wrote about the British merchant communities in Argentina during the early part of the century. In his passage commending the efforts of the women of the Postlethwaite family in promoting good relations between British merchants and Argentine elites, Robertson noted the following:

In judging of foreigners, we Englishmen are much disinclined to make any allowance for them on the score of difference of education, associations, habits, and customs. We set up a standard of our own, and woe betide the man or the woman who shall either impugn or venture to depart from it. We are sure that we are right and foreigners wrong. And in our assumed superiority, we stop at no intermediate point or position.[12]

James Wetherell also showed a critical perception of cultural stereotypes. While he, like Scully, felt that the climate had something to do with the hours kept by Bahianos, his comments were far less judgmental than Scully's. Wetherell even suggested, in his practical way, that the British merchants might do well to adapt themselves to local habits:

The manners of foreigners, and particularly Englishmen, are very unsuitable for a tropical climate. But an Englishman must not only bring his indomitable energy with him, but carry out his sturdy John Bull ideas. They have no *mid-day rest.* The Brazilians are very early risers; many are out at daybreak, and, when they can, sleep during the day, and are late in going to bed. Such a course would interfere with business, and therefore cannot be adopted, but the early rising might.[13]

Scully's and Wetherell's books were published just six years apart, so their difference in outlook is remarkable. Wetherell refers to the English merchants as *they*, signaling that he was not as invested in the group identity as Scully appeared to be. However, he appears to show an interest in improving the efficiency of the British merchant enterprise, conceding that business is indeed important enough to warrant some degree of climate-inappropriate behavior. But it is just as likely that any British merchant who decided to begin taking daytime naps during 'normal' business hours would be risking an important marker of cultural – and personal – identity. Wetherell's argument does not really hold: who, exactly, did the British merchants have to do business with, during that part of the day when most Bahianos were known to be fast asleep?

Throughout the century, British and American authors addressed the theme of why Brazilians apparently did not like to work. Thomas Ewbank, an American who visited Brazil in 1855 and collected impressions from the British residents of Rio de Janeiro, made an effort to analyze the influence of slavery in rendering almost any sort of labor distasteful to white Brazilians:

Brazilians shrink with something allied to horror from manual employments. [...] Ask a respectable native youth of a family in low circumstances why he does not learn a trade and earn an independent living; ten to one but he will tremble with indignation, and inquire if you mean to insult him! 'Work! work!' screamed one; 'we have blacks to do that.' Yes, hundreds and hundreds of families have one or two slaves, on whose earnings alone they live.[14]

Ewbank related two stories to demonstrate his point. In the first, a respectable but impoverished widow was advised by "Dr. C." (probably a British doctor, but possibly an American) to put her two adolescent sons to trades. The woman immediately left the room and never again spoke to the doctor, even though he had attended her family professionally for eight years without charge. The second story concerns the same family: the widow's eldest son accosted the doctor some time later to let him know that he had found employment as a clerk in the police department, at a salary of 300$000 per year, which Ewbank evidently considered to be a meager sum ("150 dollars!"). Ewbank explained:

> To be employed under government in the police is honorable, but to descend from an emperor's service even to a merchant's is degrading.

Despite overwhelming evidence that the socially aspirant Brazilians looked down on most kinds of work, neither British nor American observers seemed to catch on to the interpretation that Brazilians who belonged or aspired to the upper class probably looked down on all merchants, even the wealthy British wholesalers themselves. The best evidence for this possibility is found in a 1944 study by Brazilian historian Wanderley Pinho, about gentlewomen's salons in nineteenth-century Brazil.[15] Pinho apparently was piqued at Maria Graham's snobbish dismissal of Bahia's upper-crust society, whose level of civilization she considered to be far below that of Bahia's British residents.[16] Reviewing her narrative more than a century later, Pinho retorted that obviously Graham's host, Consul Pennell, did not move in the best circles: at the ball he gave in the Grahams' honor, Maria did not report the presence of any military personnel, government officials, or *senhores de engenho* (sugar plantation owners), who, as anyone should know, made up the real elite of Bahian society.[17] Furthermore, where Graham imputed the orchestra's early departure from the consul's ball to its lack of professionalism,[18] Pinho asserted that the consul obviously did not know how to put on a proper reception, as his guests were left without an orchestra.[19] Pinho's conclusion may attest more to his own view of British merchants than that of early nineteenth-century Bahian elites, but it is still apparent that the British did not quite have the access into local high society circles that they seemed to take for granted.

The likely conclusion is that the British merchants were accepted or tolerated by Brazilians on the basis of their European status, considerable wealth, and perhaps even their socially reclusive tendencies. But at the level of daily face-to-face interactions, some status jockeying would have been expected to occur. Ewbank related the story of how a

Brazilian employee of a foreign merchant firm solved an interesting problem that arose with his British employer:

> A gentleman of eighteen was induced to honor an importing house with his services at the desk. A parcel not larger than a double letter was handed him by one of the firm, with a request to take it to another house in the neighborhood. He looked at it; at the merchant; took it between a finger and thumb; gazed again at both; meditated a moment; stepped out, and, a few yards from the door, called a black, who carried it behind him to its destination![20]

Although the event took place in Rio de Janeiro, the attitude it conveyed seemed usual in Bahia. Wetherell relates that:

> [The lower class of whites] refuse to place themselves in a [...] *degrading* position, namely that of making money. Sooner than enter a store or become a shopkeeper's clerk with an ultimate or even certain hope of becoming a partner, they accept small under-paid Government situations.[21]

Clearly the Brazilian had to balance his economic against his social requirements.[22] What is interesting is that British observers viewed this practice with ridicule and contempt. If one compares it to the horror felt by the first British wholesale merchants in Brazil at the thought that they might fail at business and be forced into retail,[23] such British scoffing at the unwillingness of Brazilians to work at trades seems a bit hypocritical, and may reflect the overall attitude of benevolent condescension to perceived social inferiors that was examined in Chapter 4. The desire to avoid at all costs the diminution of social status obviously was not foreign to the British. What seems to surface from these stories is a British puzzlement as to why Brazilians preferred employment as underpaid government clerks to becoming shopkeepers. After all, the British wholesale merchant might prefer to go out of business rather than fall into retail, but the idea of turning to government employment at a low salary in order to preserve social status would not occur to him. Ewbank perceived this as a Brazilian preference to live at public expense, and implied a similarity to the other practice of living exclusively on the earnings of one's slaves rather than by one's own exertion and industry. Nevertheless, even those Brazilians who actually were shopkeepers did not have the merchants' respect, either: "The merchants will tell you that it is quite sufficient, in a general way, for a shopkeeper to be a Brazilian not to be trusted".[24]

Culturally speaking, then, it does not seem to have been possible for a British merchant to respect any Brazilian at all. These self-fulfilling stereotypes parallel the British attitude toward Bahia's mild climate examined in the last chapter: believing it to be harsh, but determined not to be cowed by it, they exposed themselves in ways that Brazilians did not; and when illness resulted, it was blamed on the peculiar toxicity of the climate to European constitutions. In other words, that which is assumed at the outset ('the climate is dangerous;' 'Brazilians have poor character') ends up as the conclusion, in a process that masquerades as reasoning, but which in fact replaces the possibility of personal openness to the unknown with a false practical certainty towards the present and future. This sub-conscious circular reasoning is a key way in which stereotypes perpetuate themselves in any situation, by appearing to offer a more predictable reality in a very complex world.

But what about those writers who made an effort to get at the reality behind the façades? Their impressions of Brazilians deserve attention, for their books were read by the English-speaking public, and could play a role in attenuating the negative impressions that dominated British images of Brazilians throughout the century.[25] At least three authors tried to give the Brazilians a fair assessment based on actual experience: Robert Dundas, who lived in Bahia for 25 years; Robert Walsh, chaplain to the British legation in Rio de Janeiro, who spent two years traveling alone through rural Brazil; and Charles Fraser, a gentleman explorer from London who traveled extensively around Brazil during the earliest years of the British presence, and communicated his discoveries to his friend, Foreign Secretary Lord Castlereagh. What did they have to say about this question?

The scientific mind of Dundas carefully worked out a description of the character of "the Brazilian". In physical terms:

> The native Brazilian is in general compact and well-formed, and of healthy organization, but not of an athletic frame. His intellectual faculties are acute, though little developed by cultivation. Descended from European ancestors, he has still a considerable admixture of African and native American blood.[26]

Noting, as did most of the writers, that the Brazilian's working habits differed from the British, he did not attempt to pin down the reasons for this perceived character fault, but merely noted that:

He is indolent by nature, and indisposed for active exertion or industry; but he is protected against the evil influence of the former on his health, by a simple and abstemious diet; and the injurious consequences of the latter to his social position are obviated by the circumstance, that the four great wants of the humbler classes in Europe press but lightly on the Brazilian. Fuel he scarcely requires; of clothing, but little; his primitive habitation is simply constructed; and one day's labour will amply provide for the moderate demands of the whole week.[27]

By comparing the Brazilian to the European laborer, Dundas drew the conclusion that the Brazilian was able to get away with an inherent and natural (i.e., racially determined) indolence because the mild climate made it possible for him to survive without having to work very much. But, in the process, Dundas unwittingly slipped in a contradictory idea: that given similar circumstances, the "humbler classes in Europe",[28] who were presumably entirely free of African and native American blood, might well behave in exactly the same way. As in his discussion of Bahia's climatic dangers for Europeans, Dundas registered his observations in neutral language. Still, benevolent though he sounded, he was reiterating many of the prejudices that he presumably sought to overcome through his scientific discourse. In this case, his reading of the Brazilian national character turned out to express his personal prejudices about class and race, and his own class inclinations favoring industry over leisure.

Later in the passage, Dundas discussed the subjective character of Brazilians:

With passions naturally quick, he is nevertheless placable; his disposition is kindly; the future never disturbs him with its doubts, nor the past with its regrets; the struggles and vicissitudes of European life are unknown ... he meets at length the inevitable doom, if not with philosophy, at least with resignation; satisfied of his claims to eternal felicity, in the confident assurance of an infallible Church.[29]

The apparent serenity and happiness of the average Brazilian seemed to have puzzled the doctor. Despite the condescension or irony in his tone, there might almost be a touch of envy in the description. Dundas did not remark on the possibility that while the problems of a cold climate were unknown to the working-class Brazilian, there could be any number of other struggles and vicissitudes making their lives difficult. He might also have interpreted their calm as an attitude associated with stoicism and intelligence, rather than Catholicism and ignorance.

A more elaborate character sketch was written by Robert Walsh, an Anglican clergyman who journeyed through the cities and countryside of Brazil in 1828 and 1829.[30] Often traveling alone or with a mulatto guide, without the benefit of letters of introduction or even a good idea of where he was going, Walsh essentially threw himself on the mercy of Brazilians as a stranger in their midst. What he learned was entirely contrary to what he had been told to expect by acquaintances in England. One of the chapters in his book carries the following subtitle: *Restrospect of Journey.– Reported, and real Character of the Brazilians. – Rudeness.– Indolence.– Ignorance.– Irritability.– Inhospitality.– Licentiousness.– Dishonesty.– Climate.* In it he presents a compellingly thorough description of the British stereotype of Brazilians:

> I had been taught to believe that I should find them rough and rude in their manners, and strongly and unreasonably prejudiced against all strangers; so indolent, that they neglected all the advantages of their fine country, and so ignorant that they not only knew nothing themselves, but were utterly indifferent in searching for any source of information; of quick and irritable temper, readily disposed to take and resent an offence, even by the assassination of the offender; of a churlish and inhospitable disposition, not inclined to admit others into their houses, and, though selfishly ready to receive, never known to return an invitation; so mercenary, that they would take all they could get, but would give nothing without more than adequate return; so sensual, that they indulged their propensities in this way without much restraint from the laws of morality or religion, and every house a family brothel; so dishonest, that nothing was safe with a traveller, and the roads so insecure, and murders so frequent, that the fatal spots were marked at every hundred yards. [...] Such was the opinion I had been taught to entertain before I left England.

This unequivocally negative image was obviously generated from anecdotal and superficial nuggets of information, and did not represent more than a caricature that gained currency in Britain and grew there to influence the minds of those who would journey to Brazil. It insinuated itself into the background of the descriptions and interpretations of the better-informed writers such as Dundas, Scully, and Wetherell. This makes Walsh's contribution all the more valuable, as he was deliberately putting himself into situations that, if the rumors were true, would be gravely dangerous to himself and to his property. In this sense, his experimental approach was far more scientific than Robert Dundas' medical discourse.

Throughout his journey, Walsh had ample opportunity to debunk such blanket condemnations of Brazilian character, as well as to discern plausible explanations as to why the British systematically misinterpreted Brazilian behaviors. With respect to the propensity to neglect reciprocity for social invitations, Walsh pointed out that:

> If they are not inclined to invite people to their houses, it is not from a churlish disposition, but because their houses are not fitted up for, or they themselves in the habit of such intercourse. Their females are retiring and domestic, and our modes of company would break in on the whole economy of their establishment. They are, however, prompt and pleased in returning the obligation by any other courtesy or civility in their power.

In other words, unlike the British, Brazilians did not socialize with superficial acquaintances inside their homes; the Brazilian home was not meant to be a locus of such activity, and it would be inappropriate to expect a Brazilian to make it so. Walsh was able to make these observations because he was taken in at many such homes in the course of his journey, having nowhere else to stay. To recall for a moment Maria Graham's feverish round of morning visits to the gentlewomen of Bahia, which appeared to have the purpose of confirming her low opinion of their housekeeping abilities and personal grooming habits, it is easy to see how negative myths surrounding the manners and character of the other side could develop and persist, depending on the prejudices brought to each situation.[31]

Walsh continued his defense of Brazilians' character and social habits at some length, always providing evidence from his own experience to support the counter-claims that he makes. "Though sometimes rough and unpolished, they are remarkably kind and good-natured; and their former prejudice against strangers never renders them hostile, or even uncivil." – "If they are indolent, it has [been due to] having all their labor performed, and their wants supplied, by slaves. Where a due incentive is applied, there are no people more active." – "If they are ignorant, it is not from any want of a desire for knowledge, or a disposition to learn." – "If they are a people of a quick or irritable temper, it is the constitutional fault of a tropical climate, and they seldom carry it to a fatal excess. Duelling [...] is never heard of in Brazil." – "But of all charges, that of dishonesty and robbery seems most unfounded, and I know no country through which I would now travel with a greater feeling of security."

Walsh took a significant risk in his two-year effort to find out whether Brazilians were as rapacious as they were said to be. In many places, he arrived dirty, disheveled, "without introduction or equipage [...] exceedingly unprepossessing, I imagine, in my appearance". He noted that the locals also believed him to be carrying a chest full of gold from the mines, which at that time would be highly illegal as well as dangerous. He felt "totally helpless and unprotected, being myself a total stranger, and having no one with me but a poor despised negro for a guide, who was held in no more estimation than the mule he led". Nevertheless, he was everywhere received with the greatest courtesy, independently of social class: "a titled Dona, a Brazilian gentleman, and the humble keeper of a poor rancho, the occupier of a small room, all equally received me with cordial hospitality, and gave up their own necessary comforts for my accommodation". On the road or in the towns, no one molested him, or attempted to overcharge him for goods or services rendered. On one occasion, the owner of a gold mine even presented him with a sheet of gold leaf and refused any payment. Walsh emphatically conveyed a belief that his passage would never have been as safe if he were traveling in this way through England or Ireland.

Why were Walsh's experiences so different from those of most of the other British subjects who had resided in, or visited, Brazil? Walsh seemed determined to observe the Brazilians as fairly as possible, perhaps even more so than Dundas and Wetherell. He must have been favorably predisposed towards them because of his willingness to throw himself on the mercy of strangers, in fact leaving himself little other recourse; so perhaps Walsh's favorable predisposition toward Brazilians may have influenced their treatment of him, as probably happened to Wetherell (see Chapter 4). Another aspect of the situation concerns the openness to the really new that is possible in a rural setting, where the general lack of contact with the outside world would have helped Walsh's goodwill to be taken at face value and lead on from there to positive experiences. In this sense, one wonders what might have happened if here were really to travel through the country roads of England and Ireland. His own fears would probably prevent him from ever attempting such a thing, fears based no doubt on hearsay of the sort that stopped British residents in Brazil from traveling alone through the interior.

In this sense, it is useful to compare the experience of Robert Walsh to that of Charles Fraser, whose 1812 manuscript narrative has been mentioned in previous chapters, and to other British subjects who kept themselves more organically connected to the merchant communities in the major cities. The independent travelers had much richer opportunities, indeed a daily necessity, for close communication and even camaraderie with Brazilians of many classes, who on their part had not had much previous contact with the British at all. Because of these circumstances, neither side had sufficient motivation or experiential knowledge to erect *a priori* barriers to understanding the other, such as negative stereotypes and the group-versus-group contexts that allow for their reinforcement.

Brazilian Views of the British

Many twentieth-century Brazilian historians have expressed the need for their national histories to reflect a deeper understanding of the British presence in their midst, especially during the nineteenth century. In the essay she wrote about this topic for the series *História Geral da Civilização Brasileira,* Olga Pantaleão mostly discussed commercial treaties, tariffs, and political tensions among the privileged British merchants and Brazilian elites. She devoted a passage of about seven pages to what the British merchants' lives were like, using as her sources Luccock and Mawe. She stated unequivocally that the nineteenth century was "the British century in Brazil", especially its first half.[32]

The renowned sociologist Gilberto Freyre undertook a more thorough study of the social history of the British living in nineteenth-century Brazil. He introduced the work acknowledging that the presence of "British culture" in Brazilian development – not only economic, but also social and mental – cannot be ignored. He agrees with Pantaleão in stating that the most influential period of the British presence was the first half of the nineteenth century.[33] Leslie Bethell, in his study of the British role in the abolition of the international slave trade to Brazil, quoted a statement by Brazilian historian José Honório Rodrigues that "[The] clash between national needs and British demands was the very essence of our history in the first fifty years of the nineteenth century".[34]

Most studies of the British presence in Brazil have emphasized economic or political factors, and any discussion of social history usually focuses on Rio de Janeiro.[35] Bahia, however, was just as important at the time of the British arrival. James Prior noted in 1813 that the Prince Regent had wanted to remain in Bahia with his entourage when it stopped there on its way to Rio, and only reluctantly bowed to political pressure to continue on to Rio de Janeiro. Prior remarked that in his opinion, Bahia's beauty and temperate climate more than justified the Prince's reaction. Freyre, too, pointed out that the most influential British communities in Brazil were those of Rio de Janeiro, Bahia, and Pernambuco.

In 1993, the prominent Bahian historian Thales de Azevedo wrote an article for Salvador's *A Tarde* newspaper (mentioned in Chapter 3) in which he supported efforts to establish the historical-monument status of Bahia's British Cemetery, and belatedly lamented the demolition, in 1975, of the English chapel in Campo Grande. The fact that the destruction of such a significant historic structure had not elicited any sort of protest from the local community demonstrated, to him, that the importance of the British presence in Bahia was insufficiently understood or appreciated:

> That monumental temple spoke of the numerous presence, in our midst, of subjects of H. British Majesty who lived and worked among us, contributing to our culture and civilization since at least the legendary opening of the ports. [...] As for Bahia, we know little or nothing, except for allusions in Freyre's *Ingleses no Brasil*. It is necessary that we study and analyze our nineteenth century from this point of view.[36]

Azevedo's high stature as a historian was illustrated in a review of his work by Gilberto Freyre in 1970, who referred to him as being one of the most prominent scholars at the University of Bahia.[37] Azevedo's view was that the British legacy to Bahia was one of civilization, industry, and mutual respect. Since he made it clear that not enough was known about what actually took place between the British and Brazilians in Bahia during the nineteenth century, his assertion regarding their positive image is probably the general impression prevalent among Bahian scholars today.

Images and Impressions

How true was the image expressed by Azevedo? Were the British
viewed by nineteenth-century Brazilians primarily as hardworking,
useful vectors of European culture and Anglo-Saxon industry? During
the mid-nineteenth century, when the new British chapel was being built
in Campo Grande, the British residents of Bahia were in fact facing the
overwhelmingly negative reactions from Brazilians of all classes
against the British government's violations of Brazilian sovereignty,
particularly after the Aberdeen Act (see Chapter 2). But to answer this
question more fully, we must return to the beginning of the period of
mutual contact. Henry Koster, possibly the only British merchant to
become a *senhor de engenho*[38] in northeastern Brazil, made a sophisticated critique of the British in his narrative, which was written before
Recife had a British chapel or cemetery. From his privileged standpoint
as a bi-cultural Portuguese-British traveler,[39] He complained of the
ragtag group that formed the British presence in Pernambuco:

> At the time of my coming away, there was no protestant chapel, no
> clergyman, nor even a burial ground for our countrymen [...] no
> steps have been taken towards [establishing these] ... although they
> are now aware that at any rate we have the forms of human beings,
> that we have the power of speech, and that we have our share of
> intellect in all the common transactions of the world, still how are
> we to look for respect from them towards a set of men, who have no
> appearance at least, of possessing any religious feelings? It should
> be recollected that we are living among a people [...] whose devoted-
> ness to their church establishment surpasses every other feeling.[40]

Koster made the point that the *appearance* of religiosity, especially
its visible, physical structures, would be enough to generate respect
from the Brazilians. Azevedo's present-day lament over the destruction
of the British chapel, and his protectiveness towards the burial ground
as a final surviving legacy of the greatnesses of British civilization in
Bahia, would suggest that Koster's recommendation had been right
on target.

Going back a bit further, a similar situation may be found. To recall
Charles Fraser's 1812 manuscript report from Bahia, describing the
state of Brazilian sentiments toward Great Britain during that politically
crucial time, he showed a response similar to Koster's:

The extreme ignorance in which the inhabitants of Brazil & of Spanish America, had been studiously kept by the old policy of their respective Governments, together with their awe of the Church & belief in its infallibility, had succeeded so well that 90 parts of 100 of the Inhabitants of Brazil are ignorant at this day that there is even a Parliament in G. Britain; and finding their interests suffering severely from the restraints & interruptions of a trade which was originally encouraged as humane & meritorious by the Church [...] *proceed[ing] from a Nation of Foreigners & Heretics* whom the same Infallible Mother Church had uniformly taught them to regard with that peculiar degree of horror & detestation with which we contemplate the Inhabitants of the Infernal Regions.[41]

Fraser did not view the Brazilians' religiosity with the same respect as Koster. He saw it more as a demonstration of Catholic backwardness and colonial isolation. Nevertheless, the same point is clear: the Brazilians largely viewed the new British arrivals as alien, odd, and spiritually (morally) inferior. Later on, of course, this impression would change, as the British did set up social and physical demarcations of status and difference that established their equality to Brazilians, and eventually their superiority.

Fraser and Koster were describing the Brazilian northeast in the 1810s. By the mid-1820s, Maria Graham found a slightly better situation in Bahia:

We went to the English chapel, and were well pleased with the manner in which the service was performed. [...] I was surprised, perhaps unreasonably, to hear [Chaplain] Synge pray for 'Don John of Portugal, Sovereign of these realms, by whose gracious permission we are enabled to meet and worship God according to our conscience,' or words to that effect.[42]

Graham added, wryly, that the British were not so polite in Rome as to pray for the Pope. The British residents of Bahia were just beginning to create a group identity that was visibly rooted (at least apparently) in religious community. They probably faced the reality that their faith was at best misunderstood, and at worst despised, by the locals. Their permission to worship was based on the requirements that they not proselytize among Brazilians in any way. The chapel had to look like a normal private residence, and no bells were to be rung to announce meetings for worship. Reverend Synge's expression of gratitude to João

VI, the prince regent, shows the British merchants' understanding of their dependence upon the goodwill of Brazilian authorities for their political and social security – survival – in Bahia.

Koster had been perceptive about the Brazilian point of view, and sympathetic to it. His alarm at the lack of unity among British expatriates in Recife was eloquently expressed in a passage where he reaffirmed the difficulty of British merchants in achieving a positive status in Brazilian eyes:

> It is not thus that the British nation is to become respectable; we may have relations of trade with these people, but we must be content to be merely regarded according to our utility; there can be no respect for our general character as a body of men, none of that regard which would make us listened to in any great question, which would make our opinions and our assertions depended upon as coming from men of steadiness, – of religious habits. Nor can we be accounted as more than residents for a time, we cannot be considered as an established community, who are thus without any common bond of union, who have not any one point to which all are directed; we have no appearance of belonging to one nation, as if we were brethren meeting in a foreign land.[43]

Koster's description rings true to Mawe's and Luccock's narratives of the *mêlée* that was the early British commercial experience in Brazil (see Chapter 3). Up until Independence, the 'community' of British merchants was no more than a set of impressions in Brazilian minds. In the early 1820s, the British began to erect deliberate representations of themselves as a unified, respectable, civilized group of foreigners, externally erasing the class distinctions that they continued to take great pains to maintain internally. That image has remained, as a historical legacy, in the minds of historians in Bahia and throughout Brazil.

Gilberto Freyre devoted most of his four hundred-page tome to exploring the stereotypes associated with the image of the *inglês*. This he often did uncritically, though with great assurance, which probably stemmed from personal understanding of Brazilian cultural stereotypes. According to Freyre, the nineteenth-century British residents were generally viewed as scrupulously honest, eminently practical, and careful with money. By turns feared and ridiculed, their layered image in Brazilian eyes may have been a way of using humor as a means of self-defense, of one-upmanship against a perceived threat.[44] A good example of this is the still current expression *prá inglês ver* (for Englishmen to see), meaning something that is being done mostly to keep up an appearance of legitimacy. Koster's reasons for building a British chapel in Recife are in fact a very good example of this, except that in that case, it was *prá brasileiro ver.*

The British reputation for honesty in business was so strong that the expression *palavra de inglês* (the word of an Englishman) was used among Brazilians as an oath. A related expression, still in vogue today, is *hora inglesa,* which means that an invitation or appointment is expected to be honored at the stated time, and overrides the usual Brazilian custom of maintaining a certain acceptable or expected degree of lateness.[45]

The Brazilian fascination with British practicality, in technological innovation as well as business acumen, was frequently expressed. Walsh encountered it repeatedly in his travels throughout the interior:

> In the [mining] province itself the people entertained some such ideas, of the summary and almost magical processes the English were to apply, to bring to light treasures which the Brazilians could not reach. Machines, they thought, would convey a river from a plain to the top of a mountain, and perform other wonders of a like miraculous nature.[46]

Great Britain's greatest technological contributions to Brazil and Bahia were made in the engineering of public works. These, however, would not occur until the second half of the nineteenth century. Construction began on the Bahia & São Francisco Railway in 1852 with its first section opened in 1860.[47] The first regular steamship line between Brazil and Europe was inaugurated in 1851, and the transatlantic cable was put into service much later, in 1874. Probably the most memorable British engineering project in the city of Bahia (Salvador) was the construction of two independent structures for managing the split-level topography of the upper and lower town, which before had to be managed either by *cadeira* or on foot. These were the construction of Ladeira da Conceição in the 1860s, which employed an ingenious system of archways to support a wide road clinging along the side of the cliff; and the massive free-standing elevator in 1883, today a familiar landmark known as the Elevador Lacerda, and used by thousands every day.

Although the British who resided in Bahia during the early nineteenth century by and large were not engineers or scientists, the

Brazilian image of British practicality, often occurring in the context of a constant lookout for a profit, is exemplified in an offhand comment by Wetherell. This note ran under the title "Fibre of Aloe Leaves":

> It is very strong, and does not easily decay in water. I believe samples have been sent to Europe, but I do not know if it has been found to answer any useful purpose in our manufactures, but I should think it might, if procurable in sufficient quantities.[48]

Freyre makes it clear that the British were considered good businessmen by the Brazilians in *Ingleses no Brasil*. In one case, a merchant named Charles Cannell advertised in Rio's *Jornal do Commercio* in 1827 that he was offering at auction "various fabrics, slightly imperfect", and "biscuits of inferior quality". Freyre observed that this happened at a time when any European article, even outdated or used, would usually be described in advertisements as new and perfect.[49] He concludes the examination of British advertisements in Brazilian newspapers from the first half of the nineteenth century with the following statement:

> With few exceptions, [these advertisements] are a lesson of good taste, sobriety, and professional ethics, and contrast with the overemphasis, the exaggeration, and occasionally the charlatanism of many other advertisements by Europeans of non-British origin and of other professions.[50]

Nevertheless, in spite of these positive attributes, or perhaps because of them, a Brazilian mythology gradually arose about the private life of this amazingly skilled, wealthy, and capable being. British engineers, railroad officials, and sailors would eventually be subsumed into the stereotype, which was expressed through linguistic expressions and jokes by Brazilians about the *ingleses*. They were variously called *missa-seca* (dry mass – a reference to Protestantism), *mister,* and *godeme* (goddammit).[51] Besides these, the Brazilians developed and adapted a large number of English words, many of which are still in use today. According to Freyre, these include *smoking* (for smoking-jacket, or tuxedo), *drink,* and *bufê* (buffet); the sporting terms *futebol* (football – soccer), *time* (team), *record, poquer* (poker), *sinuca* (snooker), and *iate* (yacht). Many people from the state of Minas Gerais trace the origin of their regional trademark exclamation *Uai!* from the English 'Why!' Still other terms include *esnobe* (snob), *gin, tênis* (tennis), and *uísque* (whisky),[52] though several of these might be traceable to the American influence as well.

The image of the Briton in Brazilian popular culture is very interesting. It was expressed early in popular comedies such as *O inglês machinista,* by Martins Pena, performed in Bahia in October of 1849.[53] The stereotype soon gained enough momentum to become a staple of café conversation, caricatures, magazines, carnival costumes, folklore, and racy jokes. It portrayed the Englishman who, despite all his worldly successes, was sexually impotent and excessively cold towards women, whom he constantly neglected in his pursuit of drinking and sports, and because of his overwhelming fascination with books and machines. By contrast, the frail-looking and unassuming Brazilian always made the best of the situation, as sexual escapades were *his* best affirmation of virile energy.[54] Freyre believes this piquant story line, repeated endlessly throughout the late nineteenth century in Brazil, was a way for Brazilian men to overcome or take revenge for what they perceived as the imperial arrogance of many British diplomatic representatives; of the insolent, violent sailors of the British navy; of bankers, missionaries, and even scientists such as Charles Darwin, who often expressed outrage at the oppressive backwardness of Brazilian slave society. In retaliation, the Brazilians came to view the Briton as "ugly and arrogant, with a pronounced overbite, blond sideburns, a pipe in the corner of his mouth, plaid clothing, and thick-soled walking shoes".[55] Such a caricature emphasized social crassness and lack of style, without denying the professional competence for which the British were so well known.

Image and Class

Despite their wealth and the desire to emulate the superiority of the upper classes in Europe, nearly all of the British merchants in Bahia worked daily at their offices in the lower town. This did nothing to diminish their views of themselves as being separate, apart, and superior to the local elites. However, the following quotes suggest that the Brazilians may have had a different idea:

> The commerce of the [Brazilian] empire is carried on chiefly [...] by foreign merchants [...] and foreign merchants are the aristocracy of its cities.[56]

> The consul appears to have socialized exclusively with merchants.[57]

The second statement, by a Brazilian historian, was meant disparagingly. The first, by a British visitor, is meant to convey the superiority of the British within the local society. It was noted earlier in this chapter that in Brazilian colonial society, merchants were not considered to be part of the elite, who were mostly landowners, military leaders, prominent lawyers or politicians, and their families. As society changed in response to political independence, the abolition of the slave trade and eventually of slavery, efforts at modernization, and increased European immigration, the status of British merchants rose. By the turn of the twentieth century, they were indeed viewed as an elite to be imitated in manners, clothing, and customs.[58] Therefore, it is useful to examine primary sources from the earliest years of the nineteenth century, before the British merchant had earned or been granted superior status in the eyes of the Brazilian elite.

James Prior's narrative is of interest for this purpose, as he was not a merchant, and recorded his impressions of Bahia in 1813, soon after the British first arrived. In the opening section, Prior attempts to convey the full experience of the filth of Praia and contrasts it, as many others have done, to the openness and tranquility of the upper city (see Chapter 3):

> The summit of the bank alone is the region of fashion; equipages, fine houses, gay people, handsome churches, and some good streets. The beach, or lower town, is the depository of commerce and filth; these the Portuguese seem to make inseparable companions. In the former appear the gay and the well-dressed, enjoying air and salubrity; in the latter, men of business intermixed with naked negroes, dragging along bales and hogsheads, both of whom, by their indifference, seem deprived of the sense of smelling. In the former are churches, balls, and operas; in the latter counting-houses, stores, and shops [...] Escaping as quickly as possible from so many impure and disagreeable objects, we ascended to the Upper Town.[59]

In Prior's perception, the stench and dirtiness of the streets resonates with the distastefulness of commerce. "Men of business" are denigrated by their vivid juxtaposition to the lowest-ranking members of society, the slaves. However, at least some of the merchants dismissed disgustedly by Prior would have been his own compatriots, who certainly did not think of themselves in such derogatory terms. Rather, they felt themselves to be continually connected with the luxuries of their Victoria homes.

But during the early years of establishing mutual relations, did the Brazilians view the British merchants as Prior suggests? Given the remarks by Koster presented earlier in this chapter, the answer is probably yes. The history of the British community of Bahia in the nineteenth century, then, becomes the history of a group of merchants gradually doing, deliberately or by accident, whatever it took to ascend in status in the eyes of elite Brazilians, whose own standards gradually changed over the century so as to give this process greater momentum.[60]

At the same time, there remained the problem of lower-class British immigrants to Brazil. In *British Exploits in South America* (1917), W. H. Koebel related a story from Rio de Janeiro in 1828, when a Brazilian political project to promote Irish immigration into Brazil's rural areas for the purpose of expanding agricultural production went badly awry. Lured by lavish promises of land and plenty, 2,400 Irish "peasants" (farmers, artisans, yeomen) set sail to Rio de Janeiro only to find, upon their arrival, that the scheme had completely fallen through. Nothing had been prepared for them; the agricultural land was still forested. The Brazilian government encouraged the Irish to make do in Rio de Janeiro as best they could. Koebel relates what happened next:

> The helpless Irish ... were soon reduced to the verge of starvation. Thus these guests of the Brazilian Government ... were to be met with at the street corners of Rio, huddled in unkempt and miserable groups ... To crown the whole business, the very Negro slaves of Rio, rejoicing in the rare spectacle of a set of human beings in a more lamentable condition than their own, took to shouting insults at the hapless immigrants, and many a jeer of *"Escravos brancos!"* – white slaves – came from the grinning African lips.[61]

For the British merchant community of Rio de Janeiro, the humiliation of this situation can only be imagined. As the tensions worsened, mob scenes ensued, and the Irishmen found to their despair that the minor officials of Rio preferred to imprison them and let the Africans go free. Once imprisoned, the Irish were seen "chained side by side with Negro prisoners, and thus set to enforced labor in the most degraded fashion".

As the century progressed, Brazilian views of the British community improved as ideas regarding modernization took hold in Brazil, and the British presence came to include scientists, engineers, and other liberal professionals. The actual relationship of these new arrivals to the existing merchant community was probably not as solid as Brazilian sources seem to suggest. In any case, their activities, attitudes, and way of life contributed to forming the Brazilian stereotype of the British man as rich, practical, not very attractive, ill-versed in the arts of love, and generally eccentric in a vaguely (but not excessively) threatening manner. Throughout the early nineteenth century, Bahianos experienced much distress due to British abolitionist activity. Therefore, regardless of whether they considered the actual merchants whom they saw in the streets to be directly responsible for the myriad problems that British abolitionism was causing, the Brazilian image of the British contained multiple internal contradictions. Nevertheless, overall it has changed over time into a generally positive perception of a homogeneous, hardworking, civilized group that has left many marks upon the geography and society of Bahia today.

Chapter 6

Crossing Boundaries: Knowledge and Sex

As mentioned in earlier chapters, it was the arrival of British women that began to give a sense and semblance of social community to the group of individual merchants and clerks who first arrived in South America during the early nineteenth century.[1] The smooth functioning of a small community was understood to depend upon the successful playing out of prescribed gender roles. This throws into relief the opposite realization that any dramatic departure from these roles would have posed a serious threat to the cohesion of the community as such. The activities of the British women were more visible, and therefore easier to control, than those of the men. Women had to stay inside or around the home most of the time in order to maintain respectability, while the men maintained theirs primarily by succeeding professionally in the public sphere, and secondarily by showing respect for the community norms by adhering to them on the surface. Discreet liaisons with Brazilian women were acceptable for British men, in fact almost expected in some cases. An interesting question arising from this is whether these gender-based differences in social conditions, expectations, and evaluations of personal success meant that the British women were better or worse off than the men whose wives and daughters they were.

As with most efforts to uncover women's history, however, documentation is scarce. With the conspicuous exception of Maria Graham, no documents written by any of the British women who witnessed and experienced Bahia during the nineteenth century appear to have survived. The occasional mention of female relatives in the consular correspondence offers only a suggestion of their presence, and the situations in which they appeared tended to be those requiring official action, which means they were probably atypical.[2] The official petitions for residency by British subjects in Bahia hardly ever mentioned women, except indirectly through the applicant's marital status. And women's travel patterns between Great Britain and Bahia are all but impossible to trace, given the lack of systematic records of passenger listings for the port of Bahia before 1851.

Therefore, the best available evidence of women's activity and experience falls roughly into the following four categories. First are the demographic records from Bahia's British chapel, showing the age at marriage, number and spacing of children, class background, and age at death for selected women.[3] The second type of documentation is the description of social life in Bahia's British community, as found in the various travel narratives written by men. Since the men spent most of their time at work, the community's social entertainments were most likely conceived, prepared, and executed by women. The observation of specific knowledge and skills required to put on, say, a successful dinner party, diplomatic reception, or weekend family retreat may provide some clue as to how women managed to carry out their expected British roles under such unfamiliar conditions. A third source for understanding women's lives is that ultimate measure of lifetime accomplishment, the tombstone – for many women still rest in peace behind the ageing walls of Bahia's British cemetery. Finally, the fourth source for documenting British women's relative success in meeting social expectations is the way in which they were treated by Brazilian and British men, as judged through the men's writings and recorded behavior. Although these sources are all indirect, they provide at least a means of comparing the female experience of Bahia's British community to the predominantly male picture seen so far.

James Wetherell wrote that as far as social life was concerned, the foreign residents of Bahia "seemed to enjoy themselves very much", frequently having small dancing parties at their homes year-round, and often putting on large picnics at the seaside during the summer.[4] But what specifically was the daily work of British women in Bahia? A closer idea is given by John Candler, whose uncritical country-squire view of the merchant community's daily life was discussed in Chapter 4. In his narrative describing a visit to Brazil in 1852, Candler wrote the following:

> On our arrival at Bahia, a clerk from [Deane, Youle, and Co.] was sent on board to meet us and facilitate our landing; and our esteemed friend, Robert Baines – 'Senhor Roberto' – one of the firm, took us in a carriage, drawn by four mules, to his country house at Victoria,

and placed us under the care of his bride, whom he had lately brought from London. [...] Here [...] we enjoyed good health, and the luxuries of a bountiful table, without cost and without care.[5]

Candler evidently had an interest in showing gratitude to his hosts, and in promoting in print their enviable graciousness and worldly comfort. Nevertheless, Mr. Baines' bride, who was probably young and inexperienced, had evidently not had much time to familiarize herself with Bahia and get her hostess act together, so to speak. Candler offers hints as to how Mrs. Baines managed this important social mission on her own, without her family or friends for support:

The wealthy merchant, and his bride [...] invited a number of their friends to meet us at their dinner-table; and the guests so invited, solicited from the party similar visits in return. By this means we were brought into acquaintance with many of our country-people, much to our enjoyment.[6]

Evidently the other British women were pooling their resources to create at least the semblance of a lively and close-knit social circle, as well as the image of fine country living that they wished to project. In so doing, they supported the newcomer and enabled her to show off Bahia and its British community to advantage in the distinguished visitor's eyes. Over the course of a few short days, not only was Candler treated to lavish hospitality and a well-conducted round of social dinners, he was also taken out to the countryside on a complicated day trip that went very well:

On one occasion we sat down, a large company, to an early dinner at three o'clock, and immediately after made an excursion, some in carriages, and some on horseback, to the foot of the proud hills that form an amphitheatre, somewhat distant, around the city, passing by several sugar-plantations, and through a country well cultivated, and of sylvan beauty.[7]

The logistics of this outing were extremely complicated. Bahia's weather is unpredictable, and a sudden deluge could render country roads impassable, possibly even stranding the party overnight. Just the scheduling and inviting of a large number of merchants and their wives for a mid-afternoon event would have taken a determined effort. The dinner itself, like any other, required the hostess to plan an acceptable menu; locate and purchase all needed supplies, either in person or through an agent, with all local transactions taking place in a language the hostess did not know well; possess the paraphernalia of a presentably British dinner service for a large party; train and supervise household slaves (or the more expensive hired servants) to prepare and serve the food acceptably; keep the conversation flowing smoothly while coordinating each detail of the dinner; and make certain the meal came to an end in time for the party to get organized into its horses and carriages, and reach its destination in good spirits, returning before the early and sudden tropical sundown. It would seem that the only way this expedition could have been so successful would have been if many British women of varied skills joined forces, both before and during the actual event.

In writing his positive review of the Baines' hospitality, John Candler was not just being nice to his hosts. Although he may have been unaware of the joint effort going on around him to improve the community's image, he was perfectly aware of the skill required to carry off such a social performance, and explicitly credited his host's bride on two occasions, though without mentioning her actual name. Candler did appreciate a good host(ess), as he had to suffer the occasional poor one. Here is his description of another day trip he took in Bahia, this one planned and conducted by a man:

> At the country-house of one English gentleman we were invited to pass a long day, and to take with him a ride among the hills, instead of stopping, as we had done before, at the foot of them. The toil of horseback at mid-day in a climate so sultry was almost too great, but the recompense was ample in delightful scenery.[8]

The merchants' standard insistence on ignoring the discomfort of Bahia's climate and topography as a means of proclaiming a British virility and strength, examined at length in Chapter 4, recurs here. However, the host's decisions in this case were not only bad for his own health, but also damaging to the well-being of his guest. Candler, along with his travelling companion Wilson Burgess, was on an official mission related to the abolition of the Brazilian slave trade,[9] and it was probably critical that he have a good impression of Bahia's British community. After all, not only did the British rent and own household slaves, but the merchants' capital was still heavily invested in the continuation of the trade.[10] Besides, Candler's narrative would be read back home by a pro-abolitionist public, and the British subjects residing in Bahia did expect to return home someday.[11] In other words, a public relations project was afoot, and a concerted effort was required to pull it off. If some men of the British community were somewhat less aware of this than the women, this may be a useful issue through which to structure the play of boundaries between them.

Women were responsible for organizing social events, running their households, being good companions for their husbands, and good British mothers to their children. The 'women's work' in this particular context seemed fairly clearly defined, and its successful execution acknowledged as critical to the survival and success of the British community as such. Perhaps the words on some of these women's tombstones would be the closest a historian can come to a performance review:[12]

After an exemplary and faithful discharge of her various duties as daughter, sister, wife and mother, departed this life for a better [...] Aged 29 years and 9 months.[13]

This monument erected as a tribute to her many virtues and as a last sad proof of the love and esteem [of] her sorrowing husband. The first best gift, that man can blame better than pomp, by crowds adored or gold immeasurably stor'd is hers: a pure and spotless name.[14]

Here lies a true and loving wife and gentle mother dear who always taught her children our Saviour's wrath to fear ... Whilst on earth we never missed her / for her loss we'd never known / like a bark without a rudder / without a mother is a home. The first best gift that man can claim is hers, a pure and spotless name. Darling rest in peace. [...] Deeply lamented in loving memory of a kind and loving mother who gave birth to 15 children and in all her troubles she trusted to the will of God.[15]

The nearly identical references to "a pure and spotless name" and the matter-of-fact reference to the woman's "various duties" may have just been Victorian set phrases. But nevertheless, there can be no real doubt that the British merchant community was keenly aware of the importance of female restraint and self-control for maintaining its reputation as a civilized enclave of competent, God-fearing, hardworking people, and that this reputation was important for its long-term commercial success (see Chapter 3). This has been true in terms of bourgeois family life down the centuries. Nevertheless, it serves to show that women were important guardians of the British community's image, to themselves and to Brazilian society at large. As Koster had realized, the community's survival depended to a large extent on how it was viewed by Brazilians – with respect? Suspicion? Warmth? Derision? All of this would affect the overall success of the merchant enterprise in Bahia, no less than the prices of commodities or the finessing of political conflict. A good deal, therefore, depended on whether a British woman could carry out all her duties while maintaining her name (reputation) pure and spotless (loyal to expected performance).[16]

In some ways these intense expectations would have been oppressive to individual women, but it could also be a point of gender pride. An example from Maria Graham's book serves to illustrate this. On November 14th, 1821, in the thick of the tensions surrounding Bahia's independence and the risk of possible outbreak of war with Portuguese troops stationed in town, Graham made an effort to help her husband carry out his mission of protecting British subjects whose lives were in danger:

> On looking out at daylight this morning, we saw artillery planted, and troops drawn up on the platform opposite to the opera house. I went on shore to see if Miss Pennell, her sister, or any of our other friends would come on board; but they naturally prefer staying to the last with their fathers and husbands.[17]

This was no simple decision. The welfare of children may have been at stake, and once Graham's ship left port, there would be no easy way to protect them if the brewing hostilities were to erupt into violence. The context of her narrative emphasizes that the situation was dangerous. Her casual use of the word "naturally" thus reinforces the idea that the women's first duty obviously was to their fathers and husbands, not to their children; and it tellingly conveys a certain pride in the promptness with which those women jumped to the correct choice, the expected courageous sacrifice. Upon reflection, it seems a bit odd that their husbands and fathers did not seem at all eager to put the safety of their wives and children before their own, for surely the men would have had sufficient authority to carry out their own wishes in this case. It would have been an ordeal to send away the women and children indefinitely, with communications as precarious as they were. If the women had left, things would have been more difficult for the men, as Graham's phrasing seems to acknowledge; and so they remained. The community held firm. Luckily, though, no war broke out.

140

But such conventional heroism may obscure the real opportunities for individual rebellion that always exist in times of war and upheaval. At least one young British woman of respectable parentage took advantage of the situation in Bahia to do exactly as it pleased her, and seems to have gotten away with it. However, she was very much *not* part of the established merchant community. She happened to be in transit, emigrating with her parents to Australia:

> We most respectfully entreat your assistance to recover our Daughter who has been stolen from us, and detained by M. Weatherby Master of the Brig *Hannah*, now lying in this Port, for the purpose of gratifying his own lustful desires, and to the utter ruin of our Daughter's character, happiness and future prospects in life.[18]

Vice-consul William Follett's cover letter to the President of Bahia, whose permission he needed in order to take action in this case, added some new information:

> The Master of the vessel bound to Europe has clandestinely and in opposition to the wishes of her Parents induced a young Woman to abandon her duty and to live with him [...] and its [*sic*] with a view of rescuing this young woman from a career of Vice and of restoring her to her disconsolate Friends that I make this representation to your Excellency.[19]

Whether or not this young woman was abducted to be forced into a life of prostitution in the streets of London, at least at this moment in Bahia she clearly wanted to stay with Captain Weatherby and return to Europe with him instead of emigrating to Australia with her parents. The parents and the consul were concerned with her future prospects, the promised payoff for good performance of duty that the daughter threw away by taking her future into her own hands. Presumably she had some vague awareness of this; and so in making her choice, she showed no less courage than the other women who remained in danger instead of fleeing to safety. Unfortunately, no other documents relating to this event are available, so we do not know how the romance turned out. The point is simply that creative choices were possible in situations where the usual social strictures were lifted and transferred to the individual wills and minds of women, and so their choices deserve credit as such.

One other point to be made concerning the women's history of the British community of Bahia has to do with how they were viewed by men. James Wetherell had candidly observed how the young British women's value to their community as high-status objects of desire made it possible for them to live much more luxuriously there than back home in Britain.[20] This represents something of a subversion of the attention to class that operated at all levels of the expatriate community. British women possessed valuable skills as household managers, instillers of national sentiment, sources of family identity and emotional support, as well as being status symbols. Since they were a crucial and scarce resource for the community, their specific class did not matter to the men who competed to court them, even if they really were "quite of the second rate of even colonial gentility".[21] Despite the hardships of foreign living and of physical and psychological distance from the homeland, British women lived well enough in Bahia for Wetherell to comment upon their tendency to prefer it over England. This was in spite of Dr. Dundas' observation that British women had a greater predisposition to dangerous illnesses in Bahia than did British men.[22]

On the whole, the women's work in the British community of Bahia was at least comparable in difficulty to that of the men, in that it required a much greater familiarity with local society as well as the constant need to translate Brazilian physical realities (such as domestic slaves and available foodstuffs) into recognizably British commodities (a dinner party or country picnic). Women were responsible for rearing identifiably British children among Brazilian slaves, settings and sounds; and they had to part with these children at a young age, when they were sent off to boarding school in Europe.[23] Furthermore, their fates depended upon the success of their merchant fathers and husbands, so the stresses associated with the merchants' career uncertainties affected them no less strongly. On the other hand, women had clearer expectations to fulfil, and these seldom conflicted with their best interests or those of the community.

With its emphasis on correct deportment and gallant self-sacrifice, the lifelong 'duty' of women dovetailed well with the overriding need to generate self-respect inside the British community and general respect by Brazilians outside of it. Their common situation as isolated expatriate wives gave them great incentive to cooperate instead of competing, so British women most likely formed a fairly close-knit group inside the enclave in which they had to spend most of their time.[24] At least some of the British wives were in fact Brazilian, with family ties to the local community, so their presence enriched the overall pool of resources available to the women more than it diluted their unified foreignness and separateness from Brazilians. Finally, it may be presumed that women, if they chose, had an escape route available to them: they could leave their husbands temporarily or permanently and return home, living with relatives as needed, without the same level of disgrace that would fall upon a man who tried to do the same (though some disgrace was inevitable, if Maria Graham is any judge). Overall, the women occupied a position of mediation between the British enclave and the host environment, and thus their lives were more rooted in external reality.

In many ways this is reminiscent of the Postlethwaite women from Chapter 4, who used their gender-specific job as hostesses to compatriots and host-country guests alike in a sort of joint project to promote mutual understanding and genuine social agreeableness for all. Robertson lavished praise upon their skilful handling of the delicate situation:

> They not only accommodated themselves to circumstances, but made the best of them; and instead of being unable, like some of our amiable John Bullish folks when they go abroad, to *endure* the people of the country, – Mrs. and the Misses Postlethwaite went beyond merely enduring the Correntinas, for they met their advances of friendship with that readiness which a conviction of the sincerity of the proffer drew forth.[25]

In that charged cross-cultural context, a certain level of trust had to be extended before the openness necessary to friendship could take root and flower. Robertson's language is somewhat unclear, but he probably meant that the Correntinas extended friendship first, and the Postlethwaites accepted it because they were convinced of its sincerity *a priori*. If correct, this interpretation implies that the Latin Americans' overtures and gestures of friendship toward the British merchants in their midst were usually treated less receptively, an idea that Robertson's remark about John Bull appears to support.[26] It is easy to see how such a pattern would result in the mutual reinforcement of negative stereotypes examined in Chapter 5. More interestingly, it becomes clear that within the urban British communities, women were in a better position than men to establish close social bonds between the British and their host societies, through their appropriately feminine receptiveness towards those around them.

Concubinage: Social Distance and Physical Intimacy

By contrast, the masculine British role was to resist being changed by the surrounding environment (Chapter 4). Nevertheless, the erotic charms of the Brazilian female – considered by them to be as much a part of the natural environment as were the local flora and fauna – were much on their minds, and it is abundantly clear from the evidence that British men succumbed to these charms again and again. The expected social reproof never quite came, so long as the merchant was discreet in his liaisons. Research in various sources revealed scattered references to many such relationships, falling mainly into three categories: socially unacceptable relations that crossed a boundary of class and/or of race in addition to that of nationality (concubinage); socially accepted but officially invisible stable unions; and licit relationships (courtship and intermarriage).

Many British merchants lived with Brazilian women in Bahia. While George Mumford remained in a long-term non-marital union with Constança Ebbe for most of his life, Andrew Comber married Maria Emilia Freitas while still very young and was proud to eulogize in the death register her performance as and exemplary British wife. Both of these merchants were engaged in legitimate, long-term, stable relationships, and produced children who were recognized and reared as British subjects. A newspaper advertisement from Rio de Janeiro around 1850, placed by "a young single Englishman", stated plainly that he desired "a colored girl to take charge of his house" – a colored girl "who is poor and to whom everything will be given to make her happy".[27] The literature of British concubinage overseas has tended to focus on issues of power relations within the white-ruling-class colonial contexts of Africa and Asia,[28] but in most of Latin America the situation was fundamentally different. British subjects residing in Brazil were understood to be privileged guests of the Portuguese and Brazilian monarchs. They were never a ruling elite by any stretch of the imagination, despite the pseudo-aristocratic aspirations discussed in Chapter 4. The gendered power dynamic operating within the Latin American context has to be considered on its own terms.

In its earliest years, the merchant settlement at Bahia was composed primarily of single men. The establishment of a settled British community as such did not occur until the arrival of British women a decade or so later, when the British businesses were more firmly established

(Chapter 3). As may have been expected, before the British women came, the issue of native concubines appeared rather frequently in *where?* British narratives of travel and residence in Brazil. However, once the community had taken root in Bahia and British families had become the backbone of social organization for the community, British–Brazilian concubinage became less visible. It continued to exist, however, and its treatment was always problematic.

The earliest and the most straightforward of denouncers of such social arrangements was John Mawe, the diplomat who also candidly connected the British merchants' genteel aspirations in Brazil to their abhorrence of going into retail trade. The following is a footnote describing the situation at Rio de Janeiro in 1812:

> [The British merchants] had set apart their hours for horse-exercise, and for going to their country seats. Delicate connections were soon formed, and females of the obscurest class appeared dressed in the most costly extreme of English fashion.[29]

Clearly the most objectionable (or to Mawe's eyes the humorous) aspect of these delicate connections was that they were made with females of "obscure" class. Satirical intent may be gleaned from the wittiness of Mawe's footnote insertion of a humorous picture: the poor Brazilian female, out in the countryside, dressed in European finery so far above her station as to make her entirely absurd and ridiculous. Surely she does not come across to him as seductive or desirable. It is worth noting, however, that these British merchants appeared desirous of having some tangible degree of well-off Englishness about the bodies of the women with whom they consorted, no matter how incongruous this might have been to the women's actual social stature.

Observers who spent many years in the British communities of Brazil viewed the reality of interracial concubinage as deeply problematic to the community. Henry Koster, writing four years after Mawe, was one such critic. Born in Lisbon of British parents and equally at ease among the English, Portuguese, and Brazilians, Koster moved to Pernambuco in 1809, published his *Travels in Brazil* in 1816, and died in Brazil in 1820.[30] In the section of his book entitled "British Residents", he discussed the need for British subjects to create some semblance of unity in order to gain the respect of Luso-Brazilians. In this context he lobbied for the establishment of an Anglican chapel at Pernambuco. Additionally, he argued, a proper religious center for the community would help to allay the dangerous proclivities of certain British men to take up immoral relations with local women. This is partly a matter of conjecture, for Koster's delicacy toward his middle-class readers forbade him from stating outright what it was that he objected to. As a result, the passage, though not clear in terms of what exactly was going on, at least illuminates how intractable and repugnant the problem was considered to be.

> To these political reasons [for having a chapel] are to be added those which are of far greater importance, those to which no Christian ought to be indifferent. I well know that it is not with the merchants that the evil arises; – but enough, I will go no farther, although I could tarry long upon this subject. I wish however that I could have avoided the mention of it altogether. I might have done so, if I had not felt that I was passing by unnoticed a subject upon which I have often spoken whilst I was upon the spot, and there my sentiments are well known to most of those persons with whom I associated.[31]

This monument of obliqueness closes Koster's chapter with the vague reassurance that he does not mean to implicate any bona fide British *merchants* in the "evil". This was in stark contradiction to Mawe, who thought the merchants' concubinage in particular was worth noting. This adds a class element to the racial element present in the situation, and each will be examined in turn.

Concubinage and Race

Implicit in the reality of concubinage was a special physical attraction that many British men seem to have felt towards Brazilian women of all classes. This kind of attraction is interesting in part because it provides one clear venue for comparison with postcolonial studies of gender relations under European imperialism. The vision of Brazilian women as extremely sexually ardent was present in European travel narratives well before the nineteenth century.[32] Though it was never quite spelled out by the more bourgeois chroniclers of Brazil's British communities (Scully, Dundas, Wetherell), it is well articulated in a narrative published by British naval officer James Prior in 1819. The volume consists of a set of letters that he wrote to a male friend during a round-the-world voyage. Prior was in Bahia in November of 1813, and left a colorful description of his impressions, several of which had to do with the allure of Brazilian females. In one passage, he describes their appearance and education:

> The dress of the fair sex is showy, resembling the French more than the English. In full dress, the bosom and arms are liberally exposed, a singular circumstance among a people, if not jealous, at least only just escaped from jealousy; yet this passion is not an unfrequent companion to voluptuousness. Flowers and precious stones ornament the head. [...] Education [...] has done little toward ornamenting the minds of the ladies; but in the happy countries of Spain and Portugal this accomplishment is not always deemed necessary.[33]

If we compare Prior's description of the women of Bahia to Edward Said's statement in *Orientalism* about the gendered nature of the European's gaze upon foreign places and people that were considered mysterious, and available for conquest, an interesting parallel occurs:

> Orientalism [...] was an exclusively male province. [...] This is especially evident in the writing of travelers and novelists: women are usually the creatures of a male power-fantasy. They express unlimited sensuality, they are more or less stupid, and above all they are willing.[34]

James Prior exerted just such a gaze upon the women of Bahia. They seemed to him sultry, exciting, voluptuous, naïve, and they met with his approval as a connoisseur. Prior seems to have restricted his own gaze to upper-class women, judging from the allusions to French fashions and jewels; perhaps this was a concession to the high status that he wished to maintain in the eyes of his readers. His objectification of foreign women is obvious when he describes his reaction to hearing the "languishing brunettes of Brazil" actually speak: "The language also, naturally soft, flows from their lips with a *naiveté* uncommonly interesting to strangers".[35] If Prior understood enough Portuguese to know what the women were saying, his remark was insulting; and if he did not, it was ridiculous. Either way, it illustrates his interest in actively exoticizing Bahian women in order to titillate his readers and raise his own status as a man.

The presence of racial difference subtly makes itself felt in Prior's narrative, as it did in that of Maria Graham. For her, darkness had signified inferiority and merited disdain: "Hair black, ill combed, and dishevelled

[…] the whole person having an unwashed appearance. […] I did not see one tolerably pretty woman to-day".[36] For Prior, this darkness also signified inferiority, but instead of being dismissed it provoked in him a reaction of desire. Despite the fact that the elite women would have been the whitest of Bahia, as they would have possessed the highest degree of European ancestry, their skin color still could not possibly have appeared to Prior to be as white as an Englishwoman's:

> The female face here may be termed animated and expressive, rather than what we call handsome. The rose and the lily do not germinate in every clime; and the languishing brunettes of Brazil have at least fine eyes, teeth, hair, and commonly good figures, if not spoiled by long waists, to compensate this neglect of nature.[37]

By emphasizing the absence of Anglo-Saxon fairness (and it is difficult to see what else this neglect could consist of), Prior's discussion of the women's faces and bodies seems to overlay with interracial overtones the implicit contemplation of sexual possibilities. The fact that this probably served to make his story more titillating also supports Said's orientalist thesis.

Almost fifty years after Prior's visit, John Codman spent ten months in Brazil and published a narrative about his experiences. Although he was American, when he decided to paint a picture of the elusive Brazilian female his words closely recalled Prior's, despite the many differences in their narrative styles. The passage below is preceded in his book by a critique of the state of female education in Brazil, and followed by a critique of the social system that allows very young women to be married to much older men, thus making mutual infidelity almost the rule. The two critiques served to provide a respectably bourgeois frame for the following remark:

> At present, even [women of] the better classes are generally proficient only in music and in dancing. Perhaps their taste for music is in a great degree attributable to the African element, and the graceful voluptuousness of their postures in the dance may be owing to the same cause. The consequences of such general ignorance among them are either a charming simplicity of manner, or an extreme of vice such as may be incredible.[38]

All the orientalist elements are present: the women of Brazil are seen by Codman as sensual, stupid, and willing. Even at elite levels, these women possessed a special power of seduction that was evidently rooted in their questionable closeness to the mysteries of the dark African continent. Although Codman must have spent a good deal of time lost in observation, he did not describe actual complexions in his report. He only gave the impression that even if Brazilian women looked and dressed like wealthy Europeans, underneath it all they were essentially as foreign, alluring, and inferior – presumably a most desirable state of affairs for a virile Western male – as the Africans with whom they cohabited so intimately through slavery. The idea that slavery was at the root of Brazilian women's sexual vices resonated with the British speculations discussed in Chapter 5 concerning the effect of slavery on the willingness of Brazilian men to work for a living. The accepted attitude of Anglo authors was that slavery was responsible for the two worst social vices of Brazilians: the women's lack of chastity and the men's lack of industry. Both of these vices would just happen to suggest to the alert British merchant an available opening for turning the situation to his own profit, through his superior personal prowess. Such travel narratives fulfilled an essential function of propaganda, and drew British ears and eyes to the opportunities available in the exotic and distant locations of Empire, informal or otherwise.[39]

And yet, the fact remains that the British merchants of Bahia owned and used slaves in their own households throughout the first half of the nineteenth century, and probably up until abolition in 1889. Maria Graham commented sarcastically on the practice in the early 1820s, Pilkington wrote a treatise in 1841 condemning the practice in no uncertain terms, and a probate inventory in the Arquivo do Estado da Bahia dating from the early 1860s confirms that George Mumford, a prominent British merchant, owned ten slaves at the time of his death, five of whom were female and six of whom were children under ten years of age.[40] In the published British travel narratives of Brazil, however, the near-total absence of observations regarding this practice (Maria Graham was the exception) is extremely interesting. It appears to support the argument that the British merchant community was powerfully invested in sustaining an image of itself as socially and morally superior to all Brazilians, even when they were engaging in practices that by their own moral standards were most contemptible.

The Reverend Robert Walsh, whose spirited defence of the Brazilian character was examined in Chapter 5, found himself having to inte just such a situation. His response was to express great shock and disillusionment at the degeneration that could be wrought upon even a British soul under the corrupting influence of slave ownership. In 1828 or 1829, he stopped at a tavern on the road to Tijuca, on the outskirts of Rio de Janeiro. In the backyard he noticed some young black boys playing with a small white boy. Walsh was charmed by the boy, who:

> ...had a soft fair face, light curling hair, blue eyes, and a skin as light as that of a European. Attracted by the very engaging little fellow, I caressed him and inquired of the man of the house, if he was his son. He said not; but that he was the son of an Englishman, and his slave, and he mentioned the name of his father. Shocked and incredulous, I denied the possibility of his father's knowing that the child was in bondage; but I was then informed, that the father not only knew it in this instance, but that, in other cases, he is known to sell his own white child along with its mother! Oh, my friend; here is a picture of slavery![41]

Walsh did not say, "Here is a picture of a despicable Englishman". Instead, he automatically resorted to the slavery explanation to make some sense of the undeniable fact that an Englishman had behaved utterly immorally.[42] If he was right to argue in 1829 that slavery wreaked havoc upon the European soul, then Scully, who published his book in 1866 after living in Rio de Janeiro for decades, may very well have been exhibiting a related sort of corruption in his sustained avoidance of the issue of British slave ownership.[43]

It is worth noting that the Reverend Walsh, when speaking of master–slave concubinage by Brazilian owners, gave a benevolently intended explanation for what he still considered a regrettable phenomenon, but did not consider it to be nearly as shocking as it was in the case of a British person.

> If [the Brazilians] indulge in illicit intercourse, we should reflect that one of the baneful effects of slavery, is to form such connexions; that a Brazilian residing by himself, insulated in a desert, and having none of the restraints which the opinions of society impose, to hinder him, readily adopts such a practice, and lives with his female slaves, as with persons who are unworthy of the rank or station of his wife.[44]

This sounds much like Scully's description of why the English clerks, isolated by their compatriots in a foreign land, readily fell into immorality and dissipation. This may be a demonstration that despite his defence of the Brazilian character, Walsh did share the overall view of them as inferior to British people in general.

The uneasy British attitude to this issue of sex and race can be traced back into the dynamics operating within the community itself. Prior had written that the Iberian countries were 'happy' insofar as their women were not educated. Maria Graham's frequent, witty, and barbed remarks about the British men whom she met in Bahia would appear to provide considerable justification for Prior's feelings. Underlying the British male fascination with Brazilian women – their irresistible combination of voluptuousness, seclusion, and ignorance – may have been an uneasy feeling about what they saw as the greater freedom, independence, and intelligence of the British woman. Her high standards for correct behavior, and the purity of her whiteness, may not have done much to make her desirable sexually, when contrasted against the orientalist Brazilian temptresses on a daily basis:

> One of the [five convents] frequently contain married women whose husbands are absent. What say our English dames to this? Tell me, for you have experience, are they not a generation too perverse to submit to this restriction?[45]

Prior's playfulness recalls the story of Mrs. C., the young English wife who danced herself to exhaustion at a picnic on the Bahian seashore. Upper-middle-class Englishwomen of the Romantic (Napoleonic) era enjoyed greater personal freedom at home and abroad than they would in the later nineteenth and early twentieth centuries. Prior's tone may have been meant to convey approval of his spirited rose-and-lily countrywomen, as he implied that they did not need to be forcibly secluded to guarantee their marital fidelity. But the very mention of the convent does seem to show his fascination with the mystery of the Brazilian female. Said's argument in *Orientalism* was mostly about British impressions of the Middle East, and of British men's attitudes toward the men and women whom they encountered there. The eight hundred-year Moorish presence in Iberia left many traces in Portuguese society, and these were transplanted to Brazil during its development as a colony. Said's theory about the British fascination with the mysterious Oriental female may thus find an interesting application in Brazil, where wealthy European-looking women moved in sensuous African-looking ways and exuded a secluded, Oriental mystery.[46]

Concubinage and Class

From comments elsewhere in his narrative, there can be no doubt that
James Prior considered himself to be well above the station of a merchant. He was a military man, and his way of describing Bahia's women
seemed to convey a consciously cultivated, worldly-wise rakishness.
This may be why his account, written to a peer, was so candidly lustful,
while those published for public consumption by British merchants and
their associates were far more oblique, with strong undertones of
shamefulness and secrecy. The anguished character of their narratives
might reasonably be said to express a typical conflict of middle-class or
bourgeois morality: the upper classes was to be imitated, but the lower
must be despised. Since concubinage happened at every level among
the British in Bahia, however, the middle-class experience of it was
likely to be somewhat tortured.

Anthropologist Ann Laura Stoler has suggested that the phenomenon
of interracial concubinage was a terrain for reaffirming or subverting
barriers of power within the ruler-ruled relationship. She states that
"colonial cultures [...] did more than reiterate middle-class European
visions and values. They were reactive to class tensions in the metropole, [creating] a 'middle-class aristocracy' that cultivated the colonials'
differences from the colonized, while maintaining social distinctions
among themselves".[47] Judging from Koster's tone, above, he had
probably been met with firm denials by British merchants as to the
extent and significance of the problem. The merchants showed a strong
tendency to distance themselves from what they considered to be a
lower form of British expatriate – the non-merchant, the clerk.

William Scully, writing fifty years after Koster, also made a point of
implying that it was only the clerks who engaged in this disreputable
behavior (Chapter 4). Unlike Koster, Scully positioned himself as concerned for the harmful circumstances which drove the poor young men
to engage in immoral practices, emphasizing the harm suffered by the
clerks more than anyone else. Still, the reality of concubinage was fully
attributed by this class-conscious author simply to the surrender of
weaker men to desires of the flesh. No reference was made to the young
men's likely need for simple emotional comfort, roots, contact, and
connection to his foreign environment. According to Scully, the clerks
were only seeking "excitement and immorality".[48] Such an interpretation probably served to cover up the pervasiveness of concubinage

with local women by colluding with the merchants in presenting it as arising uniquely from the presence of British clerks in Brazil.[49] Koster essentially did the same thing and supported the merchants in their hypocrisy, though at least he phrased his protests in such a way as to convey his distaste in having to do so.

Gilberto Freyre, well known for his benevolent and paternalistic attitude toward race mixing in the historical constitution of the Brazilian populace,[50] hardly gave a thought to the morality or immorality of cross-cultural concubinage. In *Ingleses no Brasil,* Freyre noted simply that the sexual preferences of many wealthy Englishmen were expressed through unions unsanctioned by any church. Their relationships were primarily sexual and recreational in nature and had a strong interracial component.[51] He offered no comparison between this sort of acceptable illicit liaison and those entered into by the young English clerks, whose debauchery (*libertinagem,* as Freyre referred to it in their case) he thought to have led many into illness and even suicide.[52] The elite Freyre seemed to consider merchant-class British concubinage as neutral, and clerk-class British concubinage as harmful, citing Scully uncritically throughout his book. This attitude suggests that the better-off members of the British community who engaged in concubinage were unlikely to be condemned by their contemporaries, be they other British merchants (such as Mackay regarding Mumford, in the following section), or members of the Brazilian elite such as Freyre's own family in Pernambuco. Koster's words seemed to indicate that he felt censored by the merchants for daring to suggest that their own concubinage was a problem, and by loudly acknowledging that it was *definitely not* the merchants who were doing it, left the impression that, indeed, they were.

Scully, as one might expect from the benevolently tasteful tone of his book, did not mention merchant concubinage anywhere, yet Freyre's evidence demonstrates that it had to be taking place all around him. Scully's narrative is consistent with this elision: his own attitude toward Brazilian women cannot be said to be lustful, judging from his own description of the Brazilian female:

> Many of the ladies are very attractive in their appearance and in their manners, but, as in all warm climates, their bloom is usually very evanescent, and after 25 they are apt to become very stout, a charm, however, which is not without the appreciation of their compatrio..

Among them you cannot find the blue-stocking or the strong-minded lady, for in literary pursuits the Brazilian ladies take little interest, but they are in general skilful and devoted musicians of the Italian school.[53]

Beyond this vaguely wistful glance at the non-literary character of Brazilian ladies (recalling Prior), Scully could not afford to indulge in the sexual voyeurism favoured by other British writers and readers, since his whole narrative was written from his point of view as moral guardian to the British community. Thus it is difficult to judge whether his personal feelings were stirred by the perceived exoticism of the females around him. The closest he ever got was to connect the regrettable practice of concubinage among British clerks to "this delicious and somewhat enervating climate".[54]

Another writer who appeared to be underwhelmed by the allure of Brazilian females was James Wetherell. In fact, he did something completely unique among male British observers: he made an honest effort to understand the women's perspective.

Young ladies are *smuggled* to church in cadeiras, the curtains of which are carefully drawn, and held by both hands, to preserve them from the eyes of the profane sight-seeing portion of the world. When the wind happens to overpower the curtain-holder, the recluse but often disappoints the gazer. The mothers having been taught this seclusion, endeavour to instil it into their daughters, but the *pretty* girls are becoming tired of this maternal despotism, and I do not think cadeiras *close so tightly* as they did a few years ago.[55]

The contrast between this and John Codman's interpretation of female seclusion is remarkable:

The Brazilian ladies spend most of their time in leaning upon their elbows, gazing listlessly into the streets, or exhibiting themselves coquettishly within the half-closed blinds, tantalizing those who pass.[56]

But just like Scully, Wetherell never mentioned the British merchants' liaisons with local women, except for a single anecdote about awkward-sounding married names. The situation could not possibly have escaped his notice; so he, too, or at least the friends who edited his notes for publication, must have been making an effort to avoid notice of that which ought not to have been going on.

It is unnecessary to rely exclusively on contradictory published narratives to understand whether or not concubinage was taking place in Bahia. Primary sources reveal that it was. The testament of British merchant George Mumford, for example, written five days before his death in February 1862, states that he had fathered eight illegitimate children by his Brazilian companion Constança Ebbe, all of whom he had formally recognized. In fact, five of them were being educated in Europe at the time of his death. Furthermore, Mumford had fathered a child by another unmarried Brazilian woman, Balbina, and in the will he recognized the child as his own.[57] Mumford's estate included the ten slaves mentioned earlier, three houses in and around the town, and stock in the Bahia & São Francisco Railway and Banco da Bahia companies respectively worth 5:327$539 and 5:000$000.[58] This would have been enough to establish him amongst the more successful of Bahia's British merchants. Mumford entrusted the custody of all his minor children to his business partner Francis White Mackay, who was properly married to a British wife. In fact, Mackay's own testament, written the year before Mumford's, demonstrated a high degree of moral rectitude and conjugal loyalty: departing from the usual practice, Mackay left his entire estate to his wife without restriction.[59] This would suggest that Mumford's double concubinage, or rather his officially unrecognized stable union plus a sometime mistress, did little to damage his personal status in the eyes of the merchant group.

This tacit acceptance of concubinage for higher-status individuals and condemnation of it for the others is very interesting. The higher-class the man, and the less social distance between himself and the woman, the more acceptable the relationship seemed to be to the merchants. James Prior, the most upper-class author cited in this chapter, flaunted his attraction to upper-class Brazilian women and openly admired their assets. George Mumford, a successful British merchant, had a long-term liaison with two Brazilian women simultaneously, without apparent damage to his social position in the community. William Scully, well-educated expatriate journalist, lamented the fate of weak British clerks who could not resist the temptations of Brazilian women, carefully avoiding the fact that many British merchants did the same thing without suffering adverse consequences. Henry Koster, a well-off merchant with a keen understanding of Brazilians due to his Portuguese upbringing, was irritated by the sort of hypocrisy shown by Scully, but understood the social codes well enough to make a visible effort to avoid telling an outside audience in so many words that this was going on. Male middle-class visitors to Bahia and Rio de Janeiro titillated their readers with veiled allusions to the overpowering sexuality of Brazilian women, but did not usually state that concubinage was rife among its British residents. Cross-cultural, and cross-racial, sexual contact between British men and Brazilian women took place at all levels of society in Bahia, but its acceptability depended on the parties' social class and that of the person making the judgment.

There remains the question of whether British male–Brazilian female concubinage was oppressive to the women involved. The question is difficult to answer, since virtually no attention was given to the women's perspective in the surviving sources. It is probably fair to argue that the *potential* for abuse and oppression is implicit in any intimate connection between individuals having disparate levels of power. In these cases, the disparity would have varied directly with the degree of social distance between the parties. However, the greater the acceptability of the liaison, the higher would be its level of legitimacy, and the more accountable the man would have had to be to the woman, as in the case of Mumford. It is also important to remember that a liaison with a relatively wealthy British man may have provided many Brazilian women with more status and options than they would otherwise have had, especially those coming from the lower strata of society.

Intermarriage and Stable Unions

In Walsh's efforts to redeem the Brazilians' tendency to live in sin, he had followed up his criticism of Brazilian men's slave concubinage with a statement lauding their willingness to honor the marital vow, once it had been made. "When he does form a legitimate connexion, the laws of marriage are as much respected as in any country in Europe [and their] women […] are remarkable for correctness of conduct and domestic duties." This particular concept of legitimacy suggests that illicit intercourse was problematic to a British observer because it involved the physical union of a man with a woman "unworthy of the rank or station of his wife",[60] a social judgment more than a personal one. A legitimately married woman, on the other hand, would be admirable for her correct deportment and efficient execution of duty, as her rank-worthiness could then be taken for granted. This passage is reminiscent of postcolonial studies that analyze how, in a colonial context, the concept of character could become identified (or confused) with the concept of class.[61] A legitimate relationship with a properly behaved consort had the power to improve both.

The evidence makes it clear that respectable British merchants were marrying Brazilian women, and were at pains to demonstrate the latter's acceptability as good British wives.[62] Their children were given English names, and the women were buried in Bahia's British cemetery, which probably means that they had to convert to Protestantism in order to make the marriage possible. The very fact of the easy (if superficial) Anglicization of these women may be evidence of their elite, white-enough status in the eyes of the British community, while their marriage to wealthy British wholesale merchants was by no means looked down upon by their Brazilian families and associates. Despite the anti-merchant sentiments shown by such Brazilians as Wanderley Pinho (Chapter 5), intermarriage with the British probably was not anathema to elite Brazilians, particularly as the century wore on. A casually proud remark by Scully provides an ideal demonstration of this:

> The palace of the president of [Bahia] was fast falling into decay until the distinguished administration of Mr. Sinimbu, who repaired and renovated it, and whose refined taste, seconded by the wise judgment of his accomplished wife, a lady of English origin, who superintended its internal arrangements, has made it truly a palace.[63]

The lady in question would have lost her British nationality upon marrying a Brazilian, hence the reference to her 'origin,' but the point is clear: the highest-status Brazilian in Bahia chose to marry an accomplished Englishwoman versed in upper-class tastes, and the prime representative of the British community's opinion in Brazil at mid-century was well pleased with the outcome.

These circumstances show a surprising level of mutual respect and social recognition among the Brazilian elite and the British merchants, who otherwise did so much to keep apart from them. The power relations between the British and the local elite were very different in most of Latin America than they would be elsewhere in the later British Empire. This in turn may have important implications for the continuing use of the expression 'Britain's informal empire' in Latin America, for it suggests a false analogy to the much harsher social arrangements operative in the formal British colonial empire, especially from the late nineteenth century up to the mid-twentieth century.[64]

The Case of the Widow Vital

Women were not passive participants in this continuing *pas-de-deux* of love and social progression. One unusually well-documented case gives a colorful picture of the sort of positional tactics that circumstances could throw up into a woman's path. It concerns a legal battle that took place in Salvador, Bahia, in 1860 over the estate of a deceased couple, consisting of an elderly British merchant and a woman named Marianne or Mariana Vital. They never married. Because of the opacity and mutability of her familial and national status, the ensuing debate between the relevant authorities revealed a good deal not only about how the British community was viewed in Bahia at that time, but also about the position and possibilities of women who happened to find themselves standing in the spaces between official categories.

On July 17, 1860, the widow Mariana dos Santos Vital died and was buried in the Catholic Cemitério do Campo Santo, in Salvador, Bahia. Two days later, her companion William Hooper, a British widower in his seventies, suddenly died and was buried in the Protestant British Cemetery on the other side of town. Some people suspected that Hooper may have been poisoned by Mariana's Brazilian nephew, who had claims to inherit her estate. William and Marianne had lived together for about four years in Salvador's Rua do Hospício, where she ran a boarding-house. Since they died within two days of each other, their possessions were still mixed together in the house. And since they had not left any wills, they created a considerable legal problem for the British consul.[65] He was prevented from taking charge of Hooper's estate because the widow's Brazilian nephew had immediately had the couple's possessions sealed off by the Juiz de Ausentes. In his efforts to claim the right to dispose of Hooper's estate, Consul John Morgan tried to argue from personal knowledge that Marianne herself was British; but his argument was rejected by Brazilian authorities, who in turn had evidence that she had preferred to be treated as Brazilian. In the process of formulating arguments and making demands, Morgan showed a certain arrogance and a damaging lack of confidence in the willingness of Brazilian authorities to relinquish Hooper's property in a fair and timely manner. This was probably what alienated Brazilian officials and eventually caused him to lose all power over the estate. Meanwhile, only inferences based on circumstantial evidence can reveal what Marianne Vital was up to, in this maze of relationships, nationalities, and social networks; but this is the most interesting part of the story.

The complete narrative, pieced together from police reports, legal affidavits, and diplomatic dispatches at the Arquivo Público do Estado da Bahia, tells that Marianne, or Mariana, was originally American. We do not know her maiden name, the date when she came to Bahia, nor whether she was born in Brazil of American parents. Her first marriage was to a British subject named Solinam, at which time she changed her name to Marianne Solinam and assumed British nationality. They had a son who died a grisly death, "crushed to death on the railroad", according to a police report.[66] Solinam died soon after this, and did not leave a will. She then either did or did not marry another British man, depending on whether the British consul was correct in a letter making that claim.[67] Definitely, her final marriage was to a Brazilian named João Pedro dos Santos Vital, who was employed as "Alferes do Corpo Fixo da Província da Bahia" (probably one of the "small government positions" so criticized by British observers). At this time Marianne's name and nationality were changed again, this time to Mariana dos Santos Vital, and she converted to Catholicism as well. When Vital died of cholera in 1856, also without leaving a will, Mariana continued to be known as Madame Vital; and in the four final years of her life, she lived in her boarding-house with British merchant William Hooper and brought in a niece named Alice Dawson to keep her company.[68] Vital is described by the British consul simply as Marianne's "protector", who had from Alice the affection of a daughter.

Besides running the boarding-house, Marianne / Mariana also took in washing for the military hospital of Bahia. She had two or three black live-in servants or slaves, one of whom had a boyfriend who had been stealing from her household.[69] Her multi-national extended family included the British niece, who must have been related to her first husband and at least one Brazilian nephew who depended on her for some financial support. This nephew was studying medicine and received 50$000 (fifty milréis) per month from Marianne.[70] On his part, Hooper was survived by two daughters in London and had no relatives in Bahia.

The circumstances of Hooper's death do sound rather suspect. On the day following Mariana's burial, her nephew visited the British merchant and claimed to be Mariana's sole heir. Hooper resisted. The nephew went away and returned with an officer and a document from the Juízo dos Órfãos e Ausentes supporting his claim. Property in

Hooper's home was sealed up to await legal resolution. But on the very next day, the usually robust Hooper awoke with stomach pains and sent immediately for the British doctor Alexander Paterson. Paterson was present when Hooper died that day, and at the funeral he confided his suspicions of foul play to the British consul.[71] With permission of the consul and the Brazilian police, the corpse was exhumed, and Hooper's stomach sent to the Escola de Medicina for examination. The autopsy revealed the presence of arsenic, which immediately turned all suspicions to Marianne's nephew, the medical student.[72] The ensuing investigation generated statements by police, relatives, and servants, which showed something of Marianne's daily life and history but left unsolved the question of Hooper's death. The nephew himself does not appear to have been questioned.

Consul Morgan, was not satisfied with the investigation and decided to go over the head of local authorities. He wrote a long letter to the president of Bahia, demanding immediate intervention, warning him that the British community was extremely anxious about the situation: "If such acts go unpunished, there can be no hope for the life and property of foreign residents".[73] Although he did not exactly say that the British were all afraid of being murdered in their beds by scheming Brazilians who had infiltrated their households and families, that reading would say something about the state of public and private relations among the British community and its surroundings by 1860, just a few years after the final highly unpopular destruction of the Brazilian slave trade (Chapter 2).

The president was not moved to intervene, and instead questioned the legitimacy of the consul's actions in attempting to dictate how the affair should be conducted. Morgan tried to claim jurisdiction over all of the property in Hooper's and Marianne's residence, justifying this by stating simply that Mariana was indebted to her 'protector' for what little property she owned, and therefore everything in the residence obviously belonged in reality to Hooper. Not surprisingly, the Brazilian authorities were not persuaded by this argument. Instead they impounded all of the property in the residence and explained that Mariana Vital had died intestate so a legal compromise had to be reached before the inheritance could be processed. This was in accordance not only with Brazilian custom, but also with recent treaty changes restricting the rights of British consuls to settle their subjects' estates;[74] and Morgan's strident objections probably came across as arrogant, because soon the President was refusing to receive Morgan at his office, and turned him away three times in a week.[75]

But Morgan did not give up. Rather than acknowledging the President's misgivings and accepting a procedure that would probably have involved a long wait for Hooper's heirs, he changed tactics and argued that all the property was under his own jurisdiction because Hooper *and Marianne* were both British.[76] This argument showed a certain legal daring, since Marianne was American by birth and had not been married to anyone when she died. Making a rather creative interpretation of recent Brazilian decrees, Morgan argued that because Mariana's Brazilian husband had never fathered any children, her nationality at his death had reverted to that of her former – British – husband, with whom she had had the son who died. In other words, in the game of claiming Marianne, as far as Morgan was concerned, a dead British son was worth more than a live Brazilian nephew, who in turn was admittedly worth more than a live British niece.

The offended president wrote back contesting the consul's right to reinterpret Brazilian law in this manner: "The decree is applicable only to an incontestably foreign individual residing in Brazil, who dies there intestate, and not to a woman, who, being [last] married to a Brazilian, is presumed to have been Brazilian as well, until the opposite may be proven" and suggested that the consul ought to find a lawyer to acquaint himself better with Brazilian law.[77] Morgan's next move was to resort to what was traditionally the strongest argument available to a British diplomatic representative in Brazil, that is, to bully local authorities with the power of British commerce and trade: "A minor and un-important questions such as this, finding obstacles on the part of the authorities, gives cause for concern to major foreign interests connected to the country".[78] But by 1860 this may no longer have been an effective threat, though it had been used to advantage in Bahia for decades. He went on to swear to the president that despite what may have been her legal status, he knew for a fact that Marianne had *considered herself* to be British.[79] This was virtually guaranteed to outrage the president as well as the Juiz de Órfãos e Ausentes. Negotiations ended abruptly and the Juiz de Órfãos simply placed all the property up for public auction without notifying Morgan, who read about it in the newspaper and tried desperately to stop the sale at the last minute.[80] The proceeds from Hooper's property thus probably went to the medical student in the end.

It is useful to focus on Morgan's statement concerning the widow's idea of her own nationality. In all likelihood, the consul would not lightly have sworn such a statement. His impressions concerning Marianne's Britishness must have been based on his direct interactions with her. This leads to the question of what Marianne was really doing, in her dealings with all of these different people. How did she have the consul convinced of her British identity, while the Juiz de Orfãos saw no problem in granting her entire estate to a Brazilian? She was engaged in commerce with Brazilians, lived freely as a Catholic widow with whomever she pleased, kept Brazilian servants, and appears to have maintained social contact with her extended families. But she chose to live with a British merchant and sent for a British niece to keep her company. Marianne's, or Mariana's, position was deliberately ambiguous. What *did* she consider herself to be? How did Marianne or Mariana Vital fit in to the British and the Brazilian communities? Did she choose to remain unmarried to Hooper? How did her families get along – did her British niece and Brazilian nephew view each other as cousins? How did her Brazilian husband's family, with at least one son in a prestigious medical school, feel about Marianne's living with a foreign merchant and running a boarding house? Why did she remain a practicing Catholic after her husband died and she was living with a Protestant?

It seems clear that Marianne, or Mariana, was making choices of social representation that accorded with her own interests and these developed and changed over time. She may have decided to retain her status as a Brazilian widow because of the legal, financial and social advantages this conferred, compared to becoming the wife of a British man.[81] As a Brazilian widow, she had relative freedom to live with Hooper and run her own business, when British wives could not even own property before 1882. Marianne had already experienced what it was like to be a British wife. Although her Brazilian in-laws might have objected to her living situation, but they could also have assumed that her property would flow back into the Brazilian branch of the family upon her death; at least it certainly didn't take the nephew long to act on this assumption.

Under such conditions, even if Marianne did in fact consider herself British, it would have made sense for her be Brazilian as well. This ambiguity seems to have been well tolerated by those in Marianne's life; it was her death that required a definition one way or the other. It is not clear why she did not write a will. She might not have expected her Brazilian nephew to bring suit against Hooper. Maybe she did not think much about it at all, living from day to day in the best social harmony that her complicated history would allow. Or perhaps she thought it might all be too complicated for anyone but the legal authorities to sort this out. It is nevertheless interesting to view her life in terms of active choices, and then to read those choices to see where her advantages lay in this particular social landscape.

This case illustrates the uneasy position of Bahia's British community within larger Brazilian society at mid-century. The consul's panicked reactions to the developments of the case seem to be a reflection of the larger fears of the British community with respect to their crumbling authority, not to mention their physical and legal safety in Bahia, where a Brazilian citizen appeared to be getting away with murder. It must have added to the anxiety that the consul's usual threats about the displeasure of big commercial interests were simply ignored. In hindsight, Morgan probably should have been more willing to comply with Brazilian laws. The authorities were not greedily trying to take over British property;[82] mostly they were just not as docile toward British privilege as they had been earlier in the century. Morgan was oddly slow to realize this.

Brazilian Views of British Women

This study would not be complete without giving some attention to the views that Brazilian men had of British women. As usual, very little documentation is available, as male British writers understandably did not usually touch on the subject of whether Brazilian men desired or despised British women. The evidence points to the likelihood that, due to their detachment from all aspects of their husbands' and fathers' business involvements, the women were likely to be seen as *more* admirable, more refined, and more cultured than their men. Prior's comment contrasting the uneducated Brazilian women to the perversely independent 'English dames' may be further evidence of this. And Pinho mentions that the increasing orientation of Bahian society toward northern European cultural superiority was reflected in the new demand for European tutors and governesses, especially Englishwomen.[83]

If British women were indeed viewed as the ultimate repository of European cultural refinement, and furthermore were untainted by commercial concerns, then from the perspective of elite Brazilian men a marriage to a well-off British woman would probably have been a desirable means of gaining social status. The best example of this is Scully's approval of the English wife of Bahia's highest official and her redecorating skills. Elsewhere in the literature of nineteenth-century travel narratives, occasional references are made to an elite Brazilian family sending off daughters to be educated in London in preparation for the life of a brilliant society wife in Brazil.

After reviewing the relations of British men and Brazilian women, one might wish to know whether the British women were viewed with desire by Brazilians. Freyre gives a slight clue to this, when he follows up the unflattering physical description of the stereotypical *mister* (blond sideburns and all) with a short passage about the respective *madama:* "The figure of a woman, also blond, elegant, erotic and refined, whose influence in nineteenth-century Brazilian life also needs to be studied and interpreted".[84] Keeping in mind the Brazilian stereotype of the *ingleses* as being generally unable to satisfy their women, it would not be surprising if the image were to foment a generalized Brazilian sense for the desirability of seducing the Englishman's wife, regardless of her actual charms. Possibly her usually up-to-date European fashions, refined taste and manners, and her effective seclusion within the British enclave[85] would have contributed to a desirable mystique of elite femininity, similar to British men's views of elite Brazilian women, although for somewhat different reasons.

Conclusion

South America is so essentially a Latin continent, refusing to open the doors of her intimacies to any chance knocker ignorant of her tongues, manners, and customs.

W. H. Koebel, *British Exploits in South America* (1917), p. 548

I have fought the good fight / I have finished my course / I have kept the faith.

Inscription on the gravestone of Edward Pellew Wilson,
"A British merchant resident in this city for a period of 69 years
from 1819 to 1887" (British Cemetery of Bahia)

This study has sought to shed light upon the specific, personal, unpredictable processes that gradually shaped the relationships among the British and Brazilian residents of Bahia. The British had limited, if long-term, social interactions with their host society. From its beginnings as a ragtag assortment of bachelor merchants, clerks, and adventurers, there grew an identifiably British community that maintained a fairly unified front, mainly for the benefit of Brazilians whose respect they needed in order to survive and succeed. The arrival of British women both stabilized the community and introduced a new element into the dynamic of British-Brazilian relations, for the practice of concubinage with local women thus became illegitimate and efforts were made to render it as invisible as possible. The introduction of high-profile British cultural institutions into Bahia, primarily the Anglican chapel and Protestant burial ground, served the political purpose of giving the internally divisive British group a central rallying point in the eyes of Brazilians. Gradually, the community solidified its sense of itself as a British group of expatriates expressing their cultural superiority by maintaining familiar practices in the unfamiliar landscapes of Brazil, and family linkages were formed to raise new generations. Simultaneously, cross-cultural liaisons continued to exist, many of which were legitimized by marriage. Other such unions were not officially recognized, but were acknowledged by the community as legitimate nevertheless. Unacceptable liaisons between British men and Brazilian women tended to be those in which the man, the woman, or both were of low social status in the eyes of the British merchants.

This study begins to integrate two levels of history which, though intertwined, are presently considered to be separate, at least insofar as the fields of economic and political history consider them to be so. Does history take place at the aggregate or at the personal level? If both, how do they relate or intersect? And how should the overall story be told? The gradual emergence of entrenched macro-economic systems of wealth production and distribution, though worth studying solely in terms of investment changes and economic shifts over time, still is firmly rooted in the successful establishment and daily maintenance of social relationships among real people in the past.

In collecting and arranging the various sources of information about the daily experience of the British residents of Bahia, it has been necessary to differentiate among types – by gender, class, ethnicity, and ultimately personal qualities – and from there to seek an understanding of how these types related to one another and to the Brazilians around them. On the one hand, the book analyses the daily workings of a small community of outsiders, as each person worked to survive, to improve his or her individual position, and to generate respect for the group among local residents over a period of several decades. On the other hand, it observes how the specifics of the political, economic, and social contexts of early nineteenth-century Bahia shaped the situation in which this small group of British merchant families and clerks were enmeshed. The particular relationship of Brazil and Great Britain at this time meant that many new possibilities for action and perception existed for its British residents, while many other possibilities were simultaneously cut off. Occasional deep contradictions between belief and practice arose, as in the case of domestic slave ownership (Chapter 2) or cross-racial concubinage (Chapter 6). These were handled with a certain degree of tolerance on a day-to-day basis, and were systematically concealed from the broader record of Great Britain's influence upon the old-new country of Brazil.

The British men and women who lived part or all of their lives in Bahia changed the landscape around them, in physical as well as nonphysical ways. They built houses, gardens, social circles, and codes of conduct that were self-consciously separate from the Brazilian community. Nevertheless, these could not really exist without the constant audience that was the Bahian population, who on their part gradually acquired, co-opted, or made fun of many of those practices. In erecting the walls that kept them apart, the British left a mark upon the place and upon its story. And yet, despite their adamance in maintaining control, the very process of coming to terms with Bahia caused the British to be themselves changed in unforeseeable ways, again physically (illnesses, personal habits) as well as psychologically or emotionally (self-perception, ability to cope with a changing reality).

In some instances, these changes were perceived as threatening: during the conflicts surrounding Independence, when the British merchants undermined or overruled their government's strategic position of neutrality, Consul Penell viewed their behavior as indicative of a crisis, a loss of character that placed in jeopardy the British group identity and hence its economic effectiveness, and which therefore demanded immediate intervention (Chapters 1 and 4). In other cases, though, the changes were eagerly accepted and understood as a freeing-up of cultural constraints. This was particularly true with respect to the possibilities for rapid class ascension, as minor partners in middle-class British trading firms, essentially exiled to a distant port, quickly settled into a lifestyle that reflected and embodied their own ideas of British upper-class country living (Chapter 3); or for young British women, who knew their position to be much more desirable in the expatriate community abroad than it would be if they were to return to the homeland (Chapters 4 and 6).

All the time, however, the British individual had to hold to the certainty of his or her British identity, regardless of how inaccurately their daily lives abroad reflected their true social position back home. To do otherwise would be to betray the expatriate community and lose its protective support. Thus for Maria Graham in 1821, the British residents of Bahia seemed ridiculous in their single-minded pursuit of profit and their gentlemanly poses; to her, status depended on detachment from material concerns and interest in intellectual matters, as well as a high degree of exclusionary social behavior. But by 1852, John Candler was more than impressed by the British community's self-presentation as a group at the pinnacle of the local society, and did not bother to look below the surface. Two areas were especially problematic:

cross-racial concubinage and domestic slave ownership. While many visitors uncritically accepted the British residents' rationalizations regarding their slave ownership, others were more reluctant to do so.

The subjective experience of the merchants themselves may be gleaned from the surviving documents, in particular the efforts of Dr. Robert Dundas to make sense of the illnesses and problems that systematically affected the British residents of Bahia. The new arrival was all but overwhelmed by the sheer, life, the colors, the sounds, the air, the possibilities that Bahia seemed to offer. Dundas tracked the typical British newcomer's gradual descent from this initial high, through the various diseases to which s/he was (or became) susceptible, all the way to the moment when the wrenching decision had to be made – profit versus health, your money or your life. Even when it was medically decided that the British body had had enough and it was time to go home, it might then be gripped by a terrible new disease once it re-entered the home climate. The kidneys, strained by years of expatriate living, shut down under the additional strains of readjustment to the home country – the home that had been synonymous with safety. This, more than anything else, graphically illustrates how much the average British expatriate really changed in response to a long immersion in Bahia, despite all the efforts at remaining separate in every possible way. In fact, the more tenaciously the person clung to 'British' ways of living – eating heavy meals, drinking a great deal of alcohol, walking in the noonday sun, dressing in restrictive clothing – the more likely would he or she be to succumb to the various illnesses catalogued by Dundas. Ironically, the doctor attributed these diseases to noxious aspects of Bahia's physical environment.

On the other hand, someone like James Wetherell, who laughed at his compatriots' refusal to adapt, not only was able to maintain his health and good spirits throughout his long stay, but also to appreciate better his new experiences, to reflect upon them in a more open way, improving his awareness of the changes that he may have undergone – transforming into growth that which otherwise could become a source of decay. Much of Dr. Dundas' work represented an effort to patholo-gize Bahia as hazardous *in essence* for those of northern European descent. He saw that the integrity of personal identity was as profoundly rooted in the small daily practices of bodily care as in the array of official identities and business or political activities in which the person was engaged.

The British economic expansion into newly independent Latin America, where for the most part Britain did not hold official political sway, was a fascinating compendium of improvised diplomatic strategy, business gambles, and personal dealings of greater or lesser success. In attempting to understand the overall situation, the historian must avoid the temptation to focus exclusively upon outcome, or even privileging outcome over process. Multiple possibilities are always a part of the present, and as such, were always an important part of the past, insofar as the awareness of such possibilities influenced the decisions of historical actors (and what else can any such influence consist of?). It is important to look beyond what market forces brought forth, as it were, and then to delve into the messy failures, the intangibles, the idiosyncrasies, the coincidences that made it possible for one merchant and not another to be successful and to generate the happenings that are preserved in the historical record in the form of economic figures and facts.

This study, then, attempts to take the more holistic view in accounting for the success of the ambitious business venture of the British domination of Latin American commerce in the nineteenth century. One result of this approach is that it becomes more natural to integrate, for instance, feminist theories placing an economic value upon such 'reproductive' work (opposed to 'productive' in the Marxist lexicon) as successful household maintenance and emotional support for breadwinning husbands, brothers, and sons. Such skills were critically important in the expatriate settings where most British imperial expansion took place, for a great effort was required to manage the contradictory mandates of successfully negotiating the local environment while simultaneously keeping strictly apart from it. At the same time, the deeper causes underlying the practice of native concubinage by British men, despite its condemnation by the British community, become more intelligible. A similar argument may be made about domestic slave ownership. We are thus forced to rethink the nature and value of services provided by these Brazilians, to try and account for the difficulties engendered by the prohibition against such behavior, and to draw comparisons with analogous situations in different parts of the British empire during the same period. It is simply very interesting to ask about the extent to which these deeply personal conflicts may have impacted the overall success, or ultimate failure, of British imperialism, informal or otherwise.[1]

The full story of how the British adapted or failed to adapt to Latin America has the potential to provide a useful counterfactual to what is currently known about British imperialism in the non-Western world. It would also enhance our understanding of the full British contribution to Brazil, and what its cost was to both sides. Perhaps future studies will throw additional light upon how the British in other parts of Latin America negotiated the changes in their individual and group identity, at a time when Latin Americans themselves were, in many ways, doing the same.

Notes

Acknowledgments

1   Theodore Zeldin, *An Intimate History of Humanity* (London: Minerva, 1994), p. 466.

Introduction

1   "Pois o que se procura estudar nas relações entre pessoas, ou interpessoais, não é tão diverso do que se procura estudar nos choques entre sistemas socioculturais antagônicos – choques interculturais – constituídos como são os sistemas, de pessoas, e inseparáveis como são estas pessoas dos sistemas dentro dos quais passam de indivíduos a pessoas."

2   The literature and debates are extensive on the subject of British informal imperialism in Latin America, and conversely Latin America's dependency on Great Britain from independence up until World War I. See Fernando Henrique Cardoso and Enzo Faletto, *Dependency and Development in Latin America* (Berkeley: University of California Press, 1979); H.S. Ferns, 'Britain's informal empire in Argentina, 1806–1914', *Past and Present* 4 (1953) 60–75; André Gunder Frank, *Capitalism and Underdevelopment in Latin America: Historical Studies of Chile and Brazil* (Harmondsworth, Middx.: Penguin, 1971); J. Gallagher and R. Robinson, 'The imperialism of free trade', *Economic History Review* 2nd. series 6 (1953) 1–15; Richard Graham, 'Robinson and Gallagher in Latin America: the meaning of informal imperialism' in W.R. Lewis, ed., *Imperialism: The Robinson and Gallagher Controversy* (New York: New Viewpoints, 1976); D.C.M. Platt, *Business Imperialism, 1840–1930: An Inquiry Based on British Experience in Latin America* (Oxford Clarendon Press, 1977); D.C.M. Platt, 'Dependency in nineteenth-century Latin America: an historian objects', *Latin American Research Review* 15/1 (1980) 113–30; D.C.M. Platt, 'Economic factors in British policy during the "new imperialism"', *Past and Present* 39 (1968) 120–38; D.C.M. Platt, 'Economic imperialism and the businessman: Britain and Latin America before 1914', in R. Owen and B. Sutcliffe, eds, *Studies in the Theory of Imperialism* (London: Longman, 1972).

3   See especially E. Bradford Burns, *A History of Brazil*. 3rd ed. (New York: Columbia University Press, 1993); Marshall C. Eakin, *British Enterprise in Brazil: the St. John d'El Rey Mining Company and the Morro Velho Gold Mine, 1830–1960* (Durham, NC: Duke University Press, 1989); Richard Graham, *Britain and the Onset of Modernization in Brazil, 1850–1914* (Cambridge: Cambridge University Press, 1968); Alan K. Manchester, *British Pre-Eminence in Brazil, Its Rise and Decline: A Study in European Expansion* (New York: Octagon Books, 1972); Rory Miller, *Britain and Latin America in the Nineteenth and Twentieth Centuries* (New York: Longman, 1993); J.F. Rippy, *British Investments in Latin America: A Case*

Study in the Operations of Private Enterprise in Retarded Regions (New York: Arno Press, 1959); Antônia Fernanda Pacca de Almeida Wright, *Desafio americano à preponderância britânica no Brasil, 1808–1850* (Rio de Janeiro: Imprensa Nacional, 1972).

4 Leslie Bethell, *The Abolition of the Brazilian Slave Trade: Britain, Brazil and the Slave Trade Question, 1807–1869* (Cambridge: Cambridge University Press, 1970).

5 W.H. Koebel, *British Exploits in South America: A History of British Activities in Exploration, Military Adventure, Diplomacy, Science, and Trade in Latin America* (New York: The Century Co., 1917), p. 528.

6 This is particularly true for the issue of implicit intentionality, which I believe to be embedded in much of dependency theory. The history of British political and economic decisions regarding Latin America during the early nineteenth century is too often permeated with an assumption that the agents had some form of advance knowledge of the outcome of their decisions. This assumption serves to naturalize a process that was discontinuous and not necessarily inevitable.

7 Geoffrey Jones, *Merchants to Multinationals: British Trading Companies in the Nineteenth and Twentieth Centuries* (Oxford: Oxford University Press, 2000).

8 Jeffrey Needell, *A Tropical Belle Époque: Elite Culture and Society in Turn-of-the-Century Rio de Janeiro* (Cambridge: Cambridge, 1987).

9 A significant exception to this is Gilberto Freyre's, *Ingleses no Brasil: aspectos da influência britânica sobre a vida, a paisagem e a cultura do Brasil* (Rio de Janeiro: José Olympio, 1948). Freyre's idiosyncratic approach, however, reduces the study's usefulness in reconstructing the history of any particular British community.

10 The relevant secondary literature is reviewed in Chapters 5 and 6.

11 I also visited the Arquivo Nacional (AN) in Rio de Janeiro, but with more limited results.

12 Robert Dundas. *Sketches of Brazil, Including New Views on Tropical and European Fever with Remarks on the Premature Decay of the System Incident to Europeans on Their Return from Hot Climates* (London: John Churchill, 1852).

1 British Commercial and Political Influence in Bahia

1 For the importance of sugar in the development of Bahian society, see Stuart B. Schwartz, *Sugar Plantations in the Formation of Brazilian Society: Bahia, 1550–1835* (Cambridge: Cambridge University Press, 1985); Luís Henrique Dias Tavares, *História da Bahia*. 7th ed. (São Paulo: Atica/INL/MEC, 1981).

2 James Prior, *Voyage Along the Eastern Coast of Africa to Mosambique, Johanna, and Quiloa; to St. Helena; to Rio de Janeiro, Bahia, and Pernambuco in Brazil, in the Nisus Frigate* (London: Sir Richard Phillips & Co., 1819), p. 105.

3 Leslie Bethell, 'The independence of Brazil', in Leslie Bethell, ed., *Brazil: Empire and Republic, 1822–1930* (Cambridge: Cambridge University Press, 1989), p. 19.

4 Daniel P. Kidder, *Sketches of Residence and Travels in Brazil, Embracing Historical and Geographical Notices of the Empire and its Several Provinces* (Philadelphia, PA: Sorin and Ball,1845), pp. 25–26.

5 The term 'Luso-Brazilians' is used to refer to the natives of Bahia in the period before Brazil gained its independence from Portugal.

6 British Consul Lindemann to the Earl of Bathurst, 9 February 1810, NA FO 63/87.

7 Hamilton (for Foreign Secretary Viscount Castlereagh) to British Consul Cunningham, 10 September 1817, NA FO 63/206; British Consul Pennell to the Marquis of Londonderry (Lord Castlereagh), 5 November 1821, NA FO 63/240.

8 Paulo Nogueira Batista Jr., 'Política tarifária britânica e evolução das exportações brasileiras na primeira metade do século XIX', *Revista Brasileira de Economia* 34/2 (1980) 203–39; Mansuy, 'Imperialisme britannique et les relations coloniales entre

le Portugal e le Brésil', *Cahiers des Amerigues Latines* (9–10, 1974).

9   The writer's source is presented as follows: "I am assured by a private friend from whom I procured [the data], that they are correct copies of the accounts which have been forwarded by this government to ... Rio", J. Jeffery (British official resident at Lisbon) to William Hamilton (Foreign Office), NA BT 6/64.

10   Board of Trade, NA BT 6/64.

11   Amounts are given in Portuguese currency (milréis), and in pounds sterling at 1823 equivalencies. 'One milréis' literally means 'one thousand réis' and is written as 1$000. Large values are expressed in 'contos de réis', meaning units of one thousand milréis, written as 1:000$000. One 'conto' was worth about £235 in 1823. An annual income of one conto would have been enough to secure a position in the upper class of Bahia at the time, alongside wealthy planters and the highest state and church officials of the province.

12   Exchange rates are taken from an 1823 British shipping report from Pernambuco. British consul at Pernambuco John Parkinson to Foreign Secretary George Canning, NA FO 63/262.

13   Morgan to Lima, 19 August 1855. Arquivo do Estado da Bahia (AEB), Seção de Arquivo Colonial e Provincial, Box 1190.

14   The most reliable figures are derived from the detailed annual consular shipping reports to the Foreign Office, which unfortunately only began in 1819. Information for the earlier years is gleaned from an 1812 commercial almanac and from consular tax records, those they provide an incomplete picture. Figures for 1815–1818 are calculated from consular tax records filed with the Foreign Office by the British Consulate in Bahia. Merchants were required to pay a one per cent tax on shipments, which went toward a 'contribution fund' that was used in part to pay the salaries and expenses associated with the British Consulate and Judge Conservator. The fund was also used to support a British chaplain, surgeon, and hospital in Bahia (Astley to Foreign Office, 14 September 1822, NA FO 63/249).

15   Sources: 1808 to 1810 – *Almanach para a cidade da Bahia, anno 1812* (Bahia: Typographia de Manoel Antonio da Silva Serva, 1812). 1815 to 1818 – Imports calculated using consular tax reports on British shipping in Bahia (assuming the same one per cent tax rate applied during the period 1818–1821), NA FO 63/249; 1819 – NA FO 63/230; 1820 – NA FO 63/240; 1821 – NA FO 63/249.

16   Figures in this column for the years 1808 to 1810 reflect the value of imports into Bahia from Europe excluding Portugal (*mercadorias gerais da Europa*).

17   Sent specifically to Great Britain – *Almanach 1812*.

18   Sent to European ports – *Almanach 1812*.

19   Freyre, *Ingleses no Brasil*, p. 248.

20   This colony was founded on the west African coast to provide a home for slaves freed by British naval abolitionist activity in the early part of the nineteenth century.

21   NA FO 63/230; NA FO 63/240; NA FO 63/249.

22   Manufacturing was slow to take hold in Bahia. After 1850 and the final abolition of the slave trade, there was a flurry of interest by British entrepreneurs and investors in steel mills (in Bonfim) and textile factories (in Valença), but this did not lead to industrial development of the region. The development of industry in Bahia was hampered in part because imported British manufactures were considered superior to all others, while tariff concessions kept prices relatively low. As a result, by 1855 British wholesale merchants were owed approximately twelve thousand contos (12,000:000$000) by local consumers and retailers, most of whom presumably depended on earnings from primary product exports to pay for their purchases, which reinforced the pattern. British Consul Morgan to Alvaro Tiberio do Moncorvo e Lima, President of the Province of Bahia, 19 August 1855, AEB, Seção de Arquivo Colonial e Provincial, Box 1190.

23 Ibid.

24 Mellors & Russell, 1821, NA FO 63/249.

25 Francisco Jose Pereira (representative of the Junta Provisional do Governo) to Pennell, 11 December 1821, NA FO 268/1.

26 Arquivo do Estado da Bahia (AEB). A listing of British property transactions from 1810 to 1825 is found in the Appendix.

27 The exchange rate used is from 1823. The loan's actual sterling value may have been somewhat higher.

28 A dispatch from 1839 mentions a new tax that was to be levied by the government of Brazil upon businesses employing more than one foreign clerk. Porter to Brito, 28 January 1841, AEB, Seção Colonial e Provincial, Box 1195.

29 "*Roça e casas em Brotas*," probably meaning a main residence with additional structures built on the land. Since Brotas was distant from the main town, this rental may have been intended to provide the consul with a country refuge, or a source of income.

30 Values for real estate transactions do not appear on the records, with the exception of monetary loans.

31 The Luso-Brazilian merchant community of Bahia had gradually been moving into residences in the *Cidade Alta* (Upper City), close by the commercial district. In 1754, 16 percent lived in the Cidade Alta; in 1809 the figure had increased to 25 percent, and by 1817 52 percent of Bahia's Portuguese-speaking merchants were living in the Cidade Alta. See Catherine Lugar, 'The merchant community of Salvador, Bahia, 1780–1830' unpublished Ph.D. thesis, State University of New York at Stony Brook (1980).

32 *Escrituras de Compra e Venda de Escravos* [property titles for slaves], Arquivo Municipal da Cidade de Salvador.

33 João José Reis, 'Slave resistance in Brazil: Bahia, 1807–1835', *Luso-Brazilian Review* 25/1 (1988), 111–44.

34 AEB Arquivo do Estado da Bahia, 'Devassa do levente de escravos o corrido em Salvador em 1835', *Anais do Arquivo Público do Estado da Bahia* 50 (1992). The issues surrounding British relationships to slavery and abolition during this period are discussed in Chapter 2.

35 Fraser to Foreign Secretary Viscount Castlereagh, 1 December 1812, NA FO 63/149.

36 For example, Fraser asserts that, contrary to perceptions of Brazil's British merchants, whites were not in danger of being overrun by a slave insurrection, as only in Rio de Janeiro, Pernambuco, and Bahia did black slaves outnumber the white population.

37 Arquivo do Estado da Bahia, modern index-card listing of real estate record book entries, 1800–1860. The original records were not available for direct consultation.

38 This term describes a rental in which the property will be used for profit. Payment is in the form of a set portion of profits arising from the property.

39 *Escrituras de Compra e Venda de Escravos 1834–1854*, Volume 74.2, Arquivo Municipal da Cidada da Salvador.

40 No universities or printing presses were permitted in Brazil before 1808.

41 Fraser to Castlereagh, 1 December 1812, NA FO 63/149; emphasis in original.

42 Pennell to Foreign Office, 12 July 1822, NA FO 63/249.

43 Report on consular income for 1815 to 1821, Pennell to Castlereagh, 13 September 1822, NA FO 63/249.

44 John Turnbull, *A Voyage Round the World, in the Years 1800, 1801, 1802, 1803, and 1804, in which the Author visited Madeira, the Brazils, Cape of Good Hope, the English Settlement of Botany Bay and Norfolk Island and the Principal Islands in the Pacific Ocean.* 2nd ed. (London: Maxwell, 1813), pp. 37–8.

45 Henry Brougham, House of Commons, 13 March 1817, quoted in Bethell, *The Abolition of the Brazilian Slave Trade*, p. 2.

46 Quoted in Bethell, *The Abolition of the Brazilian Slave Trade*, p. 4.

47 Pennell to Londonderry (Lord Castlereagh), 5 November 1821, NA FO 63/240.

48 "I have at all events, the satisfaction of assuring your Lordship, that the spirit of revolt has not reached this Capitania" British Consul Cunningham to Lord Castlereagh, 24 March 1817, NA FO 63/206. See also Carlos Guilharma Mota, *Nordeste 1817: estruturas e argumentas* (São Paulo: Perspectiva, 1972).

49 One interesting document shows the British Consul-General at Rio de Janeiro updating the Foreign Office on Independence conflicts in Brazil, Peru, Argentina, and Chile. The dispatch includes five original flyers distributed by rebel forces in the various countries. Cunningham to Londonderry (Lord Castlereagh), 1 October 1821, NA FO 63/240.

50 Three other unsettling events were the Malês slave rebellion of 1835, the political coup attempt known as the Sabinada in 1837, and the social convulsions associated with the ending of the slave trade. During the Sabinada, the British merchants remained neutral (trading with both sides), knowing that no real danger existed to their privileges as long as a full social revolution was averted. This also summed up their position during the independence struggle. See Luís Vianna Filho, *A sabinada* (Rio de Janeiro: José Olympio, 1938), pp. 128, 144–9; Dundas, *Sketches of Brazil*, pp. 393–7.

51 "It is my intention to avoid any further discussion on the subject with the local authorities", Pennell to Londonderry (Lord Castlereagh), 2 October 1822, NA FO 63/249.

52 See Chapter 2.

53 Elizabeth de Fiore and Ottaviano de Fiore, eds, *The British Presence in Brazil, 1808–1914.* 2nd ed. (São Paulo: Paubrasil, 1987); Brian Vale, *Independence or Death! British Sailors and Brazilian Independence, 1822–25* (London: I.B. Tauris, 1996).

54 Conselho Interino to Pennell, 24 October 1822, NA FO 268/1.

55 Cunningham served as British consul at Bahia from 1815 to 1818.

56 Cunningham to Castlereagh, 24 March 1817, NA FO 63/206.

57 "I understand their report will be extremely favorable as to [their] performance, and ultimate success against the Mother Country", Pennell to Castlereagh, 15 June 1818, NA FO 63/215.

58 Pennell to Londonderry (Lord Castlereagh), 8 December 1820, NA FO 63/230.

59 Pennell to Londonderry (Lord Castlereagh), 25 August 1821, NA FO 63/240.

60 Pennell to Londonderry (Lord Castlereagh), 5 November 1821, NA FO 63/240.

61 Pennell to Londonderry (Lord Castlereagh), 9 February 1821, NA FO 63/240.

62 Alves to Pennell, 3 September 1822, NA FO 63/249.

63 Pennell to Bathurst, 29 October 1822, NA FO 63/249.

64 Pennell to Pereira, 30 October 1821, NA FO 63/240.

65 Pennell to Londonderry, 28 August 1822, NA FO 63/249; emphasis in original.

66 *"Tenciono entrar, á viva força, nessa Capital; e por isso peço a V.S., que se passe, e toda a sua cometiva, a Villa da Caxoeira, séde do legitimo Governo desta Provincia, onde V.S. será respeitado, e dignamente tractado como Representante d'huma Nação Amiga do Hospitaleiro Brasil evitando por este modo os damnos, que os meos soldados involuntariamente lhe possão causar no momento da desordem, da dissolação, e da carnagem. Esta minha rogativa hé filha d'alta Politica do Povo Brasileiro."* [I intend to enter this Capital by force; and so I ask that you and all your followers proceed to Cachoeira, seat of the legitimate government of this province, where you will be respected and treated with dignity as representative of a foreign nation friendly to the hospitable Brazil, thus avoiding the damages that my soldiers may involuntarily cause in the moment of disorder and carnage. This my request is due to the high policy of the Brazilian People.] General Labatut (Conselho Interino) to Pennell, 26 November 1822, NA FO 63/249.

67 Governo Provisório (formerly Conselho Interino) to Follett, 10 November 1823, NA FO 268/1.

2 British Merchants and the Illegal Slave Trade to Brazil

1 While visiting Bahia in the early 1840s, American writer Daniel Kidder pointedly observed that "few slave vessels were fitted out without large credits from English houses, based on the anticipated sale of their return cargo. It was not principle that cut off these credits, but the repeated losses of the slave dealers, which left them nothing to pay. Thus English philanthropy and English cupidity came into contact with each other, and it is a happy circumstance that the former, to a great extent, triumphed. Yet the derangement of so vast a business as the slave traffic had become, has been severely felt in the commercial affairs of Bahia, not only on account of the number of persons engaged in it, but also on account of the market it had hitherto furnished for two principal products of the province – rum and tobacco." Kidder, *Sketches of Residence and Travels in Brazil*, p. 87.

2 Joseph C. Miller, *Way of Death: Merchant Capitalism and the Angolan Slave Trade, 1730–1830* (Madison: University of Wisconsin Press, 1988), pp. 505–31.

3 "In so far as its commercial and financial organization is concerned, the British slave trade is generally believed to have undergone little modification in the century-and-a-half of its existence. It is regarded as essentially a triangular trade, whereby English manufactures were exchanged for Negro slaves on the Coast of Africa, the slaves then being transported across ... the Middle Passage, to the West India or mainland colonies where they were exchanged for sugar, tobacco and other commodities. On the final leg of the triangle, colonial produce was carried to the English port from whence the voyage originated." Richard B. Sheridan, 'The commercial and financial organization of the British slave-trade, 1750–1807', *Economic History Review*, 2nd. series 11/2 (1958) 249.

4 William A. Green, *British Slave Emancipation: The Sugar Colonies and the Great Experiment, 1830–1865* (Oxford: Clarendon Press, 1976), p. 99.

5 Eric E. Williams, *Capitalism & Slavery* (Chapel Hill: University of North Carolina Press, 1944).

6 See Seymour Drescher, *Capitalism and Antislavery: British Mobilization in Comparative Perspective*. 2nd. ed. (New York: Oxford University Press, 1987); Clare Midgley, *Women Against Slavery: The British Campaigns, 1780–1870* (London: Routledge, 1992).

7 Green, *British Slave Emancipation*, p. 243.

8 Bethell, *The Abolition of the Brazilian Slave Trade*, p. 65.

9 Canning to Wellington, 30 September 1822, Cited in Bethell, *The Abolition of the Brazilian Slave Trade*, p. 31.

10 Jane Elizabeth Adams, 'The abolition of the Brazilian slave-trade', *The Journal of Negro History* 4/10 (1925) 615. This article was published almost eighty years ago. Adams' work anticipated much later scholarship – her perceptive reading of social and economic history through diplomatic documents, her material on Bahia, and a willingness to evaluate the British conflict of interest regarding the slave trade, all contribute to ensuring that her article remains relevant.

11 Bethell, *The Abolition of the Brazilian Slave Trade*, p. 82.

12 Leslie Bethell, 'The Mixed Commissions for the suppression of the transatlantic slave-trade in the nineteenth century', *Journal of African History* 7 (1966) 79.

13 Adams, 'The abolition of the Brazilian slave-trade', 620.

14 Robert Conrad, 'The contraband slave trade to Brazil, 1831–1845', *Hispanic American Historical Review* 49/4 (1969) 619.

15 Ibid, 621.

16 "*Governo da Provincia. Remetto a V. M. os Exemplares do Edital deste Governo relativamente a extinção total do vergonhoso Commercio de Escravatura, contendo a Lei o Decreto que prohibem a sua continuação com a introducção de escravos nesta Provincia, estabelece penas ao que por qualquer maneira contravierem*

aquellas *Imperiaes Ordens, afim de que V.M. lhe mande dar a maior publicidade, e observe, e faça observar de baixo de sua meior responsabilidade"*, Gazeta da Bahia, 1 August 1832, Arquivo do Estado da Bahia.

17 Bethell, *The Abolition of the Brazilian Slave Trade*; Conrad, 'The contraband slave trade to Brazil, 1831–1845'; Eltis, *Economic Growth and the Ending of the Transatlantic Slave Trade* (New York: Oxford University Press, 1987).

18 Conrad, 'The contraband slave trade to Brazil, 1831–1845', 630.

19 "In 1844 more than a quarter of the entire British Navy stood off the coasts of West Africa, Brazil, and Cuba"; Howard H. Wilson, 'Some principal aspects of British efforts to crush the African slave trade, 1807–1829', *American Journal of International Law* 44 (1950) 515.

20 Eltis, *Economic Growth and the Ending of the Transatlantic Slave Trade*, p. 243.

21 *British Foreign and State Papers*, 1845–6, pp. 760–2, cited in Adams, 'The abolition of the Brazilian slave-trade', 630.

22 Adams, 'The abolition of the Brazilian slave-trade', 631.

23 Ibid, 636.

24 Tavares, 'As soluções brasileiras no exemplo da extinção do tráfico negreiro', *Journal of Inter-American Studies* 9/3 (1967) 368.

25 *"Como ainda não se fez a história do Brasil partindo de posições brasileiras, ficou sempre a impressão de que o Brasil foi levado a acabar o tráfico negreiro unicamente por causa das repressões militares e econômicas da Inglaterra. O curioso é que essas repressões inglesas existiram para mais de quinze anos, sem, contudo, conseguir exterminar o tráfico; enquanto, nos quatro ou cinco anos depois da lei de 1850, com sua pequena Marinha de guerra e com o seu falho aparelho judiciário o Brasil realmente deteve o comércio negreiro no seu litoral. É que, naquelas alturas da segunda metade do século 19, encontrando a solução conservadora e de equilíbrio, o Brasil deixava o processo sinuoso que vinha utilizando há trinta e nove anos, afinal tranquilizado quanto a que o fim do tráfico negreiro não era o fimdo regime de trabalho escravo no qual e do qual vivia."* Tavares, 'As soluções brasileiras no exemplo da extinção do tráfico negreiro', 368.

26 Wilson, 'Some principal aspects of British efforts to crush the African slave trade, 1807–1829', 510.

27 Eltis, *Economic Growth and the Ending of the Transatlantic Slave Trade*, p. 243.

28 Conrad, 'The contraband slave trade to Brazil, 1831–1845', 620.

29 Pennell to Canning, 8 June 1827, cited in Bethell, *The Abolition of the Brazilian Slave Trade*, p. 67.

30 Cunningham to Castlereagh, 20 February 1818, NA FO 63/215.

31 Pennell to Castlereagh, 22 December 1819, NA FO 63/223.

32 Pennell to Castlereagh, 21 June 1821, NA FO 63/240.

33 Fraser to Castlereagh, 14 April 1812, NA FO 63/149.

34 British merchants of Bahia to President Viana, 14 August 1824, AEB, Seção de Arquivo Colonial e Provincial, Box 1186.

35 Acting Consul Weiss to the President of Bahia, 27 November 1829, AEB, Seção de Arquivo Colonial e Provincial, Box 1189.

36 For example, Consul Parkinson to President of Bahia, 1 October 1833, AEB, Seção de Arquivo Colonial e Provincial, Box 1187; Capt. Christie to Consul Porter, 25 January 1842, AEB, Seção de Arquivo Colonial e Provincial, Box 1195).

37 Acting Consul Weiss to President of Bahia, 24 July 1829, AEB, Seção de Arquivo Colonial e Provincial, Box 1189.

38 "This is not the first time [in] the last fifteen months. […] The numerous attrocity [*sic*] committed on myself and fellow countryman residents in the Victoria loudly calls for justice." Yonds to Weiss, 4 December 1829, AEB, Seção de Arquivo Colonial e Provincial, Box 1189.

39   The problem was that some soldiers had taken away his messenger's horse, and the President had not followed proper procedure in using the Judge Conservator to handle the case. It would appear that the consul overreacted, and could not have helped the image of the British community in the process: "I hold it to be a most important portion of my duty as British Consul, to resist infringement of the privileges, either in my own person, or in the person of the meanest British Subject [...]"; and four days later: "The discussion has now reached a point at which it becomes me to drop the correspondence and refer the whole question to higher powers". Surely this cannot be considered as skillful diplomacy at a time when the British relied so heavily on official goodwill for their physical safety, not to mention commercial interests. Parkinson to the President of Bahia, 31 July 1832 and 4 August 1832, respectively, AEB, Seção de Arquivo Colonial e Provincial, Box 1186.

40   "*O Brigue Thereza que pertende sahir amanhã para a Costa da Mina com Bandeira Portugueza, he Propiede. [propriedade] Brazileira, pertençente a Manoel Cardozo dos S.tos, e vai buscar Escravos Affricanos pa. dezembarcar nas Costas desta Provinçia, como ja o fez na Costa de Havana, O Consul de S.M.B. deve ja e já ofiçiar ao Governo desta Provinçia pa. fazer descarregar o mençionado Bre. Escuna, e como volume de fazendas achará metido dentro de hum Caixão a Caldra. pa. cozinhar a comida dos Escravos, e mais ferragens para o dito fim.*" Anonymous to Parkinson, 17 July 1832, AEB, Seção de Arquivo Colonial e Provincial, Box 1186.

41   Jackson and Grigg, no. 24, 30 September 1836, NA FO 84/199, cited in Bethell, *The Abolition of the Brazilian Slave Trade*, p. 79.

42   *Great Britain. Sessional Papers*, 1850, vol. IX, no. 53, cited in Adams, 'The abolition of the Brazilian slave-trade', 632.

43   'A politica da Inglaterra a cerca do trafico de escravos', *A Tolerancia*, 29 August 1849, AEB, Seção de Arquivo Republicano.

44   *British Foreign and State Papers*, 1845–6, pp. 760–2, cited in Adams, 'The abolition of the Brazilian slave-trade', 630.

45   Consul Morgan to President of Bahia, 24 October 1853, AEB, Seção de Arquivo Colonial e Provincial, Box 1190.

46   Consul Morgan to President of Bahia, 14 November 1856, AEB, Seção de Arquivo Colonial e Provincial, Box 1190.

47   Edward Wilberforce, *Brazil Viewed Through a Naval Glass, with Notes on Slavery and the Slave Trade* (London: Longman, Brown, Green, and Longmans, 1856), p. 69.

48   For more on the political aspects of mutual perceptions among Britons and Brazilians, see Ross G. Forman, 'Imperial intersections: imperial visions in collision and collapse in the late nineteenth and early twentieth centuries', unpublished Ph.D. thesis, Stanford University, 1998.

49   "*Pisaste uma nação, – nação tão grande / Que a loucura perdoa-te! – Cuspiste / Na face dessa que afogára em vagas, / Em rios de ouro teu paiz ingrato! / Procuraste lançar um véo de sombras / Sobre essa terra que fascina o globo / Ao clarão dos diamantes, e piedosa / Teus irmãos agazalha junto ao peito!*" Fagundes Varella, *O estandarte auri-verde: cantos sobre a questão anglo-brasileira* (São Paulo: Typografia Imparcial, 1863), pp. 10–1.

50   Sheridan, 'The commercial and financial organization of the British slave-trade', 263.

51   *The Parliamentary history of England* (1816), cited in Sheridan, 'The commercial and financial organization of the British slave-trade', 263.

52   "British law appeared unable to sever ties between the United Kingdom's economy and the slave trade." Eltis, *Economic Growth and the Ending of the Transatlantic Slave Trade*.

53   Tavares, *Comércio proibido de escravos*, p. 53.

54   Great Britain *Parliamentary Papers* 1831–2, vol. XX, cited in Tavares, *Comércio proibido de escravos*, p. 127.

55 Kidder, *Sketches of Residence and Travels in Brazil*, p. 86.
56 As early as 1925, the use of British capital in the Brazilian slave trade was well known to historians. "There was the feeling that England was not really in earnest in suppressing the slave trade … the participation of British subjects and the use of British capital in the slave trade in Brazil strengthened this idea." Adams, 'The abolition of the Brazilian slave-trade', 631. Despite this fact, many of the subsequent studies of British abolitionism do not give adequate attention to this issue.
57 For example, the management of illicit landings evoked the admiration of a British official: "The whole system of shore-signals is now brought to a degree of perfection that is quite extraordinary when you recollect the extent of the country. The boats go out to reconnoiter […] when they see the cruisers, they sound immense horns, which are heard upon the shore, and up goes a fire upon the hill as a beacon, which is repeated along the coast; it is impossible for anything to be more perfectly managed; all the appliances of this trade are brought to a degree of perfection that is astonishing and which nothing but the immense profit can explain." Report by Minister Howden. *Great Britain. Sessional Papers* 1850, vol. IX, no. 53, cited in Adams, 'The abolition of the Brazilian slave-trade', 620–1.
58 Eltis, *Economic Growth and the Ending of the Transatlantic Slave Trade*.
59 Ibid, p 156.
60 "By the late 1830s dealers were issuing bills on the security of future imports … a company in Rio de Janeiro [even] specialized in discounting these slave-trader bills." Ibid.
61 Great Britain *Parliamentary Papers* 1850, vol. IX, cited in Tavares, *Comercio proibido de escravos*, p. 129.
62 Sierra Leone, Commissioners, NA FO 84/307, cited in Tavares, *Comercio proibido de escravos*, p. 96.
63 AEB, Seção Judiciária, Testamentos e Inventários, 347.919.62 and 347.672.22, 143/7, cited in Tavares, *Comercio proibido de escravos*, p. 134.
64 *Parliamentary Papers* 1847, vol. LXVI, cited in Tavares, *Comercio proibido de escravos*, p. 132.
65 "Cash credits advanced to Brazilian buyers of slaves, mainly planters, enabled them to deploy other assets of their own, released by these loans, to buy British goods that they contributed to slaving voyages of this sort. The less direct forms of British participation tended to predominate after abolition of the legal trade in 1830 and the more direct ones earlier." Miller, *Way of Death*, p. 508.
66 British Consul John Parkinson to the President of Bahia, 6 November 1833, AEB, Seção de Arquivo Colonial e Provincial, Box 1187.
67 British Consul Edward Porter to Manoel Messias de Leão, Vice President of Bahia, 30 April 1848, AEB, Seção de Arquivo Colonial e Provincial, Box 1193.
68 Listed are five Portuguese ships in port known to be engaged in the slave trade. Capt. Homberg of HMS *Cormorant* to Consul Edward Porter, forwarded to Francisco Gonçalvez Martins, President of Bahia, 5 October 1850, AEB, Seção de Arquivo Colonial e Provincial, Box 1188.
69 For example, Consul Morgan to João Mauricio Wanderley, President of Bahia, 25 November 1853, AEB, Seção de Arquivo Colonial e Provincial, Box 1188; and Consul Morgan to João Lins Vieira Cansansão de Sinumbu, President of Bahia, 4 November 1856, AEB, Seção de Arquivo Colonial e Provincial, Box 1190.
70 Consul Pennell to José Lino Coitinho, Secretary to the Provincial Junta of the Department for Foreign Affairs, 8 November 1821, AEB, Seção de Arquivo Colonial e Provincial, Box 1191.
71 Vice Consul Follett to Francisco Vicente Viana, President of Bahia, 27 August 1824, AEB, Seção de Arquivo Colonial e Provincial, Box 1186.
72 Consul Porter to Francisco Gonçalvez Martins, President of Bahia, 4 January 1851, AEB, Seção de Arquivo Colonial e Provincial, Box 1188.

73 Captain Finlayson to Consul Pennell, 3 June 1821, NA FO 63/240.
74 Finlayson to Pennell, 3 June 1821, NA FO 63/240.
75 Pennell to Finlayson, 3 June 1821, NA FO 63/240.
76 Robert Conrad, *The destruction of Brazilian slavery, 1850–1888* (Berkeley: University of California Press, 1972), p, 14.
77 A few instances of land and home purchases in their names have, however, been found.
78 Reis, 'Slave resistance in Brazil: Bahia, 1807–1835', 111–44.
79 Ibid, 125.
80 AEB, 'Devassa do levante de escravos ocorrido em Salvador em 1835', *Anais do Arquivo do Estado da Bahia*. (Salvador, Bahia: Arquivo Publico do Estado da Bahia, 1968).
81 *"Capturei como cabeças, e Chefes de Clubes que se ajuntavão na caza do Inglez Abraham ... os seguintes Nagôs – Diogo, Daniel, Jaimes e João escravos de Abraham, cabeças do Clube, sahirão e recolherão-se pela manhã ainda com as calças com sangue ... Pedro escravo do Doutor Dundas ficou no ataque com hua perna esbandalhada de balla era cabeça do Clube."* AEB, 59.
82 AEB, 117.
83 Pierre Verger, *Notícias da Bahia: 1850* (Salvador, Bahia: Editora Corrupio, 1981), p. 117.
84 *"O Cônsul da França, Mr. Mareschaux em seu relatório de 29 de janeiro de 1835 escrevia: 'Pretende-se com certa verossimilhança que este plano nasceu entre os pretos pertencentes aos estrangeiros, os ingleses em maioria, que vivem no bairro da Victória que não exerciam sobre eles nenhum controle. Também alguns brasileiros mal intencionados querem fazer acreditar que os ingleses mesmos os ajudaram, acusação absurda que encontra, porém, um certo acolhimento."* Acrescenta ele que: 'tem que fazer notar que os donos da maior quantidade de terrenos da Victória, Sr. José de Cerqueira Lima e sua mãe, Sr. viúva Cerqueira, que moram em duas bonitas casas no coração deste bairro e que aí vivem inúmeras famílias de seus escravos, não tiveram escravo nenhum comprometido neste movimento'."* MAE CPB, T. 16, p. 21, cited in Verger, *Notícias da Bahia*, p. 117.
85 British Consul Robert Hesketh to Foreign Secretary Lord Palmerston, 12 December 1840, cited in Conrad, 'The contraband slave trade to Brazil, 1831–1845', 617–38.
86 In Minas Gerais, the Morro Velho gold mine was owned and operated by a British company which developed a hybrid slavery/blue-collar system of labor: specific transgressions (lateness, carelessness, etc.) were awarded specific, corporeal punishments of increasing severity, while good behavior was rewarded in similarly homogenized doses. This eerily impersonal relationship between employer and employed, master and slave, is another example of the odd (and sometimes unfortunate) compromises that developed historically, around the fundamental inconsistency in the British attitude toward slavery viewed by that country's social ideals, commercial interests, diplomatic policies, and actions in nineteenth-century Brazil. See Douglas Cole Libby, 'Proto-industrialization in a slave society: the case of Minas Gerais', *Journal of Latin American Studies* 23/1 (1991), 1–35 and Eakin, *British Enterprise in Brazil*.
87 *The British and Foreign Anti-Slavery Reporter* (1841), cited in Tavares, *Comercio proibido de escravos*, p. 129.
88 George Pilkington, *An Address to the English Residents in the Brazilian Empire, Urging Them to Liberate Their Slaves* (1841), pp. 6, 13–4.
89 Ibid, pp. 17–9.
90 "Yet is it not amazing, how men, in other respects, so respectable, and amongst whom several are wealthy, can accept of such a paltry sum as the difference between slave and hired labor at the expense of every principle of honesty and justice? How can you meet the judge of heaven [preceded by the mutilated figures of your victims?]" Ibid, p. 20.

91 Reis, 'Slave resistance in Brazil: Bahia, 1807–1835', 129.
92 NA FO 84/174, NA FO 84/175, cited in Bethell, *The Abolition of the Brazilian Slave Trade*, p. 78.
93 Reis, 'Slave resistance in Brazil: Bahia, 1807–1835', 114.
94 Jackson and Grigg, 30 September 1836, NA FO 84/199, cited in Bethell, *The Abolition of the Brazilian Slave Trade*, p. 79.

3 Public and Private Lives of the British Community

1   See Graham, *Britain and the Onset of Modernization in Brazil* and Manchester, *British Pre-Eminence in Brazil*.
2   This is apparent from an overview of the "professions" column in the records of Bahia's British Chapel.
3   The size of the British population during the first half of the century cannot be determined with precision, because the available records are sadly incomplete. The British consulate did not maintain systematic listings of British subjects resident in Bahia, and produced only the occasional petition signed by the most important British merchants. As a result, women, children, and minor employees are almost entirely absent from the consular record. As for Brazilian official sources, the petitions for residency submitted by some British merchants provide some 25 names, with additional information on residence, occupation, and marital status. Secondary sources give a few more clues, and the tombstone inscriptions from Bahia's British Cemetery complete the list. Bahia's port authorities did not begin to maintain systematic records of passengers arriving or departing from Bahia until the 1850s, although record-books for the second half of the century are impeccably detailed.
4   British merchants to Viscount Castlereagh, 25 April 1819, NA FO 63/249; British merchants to the President of Bahia, 12 May 1828, AEB, Seção de Arquivo Colonial e Provincial, Box 1189.
5   British Merchants of Bahia to Consul John Morgan, 20 October 1859, AEB, Seção de Arquivo Colonial e Provincial, Box 1195.
6   Turnbull, *A Voyage Round the World*, p. 30.
7   Ibid, p. 37.
8   Ibid, pp. 24, 36.
9   Ibid, p. 38.
10 Herbert Heaton, 'A Merchant Adventurer in Brazil' *Journal of Economic History* 6 (1946) 1; John Luccock, *Notes on Rio de Janeiro, and the Southern Parts of Brazil; taken during a Residence of Ten Years in that Country, from 1808 to 1818* (London: Leigh, 1820); Olga Pantaleão, 'A presença inglesa', in Sérgio Buarque de Hollanda, ed., *História geral da civilização brasileira, II/1* (São Paulo: Difusão Européia do Livro, 1965), p. 74.
11 Pantaleão, 'A presença inglesa', pp. 64–99.
12 "In 1816 [Luccock] visited England … and could now afford to take back a man-servant." Heaton, 'A Merchant Adventurer in Brazil', 23. See also José Wanderley de Aranjoh Pinho, 'A Bahia, 1808–1856', in Sérgio Buarque de Hollanda, ed., *História geral da civilização brasileira, II/1* (São Paulo: Difusão Européia do Livro, 1967), p. 291.
13 W. P. Robertson and J. P. Robertson, *Letters on South America* (London: John Murray, 1843), p. 119.
14 Charles Fraser to Viscount Castleraugh *[sic]*, 14 April 1812, NA FO 63/149.
15 Henry Koster, *Travels in Brazil* (London: Longman, Hurst, Rees, Orme, and Brown, 1816), p. 400; emphasis in original.
16 Maria Graham, *Journal of a Voyage to Brazil, and Residence There during Part of*

the Years 1821, 1822, 1823 (London: Longman, Hurst, Rees, Orme, Brown, and Green, 1824), p. 141.

17 The community numbered about 120, so approximately 60 attended regular services. Kidder, *Sketches of Residence and Travels in Brazil*, p. 25.

18 "The celebration of Marriages by the Commanders of HM's Ships of War, & others, not being clergymen, afforded also an argument, from analogy, in support of the same inference." Pennell to Canning, 22 August 1823, NA FO 63/262.

19 Pennell to Canning, 23 July 1823, NA FO 63/262.

20 Foreign Office, NA FO 63/230, FO 63/240, FO 63/249.

21 Pennell to Canning, 22 August 1823, NA FO 63/262.

22 The parchment forms were double-sided, and one quadrant of the book recording marriages had been erased by the water. As a result we have the names, dates, ages, and professions for about one half of the population, but not their fathers' names, father's occupations, or witnesses. For the other part of the population the situation is reversed.

23 This does not include sailors or their wives, who died in port or at sea and were buried in the sailors' ground, for these were not members of the resident British community. The same goes for the fairly high mortality suffered by engineers and railroad workers who came to work on the Bahia and São Francisco Railway after 1850, and who died in a yellow fever epidemic. The British community erected a plaque in its cemetery in their honor, effectively identifying them as a separate group.

24 As a result, the incidence of Protestant-to-Catholic conversions among the British of Bahia cannot readily be evaluated. Arquivo Municipal da Cidade de Salvador: *Registro de Naturalização de Estrangeiros, 1833 a 1884*, vol. 155/2.

25 James Wetherell, *Brazil: Stray Notes from Bahia: Being Extracts from Letters, &c., During a Residence of Fifteen Years* (Liverpool: Webb and Hunt, 1860), p. 93.

26 Ibid, p. 116; emphasis in original.

27 AEB, Seção Judiciária, Inventário 03-1349-1818-05, John Ligertwood Paterson, 9 May 1883. In 1887 a bust of Dr. Paterson was erected in a park near Victoria, bearing the following inscription in English and Portuguese: "As a testimony of friendship, esteem, and gratitude, this monument was erected by the public to the memory of John Ligertwood Paterson, on this site which was granted by the municipal council of the City of Bahia, President Dr. Augusto Ferreira França, and President of the Province Counsellor Pedro Luiz Pereira de Souza."

28 AEB, Seção Judiciária, Inventário 01-199-352-02, George Mumford, 29 March 1862.

29 Eakin, *British Enterprise in Brazil*, p. 243; Oliver Marshall, ed., *English-Speaking Communities in Latin America* (Basingstoke: Macmillan Press, 2000); John Mayo, *British Merchants and Chilean Development, 1851–1886* (Boulder, CO: Westview Press, 1987), p. 20; Vera Blinn Reber, *British Mercantile Houses in Buenos Aires, 1810–1880* (Cambridge, MA.: Harvard University Press, 1979), p. 48.

30 The probate inventories of the merchant John Andrews (1862), his widow Emilia Viana Andrews (1896), and later of their daughters, show that Emilia sent the girls to Paris and London soon after John's death. After returning to Bahia, one married a Brazilian, and the other the son of a German merchant. AEB, Seção Judiciária, Inventário 06-2566-3066-05, Inventário 01-70-89-02.

31 Kidder, *Sketches of Residence and Travels in Brazil*, p. 24.

32 Dundas, *Sketches of Brazil*, p. 221.

33 Graham, *Journal of a Voyage to Brazil*, p. 134. Maria Graham was the wife of a British naval officer, who was assigned to patrol the ports of Brazil during the independence battles of Brazil. She has been described by Gilberto Freyre as one of the most perspicacious of social observers, and was also politically astute and interested in women's issues. Her writings on Latin America and India have been extensively used by Pratt to study the subjective construction of the British empire;

see Mary Louise Pratt, *Imperial Eyes: Travel Writing and Transculturation* (London: Routledge, 1992).

34 Pennell to Hamilton, 2 June 1818 NA FO 63/215; Foreign Office to Pennell, 1 May 1821, NA FO 63/240.

35 "The English are all served by slaves, indeed." Graham, *Journal of a Voyage to Brazil*, p. 148.

36 Pennell's alarming health report, written by Dr. Dundas, is enclosed in Pennell to Bidwell, 8 March 1828, NA FO 13/53.

37 Outside of the city of Bahia, Graham (*Journal of a Voyage to Brazil*, p. 155) refers to an English merchant resident in Cachoeira; Charles Fraser lived near Ilhéus, on his one-man mission of civilizing the Patachó Indians (Charles Fraser to Viscount Castlereagh, 14 April 1812, NA FO 63/149); and in the late 1830s, at least two British merchants lived in Valença, one of whom had with him a wife and four children ("William Sweeney [...] has been a Resident in [Bahia] thirteen years and in the Town of Valença the last twelve months engaged in trade", Edward Porter to Thomas Xavier Garcia d'Almeida, President of Bahia, 12 December 1840, AEB, Seção de Arquivo Colonial e Provincial, Box 1195. There is also evidence that the British owned property on the island of Itaparica. However, these exceptions serve to highlight the main pattern of British settlement, which was to band together in one large enclave next to the main city, and to make efforts to remain fundamentally separate from the surrounding Brazilian society.

38 William Scully, *Brazil, Its Provinces and Chief Cities; the Manners & Customs of the People, Agricultural, Commercial, and Other Statistics, Taken by the Latest Official Documents; with a Variety of Useful and Entertaining Knowledge, Both for the Merchant and the Emigrant* (London: John Murray, 1866), p. 351; Dundas, *Sketches of Brazil*, p. 24.

39 AEB, Seção Judiciária, Inventário 03-1349-1818-05, 9 May 1883.

40 John Candler, *Narrative of a Voyage to Brazil in 1852* (London: E. Newman, 1852), p, 47.

41 Graham, *Journal of a Voyage to Brazil*, p. 134.

42 Dundas, *Sketches of Brazil*, p. 249.

43 Kidder, *Sketches of Residence and Travels in Brazil*, p. 63.

44 Ibid.

45 Wetherell, *Brazil*, p. 125.

46 Ibid, p. 82.

47 Dundas, *Sketches of Brazil*, p. 208.

48 Today the upper and lower cities (*cidade alta* and *cidade baixa*) are connected by a gigantic free-standing elevator, built by British engineers in the 1870s to solve the city's central topographical problem.

49 Kidder, *Sketches of Residence and Travels in Brazil*, p. 19.

50 James Prior, *Voyage [...] in the Nisus Frigate*, p. 101.

51 Graham, *Journal of a Voyage to Brazil*, p. 133.

52 Skill was required to ride in a *cadeira*, as balance was very important: "This mode of conveyance is very luxurious and extremely easy when once the person is accustomed to it, but strangers are very apt to lean to either one side or the other of the chair, and thereby to destroy the balance, and under the momentary apprehension of falling out, make it still worse by endeavouring to put themselves right". Wetherell, *Brazil*, p. 25. "One of our passengers who had got rather hearty, stepped into one of them, and not being able to balance himself properly, tumbled out on the street, to the no small amusement of the slaves who were carrying him and all those passing at the time." Alexander Marjoribanks, *Travels in South and North America* (London: Simpkin, Marshall and Co., 1853), p. 95.

53 Marjoribanks, *Travels in South and North America*, p. 94.

54 Wetherell, *Brazil*, p. 14; emphasis in original.
55 Ibid, p. 105.
56 Dundas, *Sketches of Brazil*, p. 217.
57 "1:000$000, Nei, Africano, com 40 annos mais ou menos, carregador de Cadeira." AEB, Seção Judiciária, Inventário 06-2566-3066-05.
58 Daniel P. Kidder and James C. Fletcher, *Brazil and the Brazilians Portrayed in Historical and Descriptive Sketches* (Boston: Little, Brown and Company, 1868), p. 477.
59 Even the anti-slavery activist John Candler was pleased with the novelty. "No one need suppose that [the use of *cadeiras*] was an oppression to the slaves: on the contrary, it was to them a coveted employment ... a kind look, and a very small gratuity added to the fare, always made us welcome". John Candler and Wilson Burgess, *Narrative of a Recent Visit to Brazil: to present an address on the slave-trade and slavery, issued by the Religious Society of Friends* (London: Edward Marsh, Friends' Book and Tract Depository, 1853), p. 48.
60 Heaton, 'A Merchant Adventurer in Brazil', 13, citing Luccock.
61 Wetherell, *Brazil*, p. 119.
62 Ibid.
63 Ibid.
64 Graham, *Journal of a Voyage to Brazil*, p. 135.
65 Ibid, p. 142.
66 Ibid; emphasis in original.
67 Wetherell, *Brazil*, p. 119.
68 Dundas, *Sketches of Brazil*, p. 51.
69 This did not happen only in Latin America. Callaway studies how the British of the Victorian period made use of clothing rituals in the African colonies to emphasize their separateness and superiority to those whom they ruled. Helen Callaway, 'Dressing for dinner in the bush: rituals of self-definition and British imperial authority', in Ruth Barnes and Joanne B. Eicher, eds, *Dress and Gender: Making and Meaning in Cultural Contexts* (Oxford: Berg Publishers, 1992).
70 Dundas, *Sketches of Brazil*, pp. 99–100.
71 Ibid.

4   Mind, Body and Perception: Health and the British Expatriate

1   Dundas, *Sketches of Brazil*, p. 109.
2   Ibid, pp. 106–7.
3   Ibid, p. 109.
4   Ibid, p. 106.
5   The future of these conflicts was far from predictable. At one point it seemed that Bahia might become independent of Portugal even if the rest of Brazil remained a colony. Pennell's mission was to ensure that British interests would remain secure no matter what the outcome; he eventually was to accomplish this difficult task very well.
6   "The Meeting [a special committee formed by Pennell, Harrison & Moir] feel[s] persuaded that [...] your Lordships [are] not fully apprised of the inconvenience & expense attending a voyage & a residence in this Country." Pennell to Castlereagh, 16 September 1820, NA FO 63/230.
7   Pennell to Londonderry (Lord Castlereagh), 10 September 1822, NA FO 63/249.
8   Pennell to Castlereagh, 20 March 1818, NA FO 63/215.
9   Merchants to Castlereagh, 25 April 1819, NA FO 63/249. The letter was signed by Moir & Co., Mellors & Russell, Arthur & Peter Lowe, Toole & Weiss, Wylie Hancock, Boothby & Co., Sam Johnston, Ralph Brown, Wm. Smith & Co., James Stewart & Co., Sealy, Duncan & Walker, Harrison Latham & Co., Gilfillan Bros. &

Co., Pringle & Astley, and Miller Nicholson & Co.

10 "[I was informed] that the Income was such as to render it advisable to risk the ill effects of climate, and the many other inconveniences attending a residence in this Country." Pennell to Castlereagh, 20 March 1818, NA FO 63/215.

11 Pennell to Londonderry (Lord Castlereagh), 10 September 1822, NA FO 63/249; emphasis mine.

12 Thomas Ewbank, *Life in Brazil: Or, a Journal of a Visit to the Land of the Cocoa and the Palm* (New York: Harper & Brothers, 1856), p. 392.

13 Ibid, p. 392.

14 Except for the abolition of the slave trade. Eventually this would cause a difficult conflict of interest for all those involved, and add to the double binds faced by the community. On double binds, see Gregory Bateson, *Steps to an Ecology of Mind: Collected Essays on Anthropology, Psychiatry, Evolution, and Epistemology* (London: Paladin, 1973).

15 The best available study of British insurance in nineteenth-century Latin America is Charles Jones, 'Insurance companies', in D.C.M. Platt, ed., *Business imperialism, 1840–1930: An Inquiry Based on British Experience in Latin America* (Oxford: Clarendon Press, 1977), pp. 53–74. This article, which begins at 1860, treats insurance as one more British business interest, without making reference to its unique significance for understanding past views of the future.

16 For a broader analysis of this problem and its significance for understanding British imperialism from a comparative perspective, see Michael Alan Mcintyre, 'British imperialism in India and Brazil, 1850–1914', unpublished Ph.D. thesis, University of Chicago, 1992.

17 Graham, *Journal of a Voyage to Brazil*, p. 256.

18 Pennell to Captain Bouchier of the HMS Blossom, 4 August 1822, NA FO 63/249.

19 See, for example, Pennell to Castlereagh, dated 19 February 1821 and marked "received" at the Foreign Office over two months later, NA FO 63/240; Pennell to Londonderry (Lord Castlereagh), dated 5 November 1821 and also received two months later, NA FO 63/240; and Pennell to Londonderry (Lord Castlereagh), dated 20 February 1822 and received on 13 May 1822, NA FO 63/249. Although these letters were dispatched in times of political unrest, and may have been delayed by associated transport complications, nevertheless they must have been handled as expeditiously as possible.

20 Jones, *Merchants to Multinationals*.

21 Graham, *Journal of a Voyage to Brazil*, p. 140.

22 Dundas *Sketches of Brazil*, pp. 39, 42, 218 furnish examples of a sudden collapse in health.

23 Ibid, p. 107.

24 Ibid, p. 105.

25 "Here, then, we have, accumulated, in almost unexampled abundance, all those physical conditions which are deemed, by the unanimous consent of physicians, to constitute the elements essential for the generation of the most deadly scourges of humanity – epidemic and endemic diseases." Dundas, *Sketches of Brazil*, p. 204.

26 Wetherell, *Brazil*, p. 7.

27 "The whole city is supplied by water carried from the fountains in large earthenware jars on the heads of blacks, or in barrels, and these are generally carried on the shoulders of men, or on mules, or in carts." Ibid, p. 90.

28 Dundas, *Sketches of Brazil*, p. 203. Early in the century, a British visitor to Bahia (who spent most of his year there under house arrest) had observed something similar: "The streets are confined and narrow, wretchedly paved, never cleaned, and therefore disgustingly dirty. The backs of several of them are the receptacles of filth, which, exposed to so extreme a heat, would affect severely the health of the inhabi-

tants, but for the salubrious air that prevails, in consequence of the elevated situation of the place." Thomas Lindley, *Narrative of a Voyage to Brasil: terminating in the seizure of a British vessel, and the imprisonment of the author and the ship's crew, by the Portuguese, with general sketches of the country, its natural productions, colonial inhabitants, &c.* (London: J. Johnson, 1805), p. 244.

29 Dundas, *Sketches of Brazil*, p. 203.

30 Ibid, p. 204.

31 Ibid, p. 206 – 72 degrees Fahrenheit in winter, or above 82.5 degrees in summer; Wetherell, *Brazil*, p. 46.

32 Dundas, *Sketches of Brazil*, p. 250. Connections such as these, between health, politics, environment, and society characterize Dundas' study: "Furthermore, in numerous instances, particular houses have suffered from similar causes: – namely, the cutting down, by order of the Portuguese general, of a tree, or the destruction of some wall or building, which had previously afforded shelter from the [...] sea-breezes".

33 Ibid, p. 346; emphasis in original.

34 Wetherell, *Brazil*, p .46.

35 Ibid, p. 82.

36 "In the middle of the day, the absence of any large number of moving beings in the streets makes everything appear dull." Ibid, p. 15.

37 Ibid, p. 123.

38 "One dish of which I have not partaken, and which I do not think, with all my curiosity, I could venture upon, is made of a species of snail – the largest land-shell there is – 'bulimus maximus'. They are brought fresh by the steamers from some of the country towns, and you frequently see them in the market for sale." Ibid, p. 116.

39 Dundas, *Sketches of Brazil*, p. 205.

40 Ibid, p. 51.

41 Wetherell, *Brazil*, p. 105.

42 Ibid, pp. 11–2; all emphases in the Wetherell quotes are present in the original.

43 This was included in Pennell's petition for a leave of absence in. Enclosed in Pennell to Bidwell, 8 March 1828, NA FO 13/53.

44 Dundas, *Sketches of Brazil*, p. 41.

45 Ibid, pp. 68–9.

46 Ibid, p. 65.

47 Wetherell, *Brazil*, p 105.

48 Dundas, *Sketches of Brazil*, p. 87.

49 Graham, *Journal of a voyage to Brazil*, p. 152. She also noted with disapproval that gambling was a common pastime among British men. Graham, *Journal of a Voyage to Brazil*, p. 148.

50 John Mawe, *Travels in the Interior of Brazil, particularly in the Gold and Diamond Districts of that Country, by Authority of the Prince Regent of Portugal* (London: Longman, Hurst, Rees, Orme, and Brown, 1812), p. 329.

51 Graham, *Journal of a Voyage to Brazil*, p. 148.

52 Candler and Burgess, *Narrative of a Recent Visit to Brazil*, p. 78.

53 James Henderson, *A History of the Brazil* (London: Longman, Hurst, Rees, Orme, and Brown, 1821), p. 346.

54 Candler and Burgess, *Narrative of a Recent Visit to Brazil*, p. 78.

55 Though the building was elegant, the performances held there were nearly always declared to be dreadful. Pedro II, Emperor of Brazil. *Diário da viagem ao norte do Brasil* (Salvador, Bahia: Universidade da Bahia, 1959); Graham, *Journal of a Voyage to Brazil*, p. 140; Wetherell, *Brazil*, p. 72.

56 John James Wild, *At Anchor: A Narrative of Experiences afloat and ashore during the Voyage of H.M.S. "Challenger", from 1872 to 1876* (London: M. Ward and Co., 1878), p. 46.

57 Dundas, *Sketches of Brazil*, p. 217; emphasis in original.
58 Ibid, p. 220.
59 Scully, *Brazil*, p. 7.
60 'Burials in the City of Bahia in the Empire of Brazil', Archives of the Igreja Episcopal Anglicana do Brasil (formerly the British Chapel), Salvador, Bahia.
61 Gilberto Freyre pointed out in 1948 that too much "immorality" could lead to venereal diseases, especially syphilis, which meant that the dream of living in an English novel quickly turned into the nightmare of living in a Russian one. Freyre, *Ingleses no Brasil*, p. 103.
62 Bourgeois Brazilian families in the early nineteenth century did not allow unmarried young men into their society, unless they had excellent personal references. Freyre, *Ingleses no Brasil*, p. 103. However, Henderson points out that the families of Bahia were more willing to socialize with strangers than those of Rio de Janeiro. Henderson, *A History of the Brazil*, p. 338.
63 A weekly newspaper published in Rio de Janeiro for the Anglo-Brazilian community, owned by William Scully and James Scobel (Biblioteca Nacional do Rio de Janeiro). See Oliver Marshall, *The English-Language Press in Latin America* (London: Institute of Latin American Studies, 1996), p. 20
64 "I accompanied Miss Pennell in a tour of visits to her Portuguese friends. As it is not their custom to visit or be visited in the forenoon, it was hardly fair to take a stranger to see them. However, my curiosity, at least, was gratified. In the first place, the houses, for the most part, are disgustingly dirty…" Graham, *Journal of a Voyage to Brazil*, p. 135.
65 Indifferent to her own role in precipitating a small crisis for her hostess, Graham saw only picturesque barbarity in the scene: "At more than one house, we waited in a passage while the servants ran to open the doors and windows of the sitting-rooms, and to call their mistresses, who were enjoying their undress in their own apartments. When at any of the houses the bustle of opening the cobwebbed windows, and assembling the family was over, in two or three instances, the servants had to remove dishes of sugar, mandioc, and other provisions, which had been left in the best rooms to dry". Graham, *Journal of a Voyage to Brazil*, p. 136.
66 Goffman describes this sort of invasion as an "onstage" – "backstage" violation. The British women were consciously onstage, that is, fully costumed and playing out the role of visitor; the Brazilian women, however, were 'backstage', unable to transform themselves accordingly on such short notice, and equally unable to refuse the visit. The fact that this seems to have been the visitors' intention overlays it with insult, in my opinion. Erving Goffman, *The Presentation of the Self in Everyday Life* (Garden City, NY: Doubleday, 1959).
67 Graham, *Journal of a Voyage to Brazil*, p. 142.
68 Elsewhere in his work, he took pains to undo the negative image that British merchants held of Brazilians, including women's indolence. Scully, *Brazil*, pp. 4–6, 10, and 121.
69 "The English society is just as one may expect. A few merchants, not of the first order, whose thoughts are engrossed by sugars and cottons, to the utter exclusion of all public matters that do not bear directly on their private trade, and of all matters of general science and information … I was completely out of patience with these incurious money-makers." Graham, *Journal of a Voyage to Brazil*, p. 148; "so in-curious are my countrymen here about what brings no profit". Ibid, p. 191.
70 Pennell's skilful handling of British interests in Bahia's transition to independence was demonstrated in Chapter 1. Freyre points out time and again how the British were scrupulously honest in their dealings, so much that the Brazilian expression *palavra de inglês* (the word of an Englishman) became a very oath. Maria Graham's character may be judged by her subsequent employment as governess to the heirs of

the Brazilian throne, even if she was soon fired for trying to meddle in affairs of state.

71 Adam Smith, *The Theory of Moral Sentiments*, Knud Haakonssen, ed. (Cambridge: Cambridge University Press, 2002), p. 249.

72 In Nancy Mitford et al., *Noblesse Oblige: An Enquiry into the Identifiable Characteristics of the English Aristocracy* (Harmondsworth, Middx: Penguin Books, 1959), pp. 71–2.

73 Keith Johnstone, *Impro: Improvisation and the Theatre* (New York: Routledge, 1981), pp. 73–4.

74 Wetherell, *Brazil*, p. 74.

75 In this respect, the British community of Bahia provides a much clearer picture of this problem, as opposed to that of Rio de Janeiro. The presence of a European crowned head of state, with all the pomp and circumstance of a royal court including the presence of upper-class diplomatic envoys from many European countries, would daily have reminded the British merchants of their subordinate position within the scope of their host society.

76 Certainly the problem of how to frame the Britishness of the destitute Irish in Brazil was experienced keenly by Consul Parkinson in this letter to Brazilian authorities: "Three irishmen, *[sic]* namely Richard Dalton, John Cavenah, and Patrick Lee belonging to the unfortunate class of so-called "Irish Colonists," were … taken up by the Municipal Guard for sleeping in the streets […] three of HBM's subjects have been treated with ignominy and severity". British consul John Parkinson to Presidente da Província, 22 September 1822, AEB, Seção de Arquivo Colonial e Provincial, Box 1186.

77 Scully, *Brazil*, p. 7. This suggestion, if correct, may open an interesting avenue for comparison among British expatriate communities in other times and places, and generate new ways for understanding their unique success in establishing and maintaining themselves within vastly different host societies throughout the nineteenth and twentieth centuries. It is just this process that gave rise to what today is increasingly known as commercial globalization.

78 Dundas, *Sketches of Brazil*, p. 109.

79 Ibid, p. 103.

80 Ibid, p. 104.

81 See, for instance, the tombstone inscription at the British Cemetery in Salvador of merchant Edward Pellew Wilson: "*A British merchant resident in this city for a period of 69 years from 1819 to 1887*".

82 This explanation may not hold as strongly in the case of a British community established in a location where the physical climate really was pestilent or otherwise extreme, and/or where cultural differences were very deep. Brazil is essentially a Western society, and though it has been informed by a rich African element since its inception, the elites have had a deeply vested interest in claiming European identity. Once again, this seems to suggest that the merchants' insistence on unnecessarily harmful physical and social behaviors shows itself here in a near-pure form.

83 Mawe, *Travels in the interior of Brazil*, p. 329.

84 Wetherell, *Brazil*, p. 150. Note especially his awareness of the real hazard presented by imagined dangers to health.

85 Ibid, p. 13.

86 Ibid, p. 145.

87 Ibid, p. 142.

88 Ibid, p. 124.

89 Ibid, p. 70.

90 Ibid, p. 54.

91 Ibid, p. 138.

92 However, there occurred in 1835 a real slave conspiracy along just such lines, which

was aborted just in time; and those who worked for the British turned out to be overwhelmingly represented among its leadership (see Chapter 2). Wetherell's benevolent interpretation in this case may have been more a reflection of his good nature than a correct interpretation of what was happening around him.

93 Wetherell, *Brazil*, p. 60.

94 Ibid, pp. v–vi.

95 *"Poderia quase afirmar-se que [James Wetherell] se enamorou da cidade onde viveu quinze anos, já que somente quem gosta mesmo de uma cidade pode dissecar de tal maneira a sua vida, reparar nos pequenos acontecimentos em geral desapercebidos da maioria dos estrangeiros, entrar nos mínimos detalhes e descrever tudo quase sempre com uma segurança absoluta ... integrando-se de corpo e alma à vida baiana."* 'Apresentação', in James Wetherell, *Brasil: apontamentos sobre a Bahia.* Miguel Paranhos do Rio-Branco, trans. (Salvador, Bahia: Edição Comemorativa do Banco da Bahia., no date) p. 8. I am indebted to the Fundação Clemente Mariani for providing a copy of this commemorative edition.

96 *"Naqueles céus quase sempre sombrios do País de Gales, as anotações do antigo vice-cônsul ... vieram trazer-me um pouco de sol de Salvador ... percorr[o] como o meu colega britânico, todas as ruas e ladeiras, entrando em cada igreja, saboreando acarajés e vatapá, procurando aproveitar de tudo ... que aquela cidade tem a sorte de poder oferecer".* 'Apresentação', in James Wetherell, *Brasil*, pp. 8–9.

97 Robertson and Robertson, *Letters on South America*, p. 60.

98 Ibid; emphasis in original.

99 See Witold Rybczynski, *Home: A Short History of an Idea* (New York: Viking, 1986).

5   Brazilians and the British: Images and Reflections

1 Henderson, *A History of the Brazil*, p. 338.

2 This may explain why their views on elite Brazilian women were generally less well supported than for other groups. During the early nineteenth century, upper-class Brazilian women were kept secluded from public view. Moema Parente Augel, *Visitantes estrangeiros na Bahia oitocentista* (São Paulo: Editora Cultrix, 1980), pp. 218–30; Freyre, *Ingleses no Brasil*, p. 609.

3 Wetherell, *Brazil*, p. 119.

4 Graham, *Journal of a Voyage to Brazil*, p. 136.

5 Gilberto Freyre wrote that "a Brazilian loved a hot bath. [...] Everywhere – in the cities and in the great as well as the humble houses of the interior – water, soap, and a large clean towel welcomed a guest [...] more than one third of the seventy-two factories existing in the empire [in the mid-nineteenth century] were soap factories". Gilberto Freyre, 'Social life in Brazil in the middle of the nineteenth century', *Hispanic American Historical Review* 5/4 (1922), 626.

6 "Master mechanics and tradesmen, with the exception of a few French and other foreigners, are Portuguese. The richest men in the country, the most industrious artisans and assiduous of store-keepers, are Lusitanians. Brazilians dislike them, perhaps as much for the competence their diligence in business realizes [*sic*] as for any thing else." Ewbank, *Life in Brazil*, p. 185.

7 Scully, *Brazil*, p. 6. Scully's comments mainly pertain to Rio de Janeiro.

8 A similar process can sometimes be observed in the attitudes of Anglo-Saxon professionals who must do business in Latin countries. According to sociologist Phyllis Harrison, "North Americans must give up the habit of scheduling full days with several appointments in the morning and several in the afternoon. Business is just not done that way in Brazil. [...] One morning appointment and one afternoon appointment may very well fill the day [...] two people need to lay the proper social groundwork before any

negotiations begin". Her insistent tone suggests that many foreign businessmen would prefer to hold to their own standards of time-use, even at the expense of business interests. Phyllis A. Harrison, *Behaving Brazilian: A Comparison of Brazilian and North American Social Behavior* (Rowley, MA: Newbury House Publishers, 1983), p. 73.

9   Scully also described Ouro Preto as "badly built, and has no buildings worthy of note". Scully, *Brazil*, p. 263.

10 Dundas, *Sketches of Brazil*, p. 211.

11 Ibid, p. 71. The poet's name is not given. Compare this description to the doctor's recommended daily schedule for optimal health, in Chapter 4.

12 Robertson and Robertson, *Letters on South America*, p. 61.

13 Wetherell, *Brazil*, p. 105; emphasis in original.

14 Ewbank, *Life in Brazil*, p. 184.

15 José Wanderley de Araújo Pinho, *Salões e damas do segundo reinado* (São Paulo: Martins, 1944).

16 Graham, *Journal of a Voyage to Brazil*, p. 142.

17 Pinho, *Salões e damas do segundo reinado*, pp. 39–40.

18 "The fiddlers, after waiting some time, went away, as they alleged, because they had not their tea early enough." Graham, *Journal of a Voyage to Brazil*, p. 143.

19 "*O cônsul não parecia acostumado a receber, pois deixou os convidados sem orquestra, por terem-se os músicos retirado com a alegação de não lhes haverem servido cedo uma parte do chá.*" Pinho, *Salões e damas do segundo reinado*, p. 40. I would point out that the details for Pennell's reception were probably planned by his daughters, who had only recently arrived in Bahia.

20 Ewbank, *Life in Brazil*, p. 184.

21 Wetherell, *Brazil*, p. 75; emphasis in original.

22 For a full study of Portuguese and Brazilian shopkeepers in Bahia during the late 18th and early 19th centuries, see Lugar, 'The merchant community of Salvador, Bahia.

23 Mawe, *Travels in the Interior of Brazil*, p. 329.

24 Wetherell, *Brazil*, p. 75.

25 The writing and reading of European accounts of non-European worlds and peoples served to construct and reinforce British ideas about their relationship to the rest of the world. To understand how this process would ultimately generate broad support the imperial project of colonial domination, see Pratt, *Imperial Eyes*.

26 Dundas, *Sketches of Brazil*, p. 209.

27 Ibid.

28 Ibid.

29 Ibid.

30 "I had now travelled seven or eight hundred miles, through remote and little frequented parts of the country, and had been every day, for several weeks, mixing with different people of every class, so as to enable me to form some estimate of the inhabitants." All quotes are from Rev. Robert Walsh, *Notices of Brazil in 1828 and 1829*. vol. 2. (Boston, MA: Richardson, Lord & Holbrook, 1831), p. 161.

31 Similar misunderstandings persist to the present day. Harrison explains that "North Americans invite people into their homes frequently and with relative ease, and interpret the lack of such invitations as a sign of unfriendliness. This interpretation is incorrect in Brazil, where the home is reserved for family and for a few very close friends". Harrison, *Behaving Brazilian*, p. 86.

32 "*O século XIX, sobretudo em sua primeira metade, foi assim, no Brasil, o século inglês por excelência*". Pantaleão, 'A presenca inglesa', p. 65.

33 "*A presença da cultura britânica no desenvolvimento do Brasil, no espaço, na paisagem, no conjunto da civilização do Brasil, é das que não podem – ou não devem? – ser ignoradas pelo brasileiro interessado na compreensão e na interpre-*

tação do Brasil." Freyre, *Ingleses no Brasil,* p. 35. *"O imperialismo britânico no Brasil ... [percorreu] os séculos XVI-XIX, especialmente a primeira metade do século XIX."* Ibid, p. 33.

34 José Honório Rodrigues, *Brazil and Africa* (Berkeley: University of California Press, 1965), p. 115. Quoted in Bethell, *The Abolition of the Brazilian Slave Trade,* epigraph, p. v.

35 One other book should be mentioned: Fiore and Fiore, eds, *The British Presence in Brazil.* Produced by Lloyds Bank in commemoration of the 125th anniversary of its presence in Brazil, the book supports the idea that current Brazilian impressions of the British influence are generally positive.

36 *"Em 1975 ocorreu o desaparecimento do mais significativo marco da presença britânica entre nós, a bela e antiga igreja anglicana do Campo Grande, a St. George's Church, derrubada para a construção de um qualquer prédio de apartamentos. Essa iniciativa roubou à Cidade do Salvador um dos seus mais valiosos monumentos, desde 1853, sem que tivesse havido na ocasião ao menos um protesto. Falava esse monumental templo da numerosa presença, como ainda agora felizmente recordada por aquele cemitério, de súditos de S. M. britânica que viveram e trabalharam conosco, contribuindo para nossa cultura e civilização desde pelo menos a lendária abertura dos portos em 1808 pela Carta Régia do príncipe dom João VI, que, continuando a secular aliança luso-britânica, criou condições comerciais privilegiadas no País, para os daquela nação. Quanto à Bahia, pouco ou nada sabemos, a não ser a lusões de Gilberto Freyre no livro Ingleses no Brasil (1948). Faz-se preciso que estudemos e analisemos nosso século XIX desse ponto de vista."* Thales de Azevedo, 'Ingleses, Arabes na Bahia', *A Tarde* (4 June 1993).

37 *"Prof. Thales de Azevedo [é] mestre ilustre de sua especialidade. É um dos mais notáveis professores da Universidade da Bahia."* Gilberto Freyre, 'Em louvor de mestre Thales de Azevedo', *Universitas* (Salvador, Bahia) 6/7 (1970) 17–9.

38 Koster leased and managed two sugar plantations during the 1810s, at Jaguaribe and Itamaracá, Pernambuco. Henry Koster, *Travels in Brazil* (Carbondale: Southern Illinois Universtity Press, 1966), p. x.

39 Koster described himself thus: "England is my country, but my native soil is Portugal. [...] I belong to both, and whether in the company of Englishmen, of Portuguese, or of Brazilians, I feel equally among my countrymen". He had been born in Lisbon of British parents. Ibid, p. viii.

40 Henry Koster, *Travels in Brazil* (1816), p. 400; emphasis in original.

41 Charles Fraser to Viscount Castleraugh *[sic],* 14 April 1812. NA FO 63/149; emphasis in original.

42 Graham, *Journal of a Voyage to Brazil,* p. 141.

43 Koster, *Travels in Brazil* (1816), p. 401.

44 This can be seen in the Brazilian tradition of *"piadas de português".* These jokes usually portray a Portuguese man as gullible and/or stupid. This tradition supposedly began around the time of independence as an effort to come to terms with what British observers called the superior thriftiness and industry of middle-class Portuguese merchants. Ewbank, *Life in Brazil,* p. 185.

45 Sociologist Phyllis Harrison describes the custom in present-day Brazil: "The North American who insists on rigid schedules and prompt behavior is frequently frustrated in Brazil. Because a Brazilian rarely arrives early, appointments are often delayed. One Brazilian businessman estimated fifteen to twenty minutes delay as standard [and] one businessman arriving precisely on time might find the other not yet ready." Harrison, *Behaving Brazilian,* pp. 72–3.

46 Walsh, *Notices of Brazil,* vol. 1, p. 78.

47 Graham, *Britain and the Onset of Modernization in Brazil,* p. 70. The railroad ultimately turned out to be a financial failure.

48 Wetherell, *Brazil*, p. 23.
49 Freyre, *Ingleses no Brasil*, p. 179.
50 *"Dos anúncios de ingleses nos jornais brasileiros da primeira metade do século XIX, pode-se dizer que, feita uma exceção ou outra, são verdadeiras lições de bom gosto, de ética profissional, contrastando com a ênfase, o exagero, o transborda-mento e às vezes as evidencias de charlatanismo de grande número de anuncios de europeus de outras procedencias e de varias profissões."* Ibid, p. 257.
51 Ibid, p. 52.
52 Ibid, p. 57.
53 *A Tolerancia*, (11 Oct 1849, Salvador, Bahia). AEB, Seção de Arquivo Republicano.
54 Freyre, *Ingleses no Brasil*, p. 53. The images of the British as expressed through Brazilian literature in the late nineteenth century, and vice versa, are discussed at length in Forman, 'Imperial intersections'.
55 Freyre, *Ingleses no Brasil*, p. 56.
56 Candler and Burgess, *Narrative of a Recent Visit to Brazil*, p. 78.
57 *"A sociedade do cônsul era, ao que parece, totalmente composta de comerciantes."* The author is referring to the British consul, William Pennell, as read through Maria Graham's narrative. Pinho, *Salões e damas do segundo reinado*, p. 40.
58 Needell, *A Tropical Belle Époque*, pp. 28 and 231.
59 Prior, *Voyage [...] in the Nisus Frigate*, p. 100.
60 For a full discussion, see Graham, *Britain and the Onset of Modernization in Brazil*; Manchester, *British Pre-Eminence in Brazil*; Needell, *A Tropical Belle Époque*.
61 All quotes are from W. H. Koebel, *British Exploits in South America*, pp. 331–4.

6   Crossing Boundaries: Knowledge and Sex

1   "The highly irregular living of unmarried Englishmen, during the first years of their settlement at Buenos Ayres gradually gave way to the softening and humanizing influence of female society; so that in 1818 or 1819 we had sobered down to a very well conducted community." Robertson and Robertson, *Letters on South America*, p. 119.
2   For example, the wife of Consul Lindeman fell sick and had to return to England only one year after they arrived in Bahia. Lindeman did not obtain permission to rejoin her until three years later. Lindeman to Foreign Office, 20 December 1814, NA FO 63/170.
3   Some records, however, have been lost due to water damage.
4   Wetherell, *Brazil*, pp. 81–2.
5   Candler and Burgess, *Narrative of a Recent Visit to Brazil*, p. 47.
6   Ibid, p. 78.
7   Ibid.
8   Ibid., 79. John Candler was in his mid-sixties at the time of his visit to Bahia.
9   "In 1852 two earnest Quakers, John Candler and William Burgess, traveled to Brazil in order to assist in the anti-slave trade campaign, and, incidentally, to present the Emperor with an address on this subject." Koebel, *British Exploits in South America*, p. 369.
10 See Chapter 2.
11 "Engaged in extensive operations, with branch trading establishments in different parts of the world, many of [the British merchants] become wealthy; and although the wealth they accumulate is obtained with the view of spending it, in after life, at home, in their native country, they are not indifferent to present enjoyment them-selves, nor do they neglect hospitality to strangers." Candler and Burgess, *Narrative of a Recent Visit to Brazil*, p. 78.

12 British Cemetery, Bahia, Brazil. The inscriptions had previously been collected and transcribed by Ms. Helen Thomas, and a copy was given to me by Mr. W. Nigel Lee, the British vice-consul at Bahia.

13 Maria Emilia Freitas Comber, 1814–1845.

14 Maria Con.stancia d'Araujo Freitas Ogilvie, 1815–1837. "Wife of Thomas Ogilvie late of this city, merchant." The first two examples are probably Brazilian women who entered the British community when they married British merchants. As such, it is possible that their eulogies would have been an almost pure description of how a good British woman was supposed to behave.

15 Elizabeth Buckingham, 1839–1895. "Born in Southampton Cants England and resided in this city 30 years. [...] The dearly departed wife of William C. Buckingham."

16 Among the many formal dedications to long-lived and successful merchants, a single gravestone stands out among the men's graves in the British cemetery for its simplicity: *"In loving memory of a good husband and father"*. The deceased, Thomas Walsh, died in poverty in 1881, leaving behind his widow Jane Ellen and their three young daughters. (AEB, Seção Judiciária, Inventário 03-1135-1604–08.) Because of their lack of financial success, Thomas and Jane were probably not among the more respected members of the British community. One can only wonder whether the more worldly-successful merchants would have preferred to be remembered for their family accomplishments rather than their career successes. At least one merchant, Andrew Comber, loved and missed his young wife enough to have it recorded in her burial record that Maria Emilia Comber died at the age of "28 years 9 months & 14 days". Her death left him as sole parent to a seven-year-old son and three daughters, ages 2, 4, and 5. (British Chapel, records of burial and baptism.)

17 Graham, *Journal of a Voyage to Brazil*, p. 150.

18 Joseph & Ellen Ward to William Follett, 6 April 1824. AEB, Scção de Arquivo Colonial e Provincial, Box 1186.

19 British Vice Consul Follett to Francisco Vicente Viana, 6 April 1824, AEB, Seção de Arquivo Colonial e Provincial, Box 1186.

20 Wetherell, *Brazil*, p. 116.

21 Graham, *Journal of a Voyage to Brazil*, p. 142.

22 Dundas, *Sketches of Brazil*, p. 100.

23 This circumstance is mentioned in a number of probate inventories of the period.

24 Evidence of this may be also found in Wetherell: "Some of the ladies fix an evening weekly to be at home, and often a sufficiently large party will meet to form a dance; quite willing to see their friends at any other time, they make it more agreeable by collecting a number together in one evening". Wetherell, *Brazil*, p. 82.

25 Robertson and Robertson, *Letters on South America*, p. 61.

26 One example of this for Brazil is Scully's remark, "On meetings [...] of more than ordinary interest – such as that of long absent friend – [the Brazilians'] mutual sympathy expresses itself in a warm and hearty embrace; one lifting the other fairly off the ground – a welcome rather embarrassing to an Englishman when first subjected to it". Scully, *Brazil,* pp. 10–1. An entertaining present-day example of a similar process, in this case related to cross-cultural misunderstandings of intentions regarding flirtation, may be found in Carlos E. Sluzki, 'The Latin lover revisited', in Monica McGoldrick, John K. Pearce and Joseph Giordano, eds, *Ethnicity and Family Therapy* (New York: Guilford Press, 1982), pp. 492–98.

27 Cited in Freyre, 'Social life in Brazil in the middle of the nineteenth century', 611.

28 Key examples include Dane Keith Kennedy, *Islands of White: Settler Society and Culture in Kenya and Southern Rhodesia, 1890–1939* (Durham, NC: Duke University Press, 1987); Ann Laura Stoler, *Race and the Education of Desire: Foucault's History of Sexuality and the Colonial Order of Things* (Durham, NC: Duke University Press, 1995); Ann Laura Stoler, 'Rethinking colonial categories: European com-

munities and the boundaries of rule', *Comparative Studies in Society and History* 31/1 (1989), 134–61; Ann Laura Stoler, 'Sexual affronts and racial frontiers: European identities and the cultural politics of exclusion in colonial southeast Asia', in Frederick Cooper and Ann Laura Stoler, eds, *Tensions of Empire: Colonial Cultures in a Bourgeois World* (Berkeley: University of California Press, 1997), pp. 198–237; Margaret Strobel, *European Women and the Second British Empire* (Bloomington: Indiana University Press, 1991).

29 Mawe, *Travels in the Interior of Brazil*, p. 329. The passage from which the footnote is drawn is discussed in Chapter 4.

30 Koster described himself thus: "England is my country, but my native soil is Portugal … I belong to both, and whether in the company of Englishmen, of Portuguese, or of Brazilians, I feel equally among my countrymen". Koster, *Travels in Brazil* (1966), p. viii.

31 Koster, *Travels in Brazil (1816)*, p. 401.

32 *"A fama de sexualmente ardentes, até mesmo depravadas, acompanhou a crónica dos viajantes estrangeiros já nos séculos anteriores"* (Their reputation for sexual ardor, and even depravity, was already present in the narratives of travelers from earlier centuries). Augel, *Visitantes estrangeiros na Bahia oitocentista*, p. 222.

33 Prior, *Voyage [...] in the Nisus Frigate*, p. 104.

34 Edward W. Said, *Orientalism* (New York: Vintage Books, 1979), p. 207.

35 Prior, *Voyage [...] in the Nisus Frigate*, p. 104; emphasis in original.

36 Graham, *Journal of a Voyage to Brazil*, p. 136.

37 Prior, *Voyage [...] in the Nisus Frigate*, p. 104.

38 John Codman, *Ten months in Brazil: with incidents of voyages and travels, descriptions of scenery and character, notes of commerce and productions, etc.* (Boston: Lee and Shepard, 1867), pp. 171–2.

39 See Pratt, *Imperial Eyes*.

40 *"1:000$000 – Serafina, criola moça, lavadeira, sem molestia; 250$000 – Graciano, cabra, filho da dita, com idade de 2 1/2 annos, sem molestia; 100$000 – Roza, criolinha irmã do dito, com idade de seis meses; 1:000$000 – Madalena, Africana, moça, lavadeira, sem molestia; 500$000 – Florencia, cabra, filha da dita, com idade de nove annos, sem molestia; 400$000 – Fermina, tão bem cabra irmã da dita, sem molestia, com idade de sete annos; 250$000 – Silvestre, cabra, com idade de tres annos; 150$000 – Luiz, criolinho, com idade de quinze mezes; 600$000 – Affonso, Africano do servisso da roça, sem molestia; 100$000 – Manoel Africano, velho, avaliado em cem mil reis por ser quebrado."* AEB, Seção Judiciária, Inventário 01-199-352-02, George Mumford, 29 March 1862.

41 Walsh, *Notices of Brazil in 1828 and 1829*, pp. 194–5.

42 "The exemplary manner in which the paternal duties are performed at home, may mark people as the most fond and affectionate of parents; but let them once go abroad, and come within the contagion of slavery, and it seems to alter the very nature of the man." Ibid, p. 195.

43 See Chapter 2, especially George Pilkington. Of course, the fact that such ownership was illegal under British law by then may have affected Scully's editorial choices.

44 Walsh, *Notices of Brazil in 1828 and 1829*, vol. II, p. 164.

45 Prior, *Voyage [...] in the Nisus Frigate*, p. 103.

46 *"As camadas sociais mais altas são, por excelência, as depositárias da mentalidade herdada da Península Ibérica, católico-romana, sobrecarregada pelo elemento árabe-muçulmano. As senhoras dessas camadas … [diferiam] da mulher negra, pois … esta última se destina, entre outras atribuições, ao entretenimento da libido dos senhores."* Augel, *Visitantes estrangeiros na Bahia oitocentista*, p. 222. For British men who missed this key distinction, upper-class Brazilian women may have represented the best of all worlds.

47 Stoler, 'Rethinking colonial categories', 137, referring to the formal Dutch and British colonies in Southeast Asia during the late 19th century. This supports my argument that the British merchant community of Bahia was keenly invested in emphasizing class distinctions among themselves.

48 Scully, *Brazil*, p. 7. See also Chapter 4.

49 Ann Laura Stoler theorizes at length upon the never-ending problems of positioning less than affluent European males within the racist imperial project of British colonialism in the late nineteenth and early twentieth centuries. Stoler 'Rethinking colonial categories'.

50 Gilberto Freyre, *The Mansions and the Shanties* (New York: Knopf, 1963); Gilberto Freyre, *The Masters and the Slaves* (New York: Knopf, 1946).

51 *"[Alguns ingleses] aquí deixaram descendencia nem sempre rigorosamente ariana. Ou nem sempre constituida legalmente ou sob as bençãos da Igreja. Ainda hoje são célebres, pelo luxo das instalações que tiveram quando moças, mulatonas ou caboclas, mantidas no Rio, no Recife, em Salvador, por negociantes, engenheiros ou gerentes ingleses de bancos poderosos:* gentlemen *que às louras preferiam as morenas e até as pretas da terra."* Freyre, *Ingleses no Brasil*, p. 111.

52 See Chapter 4.

53 Scully, *Brazil*, p. 6.

54 Ibid, p. 7. The similarity of his description of Brazilian women, above, to that of Maria Graham is interesting: "They marry very early, and soon lose their bloom". Graham, *Journal of a Voyage to Brazil*, p. 137.

55 Wetherell, *Brazil*, p. 149; emphasis in original.

56 Codman, *Ten Months in Brazil*, p. 171.

57 *"Eu Jorge Mumford ... declaro que sou natural da Inglaterra, e meus Pais são fallecidos; nomeio meus testamenteiros Snr. Francisco White Mackay, socio da minha casa commercial, e snr. E. Munford, meu Irmão, residente em Liverpool ... Declaro que sempre me conservei no estado de Solteiro; mas tenho de Dona Constança Ebbe[,] mulher desempedida, oito filhos cujos nomes constão da Escriptura de reconhecimento.... Declaro que igualmente tive de Balbina, mulher solteira, desempedida, uma filha de nome Maria Amalia, a qual pela presente verba a reconheço como tal para o fim de ser minha herdeira, conjuntamente com os demais declarados na anterior verba. Nomeio para Tutor dos menores meus Filhos ao meu Socio e 1º testamenteiro o Snr. Francisco White Mackay, de quem espero um satisfatorio desempenho da comissão que lhe encarrego. Declaro que dos meus filhos reconhecidos na Escriptura publica de que já tratei, cinco se achão educando na Europa."* AEB, Seção Judiciária, Testamento 7-3048-0-2, 12 February 1862.

58 AEB, Seção Judiciária, Inventário 01-199-352-02, 29 March 1862.

59 AEB, Seção Judiciária, Testamento 05-2200-2669-21, Francis White Mackay, 8 August 1861. Mackay died in 1869. Muriel Nazzari, 'Widows as obstacles to business: British objections to Brazilian marriage and inheritance laws', *Comparative Studies in Society and History* (1995), 781–802.

60 Ibid. This also recalls the discussion of the accidentally illegal British marriages in Chapter 3.

61 See, for example, Stoler 'Rethinking colonial categories', p. 141: "The relative importance of 'character' vs. 'class' in determining colonial status is something that apparently varied in different colonial contexts. References to character pervade the colonial literature but with often contradictory formulations".

62 When dealing with documentary sources for studying the specific details of British-Brazilian intermarriage in Bahia, the problem of the damaged marriage records from Bahia's British chapel recurs. It is all but impossible to generate an accurate reconstruction of the incidence of cross-cultural intermarriages. The following is an overview of the few families whose histories the sources allow one to reconstruct

with some accuracy. Maria Emilia Freitas Comber (1814–1845) married British merchant Andrew Comber. They proceeded to have a son, Charles William, followed closely by three daughters, Constantia, Elisabeth, and Adelaide Emily. Maria Emilia died while their children were all under the age of seven. Her son grew up to marry Eleanor Porter, the daughter of another British merchant (Joseph Porter), who in turn had connections to the Bielby family (of the most prominent firms of the British community at the time) through his other child, a son. The second example is that of Maria Constancia d'Araujo Freitas Ogilvie (1815–1837). Her tombstone says simply, "Wife of Thomas Ogilvie late of this city, merchant", and eulogizes her reputation as well as registering the affection of her widowed husband. Baptism records show that they had had a daughter in November 1836, a few months before her death; so it is possible that she died of complications associated with childbirth.

63 Scully, *Brazil*, p. 351.

64 This term has mostly been used to refer to an economic relationship privileging European interests over those of Latin American governments and society from Independence up until World War I, the implicit categorization of on-the-ground British-Latin American personal relationships as 'colonial' or 'informally imperial' is insufficiently grounded in evidence of the social-history variety that this study aims to achieve. This problem becomes more evident as scholarly understanding of colonial interpersonal power dynamics and daily boundary negotiation advances. On informal imperialism, see the Introduction to this volume. For postcolonial deconstructions of the politically motivated negotiations of boundaries of power and identity, see Hilary Callan and Shirley Ardener, eds, *The Incorporated Wife* (London: Croom Helm, 1984); John L. Comaroff, 'Images of empire, contests of conscience: models of colonial domination in South Africa', *American Ethnologist* 16 (1989) 661–85; Frederick Cooper and Ann Laura Stoler, eds, *Tensions of Empire: Colonial Cultures in a Bourgeois World* (Berkeley: University of California Press, 1997); Karen Tranberg Hansen, ed., *African Encounters with Domesticity* (New Brunswick, NJ: Rutgers University Press, 1992); Kennedy, *Islands of White*; Nancy Stepan, *The Idea of Race in Science: Great Britain, 1800–1960* (London: Macmillan, 1982); Stoler, 'Rethinking colonial categories'; Stoler, *Race and Education of Desire*; Strobel, *European Women and the Second British Empire*.

65 The consul's power of execution over the estates of deceased British subjects in Brazil was a key point in all commercial treaties signed between the two countries in the nineteenth century. After 1844 there followed a period of ambiguity and contestation, until full testamentary rights were restored in 1873. Nazzari ('Widows as obstacles to business') suggests that one reason for this demand was the need to protect the rights of male British subjects to prevent their wives from inheriting, in part because this would save British estates from prolonged legal wrangling and the forced liquidation of business enterprises upon a partner's death.

66 Germano Mendes Barreto to Antonio da Costa Pinto, President of Bahia, 5 September 1860, AEB, Seção de Arquivo Colonial e Provincial, Box 1195.

67 Morgan to Costa Pinto, 12 October 1860, AEB, Seção de Arquivo Colonial e Provincial, Box 1195.

68 Morgan to Costa Pinto, 20 August 1860, AEB, Seção de Arquivo Colonial e Provincial, Box 1195.

69 Castro (*Delegado*) to Chefe da Policia da Bahia, 6 September 1860, AEB, Seção de Arquivo Colonial e Provincial, Box 1195.

70 "*Pela cobrança da importancia da lavagem de roupa para o Hospital da Misericordia.*" Castro to Chefe da Policia da Bahia, 6 September 1860, AEB, Seção de Arquivo Colonial e Provincial, Box 1195.

71 Morgan to Costa Pinto, 20 August 1860, AEB, Seção de Arquivo Colonial e Provincial, Box 1195.

72 Castro to Chefe da Policia da Bahia, 6 September 1860, AEB, Seção de Arquivo Colonial e Provincial, Box 1195.

73 *"A passar impune actos destes, não haverá esperança de vida ou da propriedade dos estrangeiros."* Morgan to Costa Pinto, 20 August 1860, AEB, Seção de Arquivo Colonial e Provincial, Box 1195.

74 Nazzari, 'Widows as obstacles to business', p. 784.

75 Morgan to Costa Pinto, 2 October 1860, AEB, Seção de Arquivo Colonial e Provincial, Box 1195.

76 *"Mas eu o faço agora por ter sido Madame Vidal, subdita Britannica [...]"* Morgan to Costa Pinto, 6 October 1860, AEB, Seção de Arquivo Colonial e Provincial, Box 1195.

77 *"[O] decreto ... é applicavel ao individuo, incontestavelmente estrangeiro, domiciliado no Brasil, que ahi faleceu intestado, e não a uma mulher, que ... cazada com um Brasileiro, presume-se, que era tão bem Brasileira, ate q. se mostre o contrario."* President's pencil notes in the margin of a letter from British Consul John Morgan to Antonio da Costa Pinto, President of Bahia, 2 October 1860, AEB, Seção de Arquivo Colonial e Provincial, Box 1195.

78 *"Uma questão pequena e de nenhuma importancia, achando embaraços da parte da authoridade, assusta grandes interesses estrangeiros que se achão ligados ao Paiz."* Morgan to Costa Pinto, 12 October 1860, AEB, Seção de Arquivo Colonial e Provincial, Box 1195.

79 *"Certifico que sempre se considerava subdita Britannica."* Morgan to Costa Pinto, 12 October 1860, AEB, Seção de Arquivo Colonial e Provincial, Box 1195.

80 Morgan to Costa Pinto, 14 October 1860, AEB, Seção de Arquivo Colonial e Provincial, Box 1195.

81 Nazzari, 'Widows as obstacles to business', p. 781.

82 At least this is suggested in the language used by the Juiz de Orphãos when he wrote, *"Se entre os bens apprehendidos como pertencentes á finada Marianna Vidal forão comtemplados alguns, que sejão do finado Hooper, o Consul de S. M. Britanica, que pel-os meios competentes faça constar ao Juizo quaes elles sejão, por que tratando-se só de assegurar o espolio d'aquella, não haverá a menor duvida ou embaraço em separar do acervo os que forem reconhecidos alheios".* Carvalho to Costa Pinto, 15 September 1860, AEB, Seção de Arquivo Colonial e Provincial, Box 1195.

83 "Um costume nôvo, ou de que não se tem notícia no século anterior, é a admissão nas casas ricas de 'damas de companhia,' professôras, *institutrices* e *frauleins*, e também mestres, todos estrangeiros, especialmente inglêses, franceses e alemães." Pinho, 'A Bahia, 1808–1856', p. 291; emphasis in the original.

84 *"Figura de mulher também loura, requintadamente elegante, finamente erótica, cuja influencia sobre a vida brasileira do século passado precisa também de ser estudada e interpretada."* Unfortunately his use of the expression "madama ou francesa" to define this image muddles the issue. The phrase is embedded in a long discussion of British images and influences upon Brazil; the French are not mentioned at all, except for a single word in the quote, so the "madama" in this case was probably British. Freyre also does not cite any sources for this assertion. Freyre, *Ingleses no Brasil*, p. 56.

85 Augel (*Visitantes estrangeiros na Bahia oitocentista*, p. 219) points out that European women who attempted to walk in public streets were jeered at and otherwise harassed.

Conclusion

1 One study that takes such an approach is McIntyre's 'British Imperialism in India and Brazil, 1850–1914'. He concludes that the British were unable to maintain

hegemony either in Brazil or in India because of their failure to adequately accept and co-opt local elites. Nevertheless, in order to understand why there was such a deep-seated resistance to integrating with the locals in any significant respect, one must ask questions about risks to personal identity, a socio-psychological theme that cannot easily be supported by most economic or political studies.

Bibliography

Archives Consulted:

Arquivo da Cúria Metropolitana da Salvador, Salvador, Bahia
Arquivo do Estado da Bahia (AEB), Salvador, Bahia
Arquivo Municipal (AM), Salvador, Bahia
Arquivo Nacional (AN), Rio de Janeiro
Igreja Episcopal Anglicana do Brasil, Salvador, Bahia
National Archives (NA) [Public Record Office], London
    Foreign Office (FO) and Board of Trade (BT)

Published Primary Sources

Almanach para a cidade da Bahia, Anno 1812 (Bahia: Typographia de Manoel Antonio da Silva Serva, 1812).

AEB, Arquivo do Estado da Bahia, 'Devassa do Levante de Escravos Ocorrido em Salvador em 1835', *Anais do Arquivo Publico do Estado da Bahia* 50 (1992) 243.

Candler, John and Wilson Burgess, *Narrative of a Recent Visit to Brazil; To Present an Address on the Slave-Trade and Slavery, Issued by the Religious Society of Friends* (London: Edward Marsh, Friends' Book and Tract Depository, 1853).

Codman, John, *Ten Months in Brazil: With Incidents of Voyages and Travels, Descriptions of Scenery and Character, Notes of Commerce and Productions, etc.* (Boston: Lee and Shepard, 1867).

Dundas, Robert, *Sketches of Brazil, Including New Views on Tropical and European Fever with Remarks on a Premature Decay of the System Incident to Europeans on Their Return from Hot Climates* (London: John Churchill, 1852).

Ewbank, Thomas, *Life in Brazil: Or, a Journal of a Visit to the Land of the Cocoa and the Palm* (New York: Harper & Brothers, 1856).

Graham, Maria, née Dundas, afterwards Lady Calcott, *Journal of a Voyage to Brazil, and Residence there During the part of the years 1821, 1822, 1823* (London: Longman, Hurst, Rees, Orme, Brown, and Green, 1824).

Henderson, James, *A History of the Brazil* (London: Longman, Hurst, Rees, Orme, Brown, and Brown, 1821).

Kidder, Daniel P., *Sketches of Residence and Travels in Brazil, Embracing Historical and Geographical Notices of the Empire and Its Several Provinces*, 2 vols. (Philadelphia, PA: Sorin & Ball, 1845).

Kidder, Daniel P. and James C. Fletcher, *Brazil and the Brazilians Portrayed in Historical and Descriptive Sketches*, 8th, revised ed. (Boston MA: Little, Brown and Company, 1868).

Koster, Henry, *Travels in Brazil* (London: Longman, Hurst, Rees, Orme, and Brown, 1816).

Koster, Henry, *Travels in Brazil* (Carbondale: Southern Illinois University Press, 1966).

Lindley, Thomas, *Narrative of a Voyage to Brasil: Terminating in the Seizure of a British Vessel, and the Imprisonment of the Author and the Ship's Crew, by the Portuguese, With General Sketches of the Country, its Natural Productions, Colonial Inhabitants, &c.* (London: J. Johnson, 1805).

Luccock, John, *Notes on Rio de Janeiro and the Southern Parts of Brazil; Taken During a Residence of Ten Years in that Country from 1808 to 1818* (London: Leigh, 1820).

Marjoribanks, Alexander, *Travels in South and North America* (London: Simpkin, Marshall and Co., 1853).

Mawe, John, *Travels in the Interior of Brazil, Particularly in the Gold and Diamond Districts of that Country, by Authority of the Prince Regent of Portugal* (London: Longman, Hurst, Rees, Orme, and Brown, 1812).

Pedro II, Emperor of Brazil, *Diário da viagem ao norte do Brasil* (Salvador, Bahia: Universidade da Bahia, 1959).

Pilkington, George. *An Address to the English Residents in the Brazilian Empire, Urging Them to Liberate Their Slaves* (Rio de Janeiro, 1841).

Prior, James, *Voyage Along the Eastern Coast of Africa to Mosambique, Johanna, and Quiloa to St. Helena, Rio de Janeiro, Bahia, and Pernambuco in Brazil, in the Nisus Frigate* (London: Sir Richard Phillips & Co., 1819).

Robertson, W. P., and J. P. Robertson, *Letters on South America* (London: John Murray, 1843).

Scully, William *Brazil, Its Provinces and Chief Cities; the Manners & Customs of the People, Agricultural, Commercial and Other Statistics Taken by the Latest Official Documents with a Variety of Useful and Entertaining Knowledge, Both for the Merchant and the Emigrant* (London: John Murray, 1866).

Turnbull, John, *A Voyage Round the World, in the Years 1800, 1801, 1802, 1803, and 1804, in Which the Author Visited Madeira, the Brazils, Cape of Good Hope, the English Settlement of Botany Bay and Norfolk Island; and the Principal Islands in the Pacific Ocean.* 2nd. ed. (London: Maxwell, 1813).

Varella, Fagundes, *O Estandarte Auri-Verde: cantos sobre a questão anglo-brasileira* (São Paulo: Typografia Imparcial, 1863).

Walsh, Robert, *Notices of Brazil in 1828 and 1829*, 2 vols. (Boston, MA: Richardson, Lord & Holbrook, 1831).

Wetherell, James, *Brazil: Stray Notes from Bahia: Being Extracts from Letters, etc., During a Residence of Fifteen Years* (Liverpool: Webb and Hunt, 1860).

Wetherell, James, *Brasil: Apontamentos Sobre a Bahia*, Miguel Paranhos do Rio-Branco, trans. (Salvador, Bahia: Edição Comemorativa do Banco da Bahia, no date).

Wilberforce, Edward, *Brazil Viewed Through a Naval Glass, with Notes on Slavery and the Slave Trade* (London: Longman, Brown, Green, and Longmans, 1856).

Wild, John James, *At Anchor: A Narrative of Experiences Afloat and Ashore During the Voyage of H.M.S. "Challenger", from 1872 to 1876* (London: M. Ward and Co., 1878).

Secondary Sources

Adams, Jane Elizabeth, 'The abolition of the Brazilian slave-trade', *The Journal of Negro History* 41:10 (1925) 607–37.

Augel, Moema Parente, *Visitantes estrangeiros na Bahia oitocentista* (São Paulo: Editora Cultrix, 1980).

Azevedo, Thales de, 'Ingleses, Arabes na Bahia', *A Tarde*, 4 June 1993.

Anderson, Benedict, *Imagined Communities: Reflections on the Origins and Spread of Nationalism*, 2nd ed. (London : Verso, 1991).

Barnes, Ruth, and Joanne B. Eicher, eds., *Dress and Gender: Making and Meaning in Cultural Contents* (Oxford: Berg Publishers, 1992).

Bateson, Gregory, *Steps to an Ecology of Mind: Collected Essays on Anthropology, Psychiatry, Evolution, and Epistemology* (London: Paladin, 1973).

Batista, Paulo Nogueira, Jr., 'Politica tarifária britânica e evolução das exportacões brasileiras na primeira metade do seculo XIX', *Revista Brasileira de Economia* 34/2 (1980) 203–39.

Bethell, Leslie, 'The Mixed Commissions for the suppression of the transatlantic slave-trade in the nineteenth century', *Journal of African History* 7 (1966) 79–93.

_____ *The Abolition of the Brazilian Slave Trade: Britain, Brazil and the Slave Trade Question, 1807–1869* (Cambridge: Cambridge University Press, 1970).

_____ 'The independence of Brazil', in Leslie Bethell, ed., *Brazil: Empire and Republic, 1822–1930* (Cambridge: Cambridge University Press, 1989), pp. 3–42.

Burns, E. Bradford, *A History of Brazil*. 3rd. ed. (New York: Columbia University Press, 1993).

Callan, Hilary, and Shirley Ardener, eds, *The Incorporated Wife* (London: Croom Helm, 1984).

Callaway, Helen, 'Dressing for dinner in the bush: rituals of self-definition and British imperial authority' in Ruth Barnes and Joanne B. Eicher, eds, *Dress and Gender: Making and Meaning in Cultural Contexts* (Oxford: Berg Publishers, 1992), pp. ???–???.

Cardoso, Fernando Henrique, and Enzo Faletto, *Dependency and Development in Latin America* (Berkeley: University of California Press, 1979).

Comaroff, John L., 'Images of empire, contests of conscience: models of colonial domination in South Africa', *American Ethnologist* 16 (November 1989) 661–85.

Conrad, Robert. 'The contraband slave trade to Brazil, 1831–1845', *Hispanic American Historical Review* 49/4 (1969) 617–38.

_____ *The Destruction of Brazilian Slavery, 1850–1888* (Berkeley: University of California Press, 1972).

Cooper, Frederick and Ann Laura Stoler, eds., *Tensions of Empire: Colonial Cultures in a Bourgeois World* (Berkeley: University of California Press, 1997).

Cunnington, C. Willett, and Phyllis Cunnington, *Handbook of English Costume in the Nineteenth Century*, 2nd ed. (London: Faber and Faber, 1966).

Drescher, Seymour, *Capitalism and Antislavery: British Mobilization in Comparative Perspective*, 2nd ed. (New York: Oxford University Press, 1987).

Eakin, Marshall C., *British Enterprise in Brazil: the St. John d'El Rey Mining Company and the Morro Velho Gold Mine, 1830–1960* (Durham, NC: Duke University Press, 1989).

Eltis, David, *Economic Growth and the Ending of the Transatlantic Slave Trade* (New York: Oxford University Press, 1987).

Ferns, H.S., 'Britain's informal empire in Argentina, 1806–1914', *Past and Present* 4 (1953) 60–75.

De Fiore, Elizabeth, and Ottaviano de Fiore, eds, *The British Presence in Brazil, 1808–1914*, 2nd ed. (São Paulo: Paubrasil, 1987).

Forman, Ross G., 'Imperial intersections: imperial visions in collision and collapse in the late nineteenth and early twentieth centuries', unpublished Ph.D. thesis, Stanford University, 1998.

Frank, André Gunder *Capitalism and Underdevelopment in Latin America: Historical Studies of Chile and Brazil* (Harmondsworth, Middx.: Penguin, 1971).

Freyre, Gilberto, 'Social life in Brazil in the middle of the nineteenth century', *Hispanic American Historical Review* 5/4 (1922) 597–630.

_____ *The Masters and the Slaves (Casa grande e senzala)* (New York: Knopf, 1946).

_____ *Ingleses no Brasil: aspectos da influência britânica sobre a vida, a paisagem e a cultura do Brasil* (Rio de Janeiro: José Olympio, 1948).

_____ *The Mansions and the Shanties (Sobrados e mucambos)* (New York: Knopf, 1963).

_____ 'Em louvor de mestre Thales de Azevedo', *Universitas* (Salvador, Bahia) 6/7 (1970), 17–19.

Gallagher, J. and R. Robinson, 'The imperialism of free trade', *Economic History Review*, 2nd series 6 (1953) 1–15.

Goffman, Erving, *The Presentation of the Self in Everyday Life* (Garden City, NY: Doubleday, 1959).

Graham, Richard, *Britain and the Onset of Modernization in Brazil, 1850–1914* (Cambridge: Cambridge University Press, 1968).

_____ 'Robinson and Gallagher in Latin America: the meaning of informal imperialism', in W. R. Louis, ed., *Imperialism: The Robinson and Gallagher Controversy* (New York: New Viewpoints, 1976).

Green, William A., *British Slave Emancipation: The Sugar Colonies and the Great Experiment, 1830–1865* (Oxford: Clarendon Press, 1976).

Hansen, Karen Tranberg, ed., *African Encounters with Domesticity* (New Brunswick, NJ: Rutgers University Press, 1992).

Harrison, Phyllis A., *Behaving Brazilian: A Comparison of Brazilian and North American Social Behavior* (Rowley, MA: Newbury House Publishers, 1983).

Heaton, Herbert, 'A merchant adventurer in Brazil', *Journal of Economic History* 6 (1946) 1–23.

Johnstone, Keith, *Impro: Improvisation and the Theatre* (New York: Routledge, 1981).

Jones, Charles, 'Insurance companies', in D.C.M. Platt, ed., *Business Imperialism, 1840–1930: An Inquiry Based on British Experience in Latin America* (Oxford: Clarendon Press, 1977), pp. 53–74.

Jones, Geoffrey, *Merchants to Multinationals: British Trading Companies in the Nineteenth and Twentieth Centuries* (Oxford: Oxford University Press, 2000).

Kennedy, Dane Keith, *Islands of White: Settler Society and Culture in Kenya and Southern Rhodesia, 1890–1939* (Durham, NC: Duke University Press, 1987).

_____ 'The peril of the midday sun: climatic anxieties in the colonial tropics', in John M. Mackenzie, ed., *Imperialism and the Natural World* (Manchester: Manchester University Press, 1990), pp. 118–40.

Koebel, W. H., *British Exploits in South America: A History of British Activities in Exploration, Military Adventure, Diplomacy, Science, and Trade, in Latin-America* (New York: The Century Co., 1917).

Libby, Douglas Cole, 'Proto-industrialization in a slave society: the case of Minas Gerais' *Journal of Latin American Studies* 231 (February 1991) 1–35.

Lugar, Catherine, 'The merchant community of Salvador, Bahia, 1780–1830', unpublished Ph.D. thesis, State University of New York at Stony Brook, 1980.

Mcintyre, Michael Alan, 'British imperialism in India and Brazil, 1850–1914', unpublished Ph.D. thesis, University of Chicago, 1992.

Manchester, Alan K., *British Pre-Eminence in Brazil, Its Rise and Decline: A Study in European Expansion* (New York: Octagon Books, 1973).

Mansuy, André, 'Imperialism britannique et les relations coloniales entre le Portugal et la Brésil: Un rapport de l'Admiral Campbell au Foreign Office, 14 août 1804', *Cahiers des Amerigues Latines* no. 9–10 (1974).

Marshall, Oliver, *The English-Language Press in Latin America* (London: Institute of Latin American Studies, 1996).

_____ ed., *English-Speaking Communities in Latin America* (Basingstoke: Macmillan, 2000).

Mattoso, Katia M. de Queirós, *Bahia, século XIX: uma província do Império* (Rio de Janeiro: Editora Nova Fronteira, 1992).

Mayo, John, *British Merchants and Chilean Development, 1851–1886* (Boulder, CO: Westview Press, 1987).

Mello, José Antonio Gonsalves de, *Ingleses em Pernambuco: história do Cemitério Britânico do Recife e da participação de ingleses e outros estrangeiros na vida e na cultura de Pernambuco, no período de 1813 a 1909* (Recife: Instituto Arqueológico, Histórico e Geográfico Pernambucano, 1972).

Midgley, Clare, *Women Against Slavery: The British Campaigns, 1780–1870* (London: Routledge, 1992).

Miller, Joseph C., *Way of Death: Merchant Capitalism and the Angolan Slave Trade 1730–1830* (Madison: University of Wisconsin Press, 1988).

Miller, Rory, *Britain and Latin America in the Nineteenth and Twentieth Centuries* (New York: Longman, 1993).

Mitford, Nancy, et al., *Noblesse Oblige: An Inquiry Into the Identifiable Characteristics of the English Aristocracy* (Harmondsworth, Middx.: Penguin, 1959).

Mota, Carlos Guilherme, *Nordeste 1817: estruturas e argumentos* (São Paulo: Perspectiva & Editora da Universidade de São Paulo, 1972).

Nazzari, Muriel, 'Widows as obstacles to business: British objections to Brazilian marriage and inheritance Laws', *Comparative Studies in Society and History* 37/4 (1995) 781–802.

Needell, Jeffrey, *A Tropical Belle Epoque: Elite Culture and Society in Turn-of-the-Century Rio de Janeiro* (Cambridge: Cambridge University Press, 1987).

Pantaleão, Olga, 'A presença inglesa', in Sérgio Buarque de Hollanda, ed., *História Geral da Civilização Brasileira* II/1 (São Paulo: Difusão Européia do Livro, 1965), pp. 64–99.

Pinho, José Wanderley de Araújo, *Salões e damas do segundo reinado* (São Paulo: Martins, 1944).

_____ 'A Bahia, 1808–1856', in Sérgio Buarque de Hollanda, ed., *História Geral da Civilização Brasileira, III* (São Paulo: Difusão Européia do Livro, 1967), pp. 242–311.

Platt, D.C.M., 'Economic factors in British policy during the "new imperialism"', *Past and Present* 39 (1968) 120–38.

_____ *Business Imperialism, 1840–1930: An Inquiry Based on British Experience in Latin America* (Oxford: Clarendon Press, 1977).

_____ "Dependency in nineteenth-century Latin America: an historian objects', *Latin American Research Review* 15/1 (1980) 113–30.

_____ 'Economic imperialism and the businessman: Britain and Latin America before 1914', in R. Owen and B. Sutcliffe, eds, *Studies in the Theory of Imperialism* (London: Longman, 1972), pp. 295–310.

Pratt, Mary Louise, *Imperial Eyes: Travel Writing and Transculturation* (London: Routledge, 1992).

Reber, Vera Blinn, *British Mercantile Houses in Buenos Aires, 1810–1880* (Cambridge, MA: Harvard University Press, 1979).

Reis, João José, 'Slave resistance in Brazil: Bahia, 1807–1835', *Luso-Brazilian Review* 25/1 (1988) 111–44.

Ridings, Eugene, *Business Interest Groups in Nineteenth-Century Brazil* (New York: Cambridge University Press, 1994).

Rippy, J. Fred, *British Investments in Latin America, 1822–1949: A Case Study in the Operations of Private Enterprise in Retarded Regions* (New York: Arno Press, 1959).

Rybczynski, Witold, *Home: A Short History of an Idea* (New York: Viking, 1986).

Said, Edward W., *Orientalism* (New York: Vintage Books, 1979).

Schwartz, Stuart B., *Sugar Plantations in the Formation of Brazilian Society: Bahia, 1550–1835* (Cambridge: Cambridge University Press, 1985).

Sheridan, Richard B., 'The commercial and financial organization of the British slave-trade: 1750–1807', *Economic History Review* 2nd series 11/2 (1958) 249–63.

Sluzki, Carlos E., 'The Latin lover revisited', in Monica McGoldrick, John K. Pearce, and Joseph Giordano, eds, *Ethnicity and Family Therapy* (New York: Guilford Press, 1982), pp. 492–98.

Smith, Adam, *The Theory of Moral Sentiments,* Knud Haakonssen, ed. (Cambridge: Cambridge University Press, 2002).

Socolow, Susan Midgen, *The Merchants of Buenos Aires, 1778–1810: Family and Commerce* (Cambridge: Cambridge University Press, 1978).

Stepan, Nancy, *The Idea of Race in Science: Great Britain, 1800–1960* (London: Macmillan, 1982).

Stoler, Ann Laura, 'Rethinking colonial categories: European communities and the boundaries of rule', *Comparative Studies in Society and History* 31/1 (1989) 134–61.

_____ *Race and the Education of Desire: Foucault's History of Sexuality and the Colonial Order of Things* (Durham, NC: Duke University Press, 1995).

_____ 'Sexual affronts and racial frontiers: European identities and the cultural politics of exclusion in colonial southeast Asia', in Frederick Cooper and Ann Laura Stoler, eds, *Tensions of Empire: Colonial Cultures in a Bourgeois World* (Berkeley: University of California Press, 1997), 198–237.

Strobel, Margaret, *European Women and the Second British Empire* (Bloomington: Indiana University Press, 1991).

Tavares, Luís Henrique Dias, 'As soluções brasileiras no exemplo da extinção do tráfico negreiro', *Journal of Inter-American Studies* 9/3 (1967) 367–82.

_____ *História da Bahia*, 7th ed. (São Paulo: Atica/ INL/ MEC, 1981).

_____ *Comércio proibido de escravos* (São Paulo: Editora Atica, 1988).

Tenenbaum, Barbara, 'Merchants, money, and mischief: the British in Mexico, 1821–1862', *The Americas* 35/5 (1979) 317–39.

Vale, Brian, *Independence or Death! British Sailors and Brazilian Independence, 1822–25* (London: I. B. Tauris, 1996).

Verger, Pierre, *Notícias da Bahia: 1850* (Salvador, Bahia: Editora Corrupio, 1981).

Vianna Filho, Luis, *A sabinada* (Rio de Janeiro: José Olympio, 1938).

Wallerstein, Immanuel, *Unthinking Social Science: The Limits of Nineteenth-Century Paradigms* (Cambridge, MA: Polity Press, 1991).

Williams, Eric E., *Capitalism and Slavery* (Chapel Hill: University of North Carolina Press, 1944).

Wilson, Howard H., 'Some principal aspects of British efforts to crush the African slave trade, 1807–1829', *American Journal of International Law* 44 (1950) 505–26.

Wright, Antônia Fernanda Pacca de Almeida, *Desafio americano à preponderância britânica no Brasil, 1808–1850* (Rio de Janeiro: Imprensa Nacional, 1972).

Zeldin, Theodore, *An Intimate History of Humanity* (London: Minerva, 1994).

Index

Printed in the United States
61789LVS00003B/142

9 780954 407032